Grade 1

英検®1級
最短合格!
英作文問題
完全制覇

ジャパンタイムズ & ロゴポート 編

無料音声アプリ
PCでもダウンロードできる

the japan times 出版

英検®は、公益財団法人日本英語検定協会の登録商標です。

はじめに

　英検®1級の筆記試験の中でも、筆記大問4の英作文問題は受験者のみなさんにとって悩みの種ではないでしょうか。日本の少子高齢化から世界の食糧不足やテロ、クローン研究や宇宙開発の是非、未成年犯罪、大学教育の必要性といったものまで、ほとんどありとあらゆる時事問題や社会問題について、英語で自分の考えを述べなければなりません。しかも、2016年度第1回の試験からは、それまで解答の手がかりとなっていたPOINTSもなくなり、自力で議論を組み立てなければならなくなりました。

　しかし、過去問のTOPICやPOINTSを詳細に分析してみると、互いに関連し合う論点が繰り返し出題されていることがわかります。例えば、環境や気候変動に関する論点が、食糧や水の供給、遺伝子組み換え作物といったテーマだけでなく、都市化や自由貿易、多国籍企業の役割といったさまざまなテーマを論じる際にも使われる、といった具合です。つまり、限られた数の議論を頭に入れておけば、多くのテーマについて書くためのパーツとして使える可能性が高いのです。

　本書『最短合格！ 英検®1級 英作文問題完全制覇』では、このような観点からChapter 1で英作文問題の概要を確認したあと、Chapter 2において、答案の本論（body）の各段落になるパッセージ（本書では「内容の塊」という意味で「コンテンツブロック」と呼んでいます）を、分野別に200以上紹介しています。これだけのコンテンツが頭に入っていれば、非常に幅広いテーマに応用することができるはずです。またChapter 3では30問のオリジナル問題とそれに対する肯定・否定60の答案例を挙げ、Chapter 2のコンテンツブロックの具体的な使用例を示しています。Chapter 3で初登場するオリジナルのものを合わせると、本書に掲載されているコンテンツブロックは実に270を数えます。

　二次試験の面接は出題形式は多少異なりますが、それでも本書の内容が英作文問題だけでなく、二次面接の即戦力にもなることは言うまでもありません。

　本書を活用され、みなさんが合格の栄冠を手にされることを、心よりお祈りしています！

編者

はじめに		3
本書の構成と使いかた		6
音声のご利用案内		8

CHAPTER 1
英作文問題を攻略する

1	英作文問題の出題形式と採点基準	10
2	テーマ文の内容とタイプ	12
3	解答時間とメモ	13
4	全体の構成と語数	14
5	メモの取りかた	16
6	導入の形式	18
7	本論の形式	20
8	結論のまとめかた	22
9	パラフレージング（言い換え）	23
10	説得力ある文を書くためのテクニック	25

CHAPTER 2
分野別 コンテンツブロック212

1	現代日本社会	28
2	人権	36

| 3 | 犯罪 …………………………………… 46
| 4 | 世界の問題 ……………………… 56
| 5 | 戦争・核兵器・テロリズム …… 68
| 6 | 世界経済 ………………………… 78
| 7 | 世界の中の日本 ………………… 86
| 8 | 環境保護 ………………………… 92
| 9 | 教育・文化・スポーツ ………… 106
| 10 | テクノロジー …………………… 120
| 11 | 医療・生命倫理 ………………… 134
| 12 | 経済・ビジネス ………………… 144

CHAPTER 3

実践問題30

| 1 | 社会問題 ………………………… 160
| 2 | 国際問題 ………………………… 202
| 3 | サイエンス ……………………… 228
| 4 | 教育・IT・ビジネス …………… 266

装丁　清水裕久(Pesco Paint)
本文デザイン　高橋明香(おかっぱ製作所)
組版　株式会社創樹
ナレーション　Rachel Walzer／Chris Koprowski
音声収録　ELEC録音スタジオ

本書の構成と使いかた

本書は、1級筆記大問4の英作文問題で高得点を獲得するための対策書です。「Chapter 1 英作文問題を攻略する」「Chapter 2 分野別コンテンツブロック212」「Chapter 3 実践問題30」の3章で構成されています。

Chapter 1　英作文問題を攻略する

1級英作文問題とはどんな問題で、どのようなテーマが出題されるのか、また、英文エッセイの構成や答案作成のプロセスを解説しています。

Chapter 2　分野別コンテンツブロック212

「現代日本社会」「人権」「環境保護」など、英作文問題で出題される可能性の高い12の分野に関する**概要**とキーワード、そして答案作成に使うことができるパラグラフ単位の英文（コンテンツブロック）を掲載しています。

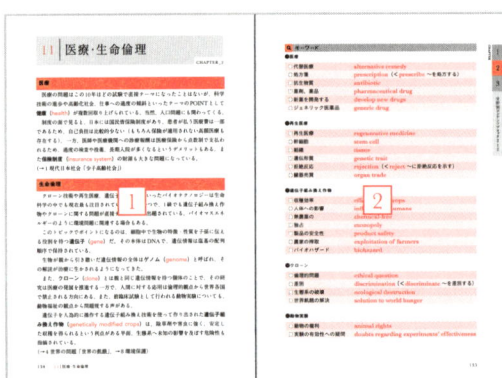

① 分野解説
出題される可能性が高い分野の概要を解説しています。

② キーワード
各分野の覚えておきたい表現をリストアップしています。

③ トピック名
コンテンツブロックの内容を示しています。

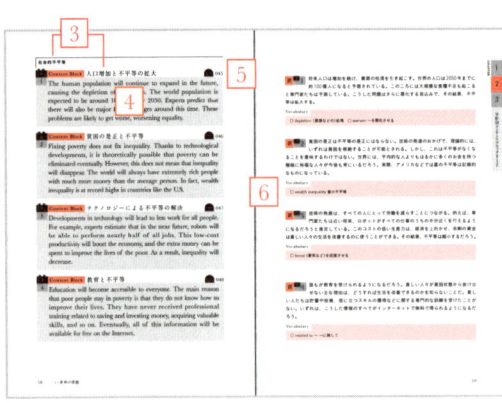

④ コンテンツブロック
答案本論（body）に使えるパラグラフ単位の英文です。12の分野にわたり212のコンテンツブロックを掲載しています。
※本書では、自然な英文にするために総称人称のyou（人一般を表すyou）、singular they（he or sheの代用）を使っている場合があります。

⑤ MP3ファイル番号
無料ダウンロードできるMP3音声のファイル番号を示しています。

⑥ Vocabulary
コンテンツブロック内で覚えておきたい語句です。

How to Use

Chapter 3　実践問題30

本番同様の英作文問題30問を収録しています。各問題にはAffirmative（肯定）とNegative（否定）それぞれの立場で書かれたモデルエッセイを掲載しました。

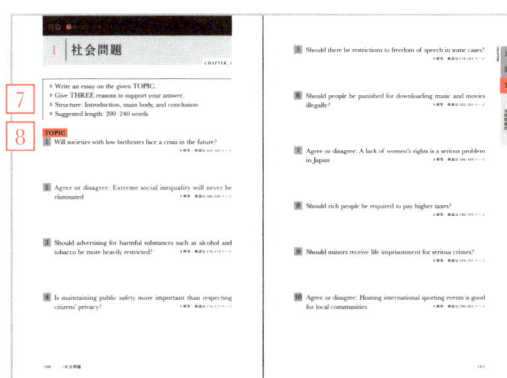

7 **指示文**
エッセイの構成や語数など、解答に関する指示が書かれています。

8 **TOPIC**
エッセイで論じるべきテーマです。

9 **モデルエッセイの立場**
モデルエッセイがTOPICに対してどちらの立場（AffirmativeかNegativeか）で書かれているかを示しています。

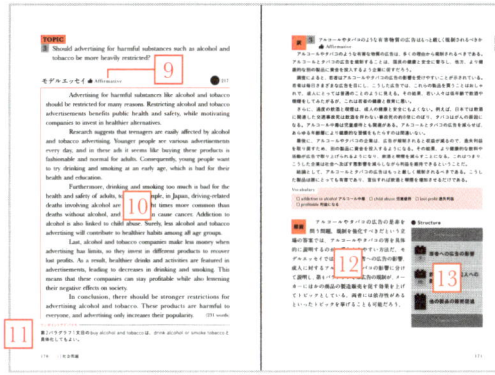

10 **モデルエッセイ**
TOPICに対するモデルエッセイです。introduction（導入）、3段落から成るbody（本論）、conclusion（結論）の5段落構成です。

11 **ワンポイントアドバイス**
言い換え表現などに関するアドバイスです。

12 **解説**
解答のポイントや、ほかにどんなトピックで書くことができるかなどを示した解説です。

13 **Structure**
エッセイがChapter 2のどのコンテンツブロックから構成されているかを図示しています。Chapter 3で初めて登場するコンテンツブロックは「オリジナル」と示されています。

音声のご利用案内

本書に対応する音声は、スマートフォン（アプリ）やパソコンを通じてMP3形式でダウンロードし、ご利用いただくことができます。

スマートフォン

1. ジャパンタイムズ出版の音声アプリ「OTO Navi」をインストール

2. OTO Naviで本書を検索
3. OTO Naviで音声をダウンロードし、再生

3秒早送り・早戻し、繰り返し再生などの便利機能つき。学習にお役立てください。

パソコン

1. ブラウザからジャパンタイムズ出版のサイト「BOOK CLUB」にアクセス

   https://bookclub.japantimes.co.jp/book/b309521.html

2. 「ダウンロード」ボタンをクリック

3. 音声をダウンロードし、iTunesなどに取り込んで再生

※音声はzipファイルを展開（解凍）してご利用ください。

英作文問題を攻略する

CHAPTER 1

このChapterでは、
1級英作文とはどんな問題か、
どう時間を使い、
どのような手順で考え、
答案全体をどう組み立てていったらいいか、
そして具体的にどのように書き始めればいいか
といったことを見ていこう。

1 英作文問題の出題形式と採点基準

CHAPTER_1

英作文問題の出題形式

一次試験は筆記とリスニングから成り、筆記はさらに四つの形式の大問に分かれています。大問1が短文の語句空所補充、大問2が長文の語句空所補充、大問3が長文の内容一致選択、そして大問4が本書で取り上げる英作文です。技能別に考えると、大問1〜3がリーディング、大問4がライティングになります。

筆記大問4の英作文では、2016年度第1回より、以下の形式の問題が出題されています（便宜上、和訳も添えてありますが、実際の問題に和訳はついていません）。

・Write an essay on the given TOPIC.
・Give THREE reasons to support your answer.
・Structure：Instruction, main body, and conclusion
・Suggested length：200-240 words

TOPIC
Should economic development be a higher priority for developing countries than environmental protection?

（以上、日本英語検定協会発表のサンプル問題）

・与えられたテーマについてエッセイを書きなさい。
・あなたの答えを支持するために三つの理由を挙げなさい。
・構成：導入、本論、結論
・推奨される長さ：200〜240語

テーマ
途上国にとっては、経済発展は環境保護よりも優先度が高くあるべきか

上のTOPICとはこの問題で論じるべき「テーマ」、エッセイとは「自分の意見を述べた文章」のこと。つまり、**筆記大問4は、与えられたテーマに関して英語で自分の意見を文章にまとめる問題です**。

なお、エッセイは〈introduction（序論）→ main body（本論）→ conclusion（結論）〉で構成し、200語〜240語でまとめるように指示されています。

> 採点のポイント

日本英語検定協会の発表によると、エッセイは「内容」、「構成」、「語彙」、「文法」の四つの観点で採点されます。

① **内容　課題で求められている内容（意見とそれに沿った理由）が含まれているか**
- 与えられたTOPICについて、自分の意見とそれを支持する具体的な理由を述べましょう。TOPICから外れた内容は、基本的に評価の対象になりません。

② **構成　英文の構成や流れがわかりやすく論理的であるか**
- 自分の意見とそれを支持する理由を、わかりやすく論理的に展開します。As a result（その結果）、However（しかしながら）といった表現を適宜使い、議論の流れや展開がわかりやすくなるようにしましょう。

③ **語彙　課題にふさわしい語彙を正しく使えているか**
- テーマに関する自分の意見を述べるのにふさわしい語句を使いましょう。同じ語句を何度も繰り返すことはできるだけ避け、1級にふさわしい語彙力があることを示しましょう。

④ **文法　文構造のバリエーションやそれらを正しく使えているか**
- 文法的に誤りのない文を書くことを心がけましょう。同じ内容を表す場合でも、異なる構文を使って書けると、表現力の広さをアピールすることができます。

> 合格基準スコアから見たライティングの重要性

英検1級一次試験の技能ごとのスコアは、リーディング、リスニング、ライティング、それぞれ850点（一次試験の満点はこれらを合計した2550点）。そして、合格基準スコアは2028点となっています。つまり、リーディングとリスニングで満点（850点＋850点＝1700点）を取ったとしても、それだけでは合格点には達しません。一方、三つの技能を700点ずつ取れば、2100点になるわけです。**ライティングでどれだけスコアをとれるかが、一次試験突破の重要なカギを握っている**と言うことができます。

2 テーマ文の内容とタイプ

 最近10年ほどの問題を振り返ると、世界の人口・食糧問題やグローバリゼーションの是非、移民、感染症といった世界規模のテーマを扱う問題が増えています。経済制裁や自由貿易といった経済面での出題もあります。また、日本に関する問題でも、アメリカやアジア諸国との関係について問うテーマが出題されており、日本の世界における立ち位置について考えることが求められていると言えるでしょう。その他のテーマとしては、死刑や言論の自由、プライバシーの保護といった人権問題、大学教育あるいは人文科学の意義といった教育問題、宇宙開発の是非に関する問題などが出題されています。化石燃料と再生可能エネルギーのような環境に関するものも、定番のテーマと言えます。

 一方、テーマ文のタイプは2種類あります。

タイプ① Yes / No 疑問文
タイプ② Agree or disagree 問題

 先に挙げた Should economic development be a higher priority for developing countries than environmental protection? は、タイプ①のテーマ文ですね。疑問文と言っても、基本的に What や Where、When などで始まる疑問文は出題されません。こうした疑問詞疑問文では、答えが一義的に決まってしまい、広がりのある議論が展開しづらいからです。過去の問題では、動詞 outweigh(〜を上回る)を使った

Do the benefits of free trade outweigh the disadvantages?
 訳 自由貿易のメリットはデメリットを上回るか

の形の疑問文も何回か出題されています。
 一方、タイプ②には、例えば、次のような文が出題されます。

Agree or disagree: Gambling has a negative effect on society
 訳 賛成か反対か:ギャンブルは社会にマイナスの影響がある

3 解答時間とメモ

　筆記試験全体の解答時間は100分で、そのうち英作文問題（筆記大問4）にかける時間は指定されていません。しかし、語彙問題や読解問題にかける時間を確保することを考えると、筆記大問4は、25分で解答することを目標にするとよいでしょう。

　ところで、ここで注意すべきことがあります。それは、いきなり答案を書き始めてはいけないということです。「早く書き始めないと」と気持ちが焦るかもしれませんが、はじめに必ずエッセイ全体の概要をメモするようにしてください。解答ではないので自分にわかるように書けばOK。もちろん日本語の簡単な箇条書きでも構いません。メモの作成にかける時間は3〜5分を目安にしましょう。

　概要を決めるときのポイントは二つあります。

- 自分の立場を決める（YesかNoか、AgreeかDisagreeか）
- 主張をサポートする論点（この先、本書では「トピック」と呼びます）を三つ挙げる

　この2点が明確に決まったら、それを基に、導入、本論、結論と書き進めます。18〜20分を目安に書きましょう。

　そして書き終わったら、最後に2分ほど使って見直しをしましょう。文法的な誤りがないか、特に主語と動詞が呼応しているか、名詞の複数形のsを忘れていないか、またつづりのミスをしていないかを確認します。せっかくの答案がケアレスミスで減点されないようにしましょう。また、見直していて同じ語句を繰り返し使っていることに気づく場合もあります。そのような場合はパラフレージング（言い換え）を考えましょう。

　ただし見直しの段階では、ケアレスミスを直したりパラフレージングをしたりすることはできても、議論の流れを変えるような修正を行うのは困難です。書き始める前の段階で、全体の構成をきちんと決める。それが一番大切です。

4　全体の構成と語数

CHAPTER_1

　前述の見本問題の指示にもありましたが、何よりも「与えられたテーマ」について書くことが大切です。全体の構成を決めるときには、まずそのことを念頭に置いてください。当たり前のことのように思えるかもしれませんが、あれこれと考えているうちに思考が脱線し、テーマからずれたトピックを考えてしまうことも十分にあり得ることなのです。英文としていくらすぐれたものを書いても、テーマからずれた内容であれば点数には結びつきません。

　全体の構成は「導入、本論、結論」と指定されています。そして「答えを支持する三つの理由を挙げる」ことが求められています。したがって、エッセイ全体の構成は必然的に次のようになります。

❷ エッセイの構成

Introduction	導入
Body 1	本論1
Body 2	本論2
Body 3	本論3
Conclusion	結論

　答案は5段落構成にし、段落の始めは必ず字下げして、新しい段落であることを明示します。字下げ幅は1.2〜1.5センチ（半角文字5文字分）くらいを目安にしましょう。段落と段落の間に空行を入れる必要はありません。

　語数は200〜240語と指定されていますが、210〜220語くらいを目安に書き、結論で語数を調整するといいでしょう。語数が多いからといって点数が上がるわけではありません。長く書けばその分時間も消費することになるので、上記の語数を目安にし、予定よりも多少長くなっても短くなっても対処できるようにしましょう。

導入

　導入と結論を合わせて50語から60語程度を目安にしましょう。

具体的な書き方については後述しますが、導入では、テーマに関してYesなのかNoなのか、あるいはAgreeなのかDisagreeなのか、あなたの立場を明示します。これはある意味で結論を最初に明示するということです。「エッセイ」と言っても英語のessayは「小論文」のことであり、「随筆」とは異なります。導入とは基本的に、テーマに対するあなたの立場、つまり結論を明示するための段落だと割り切ってください。

本論

　本論は、テーマに対してなぜ導入で述べた立場を取るのかを説明する部分で、三つの理由を挙げて（つまり三つの段落を使って）説明します。英語でbody（本文、主文）と呼ばれるように、解答全体のメインパートであり、ここでいかに効果的な説明ができるかが答案の成否を分けます。語数は内容によって変わりますが、一つの段落につき、50〜60語くらいを目安にまとめるようにしましょう。

結論

　結論では導入で述べた主張をもう一度繰り返します。導入と多少表現を変えることが望ましいですが、内容的に新しいことを述べる必要はありません。語数に余裕があれば本論の簡単な要約を添えると結論として締まります。語数に余裕がなければ、結論を1文でまとめて答案全体を240語に収めます。

---

column

どちらの立場が有利？

　テーマに対する立場を決める際、あなたがどちらの立場を取るかは、採点には一切影響しません。「この問題にはYesで答えておいたほうが、採点官の印象がいいだろう」といったことを考える必要はありませんし、それが本当にあなたの考えに即したものであるかも、点数には関係ありません。英作文の問題は、あなたの主義主張を問うのではなく、あなたが自分の主張を述べる説得力のある英文を書けるかを試験するためのものです。あなたが書きやすい立場を選ぶことが大切です。

　ちなみに、物事には常に両面の見方があります。普段何かについて考えるときに、一つの立場だけでなく、別の、あるいは逆の立場でも考えてみる習慣をつけましょう。こうした習慣は英作文や面接の解答力に直結するだけでなく、実際のビジネスなどの場面で、自分の発言に客観性や説得力を持たせる訓練にもなります。

5 メモの取りかた

CHAPTER_1

「解答時間とメモ」のところで、答案を書き始める前にエッセイ全体の概要をメモしましょうと述べました。限られた時間の中でなぜそんなことをするかといえば、書きながらトピックをひねり出そうとすると、考えに詰まって時間を大幅にロスしたり、途中で主張が変わって首尾一貫しない答案になったりする可能性があるからです。答案を書く前にポイントをメモするのは、一貫性のある答案を書く最も効率的な方法です。少し大げさに言えば、このメモがきちんとできた時点で、解答は半分できたようなものと言ってもいいでしょう。

ここで少し具体的に考えるために、いくつかのテーマを見てみましょう。あなたは次のようなテーマが出題されたら、どんなトピックで答案を書きますか？

> Do the benefits of economic development outweigh the damage caused to the environment?
> 訳 経済発展のメリットは環境に及ぼすダメージにまさるか
>
> Is it unethical for companies to collect personal information about customers?
> 訳 企業が顧客の個人情報を収集することは道義にもとるか
>
> Should the number of nuclear power plants be increased?
> 訳 原子力発電所の数は増やすべきか
>
> Agree or disagree: Wealthy nations should provide more funding for global poverty relief efforts
> 訳 賛成か反対か：裕福な国は世界の貧困救済のためにより多くの資金提供を行うべきだ
>
> Should artificial intelligence continue to be improved?
> 訳 人工知能は改良され続けるべきか

どうでしょう。こうした多岐にわたるテーマに対して、Yes / No、あるいは Agree / Disagree のいずれの立場を取るにしても、それをサポートするトピック

を三つ考えるのはなかなか大変だと思います。したがって、メモを取るときには「自分の立場を決める（YesかNoか、AgreeかDisagreeか）」「主張をサポートするトピックを三つ挙げる」の2点を決めなければならないと述べましたが、立場を決める前に、自分ならどういったトピックを出せるかを考えることが大切です。つまり、立場を決めたうえでそれをサポートするトピックを考えるのではなく、トピックが三つ挙げられる立場を選んで解答するべきなのです。

● メモの手順

テーマに関するトピックを（できるだけ多く）書き出す
∨
トピックを三つ選ぶ
∨
立場を決める

繰り返しになりますが、英作文問題ではあなたの主義主張を問うているわけではありません。テーマを見たら、まずはそれに対して思いつくトピックをできるだけ多く書き出してみましょう。そしてその中で矛盾なく提起できる三つのトピックを選び、YesかNoか、あるいはAgreeかDisagreeかの立場を決めましょう。

例 Agree or disagree: Online learning is just as effective as face-to-face learning

訳 賛成か反対か：オンライン学習は対面型の学習と同じくらいの効果がある

☑ 自分のペースで学習できる
☐ 直接質問ができない
☑ 費用が安い
☑ 効果が実証されている
☐ グループ学習ができない

Agreeで答える！

このあと、箇条書きのわきにさらに具体的な事例などを加えてから書き始めれば、答案を書く作業は、事実上メモの肉付け作業のようなものになるはずです。

6　導入の形式

　立場をサポートするトピックを三つ決め、立場が決まったら、いよいよ答案作成開始です。
　Yes / No 疑問文のタイプの問題では、テーマの文を疑問文から平叙文にするか、I think [believe] ...（否定する場合は I don't think [believe] ...）の後ろにテーマの文を続ける、また Agree or disagree タイプの問題では、I agree [disagree] that ... で書き始めるのが、一番オーソドックスな書き方です。
　いずれにしても、最初に自分の立場を明示する、それが英文エッセイの基本です。そしてその後ろに、本論を踏まえた理由を、要約する形で続けます。

> 例　Smoking in restaurants should not be banned. A number of restaurants already have separate sections for smokers. Also, individual restaurants can decide their own smoking policy.
>
> 訳　レストランでの喫煙は禁止されるべきではない。多くのレストランではすでに喫煙者のための隔てられたスペースがある。また、個々のレストランは独自の喫煙方針を決めるべきだ。

> 例　I do not think that recycling should be required by law. Recycling is a complicated issue, and often it is difficult to know which items are recyclable.
>
> 訳　リサイクルは法によって強制されるべきではないと思う。リサイクルは複雑な問題であり、どの製品がリサイクルできるかを知るのが難しいことも多い。

> 例　I agree that online learning is just as effective as face-to-face learning. In fact, it has many advantages, such as customizable pacing and time-saving benefits.
>
> 訳　オンライン学習は対面型の学習と同じくらい効果があるという意見に賛成だ。実際、人それぞれにペースを決められる、時間の節約になるといったメリットなど、多くの利点がある。

　理由を先に述べたうえで、自分の立場を表明することもできます。その場合は、間に Thus、Therefore（したがって）、For these reasons（そのようなわけで）といった語句をはさむとよいでしょう。

を三つ考えるのはなかなか大変だと思います。したがって、メモを取るときには「自分の立場を決める（YesかNoか、AgreeかDisagreeか）」「主張をサポートするトピックを三つ挙げる」の2点を決めなければならないと述べましたが、立場を決める前に、自分ならどういったトピックを出せるかを考えることが大切です。つまり、立場を決めたうえでそれをサポートするトピックを考えるのではなく、トピックが三つ挙げられる立場を選んで解答するべきなのです。

メモの手順

テーマに関するトピックを（できるだけ多く）書き出す
∨
トピックを三つ選ぶ
∨
立場を決める

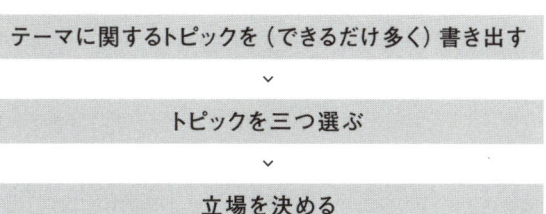

繰り返しになりますが、英作文問題ではあなたの主義主張を問うているわけではありません。テーマを見たら、まずはそれに対して思いつくトピックをできるだけ多く書き出してみましょう。そしてその中で矛盾なく提起できる三つのトピックを選び、YesかNoか、あるいはAgreeかDisagreeかの立場を決めましょう。

例 Agree or disagree: Online learning is just as effective as face-to-face learning

訳 賛成か反対か：オンライン学習は対面型の学習と同じくらいの効果がある

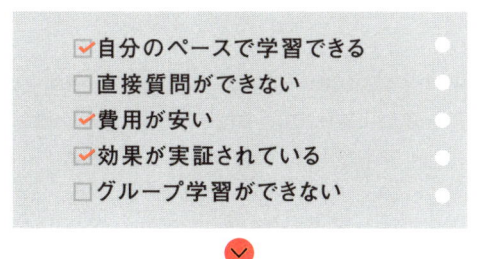

☑ 自分のペースで学習できる
☐ 直接質問ができない
☑ 費用が安い
☑ 効果が実証されている
☐ グループ学習ができない

∨
Agreeで答える!

このあと、箇条書きのわきにさらに具体的な事例などを加えてから書き始めれば、答案を書く作業は、事実上メモの肉付け作業のようなものになるはずです。

6 導入の形式

　立場をサポートするトピックを三つ決め、立場が決まったら、いよいよ答案作成開始です。
　Yes / No疑問文のタイプの問題では、テーマの文を疑問文から平叙文にするか、I think [believe] ...（否定する場合はI don't think [believe] ...）の後ろにテーマの文を続ける、またAgree or disagreeタイプの問題では、I agree [disagree] that ...で書き始めるのが、一番オーソドックスな書き方です。
　いずれにしても、最初に自分の立場を明示する、それが英文エッセイの基本です。そしてその後ろに、本論を踏まえた理由を、要約する形で続けます。

例　Smoking in restaurants should not be banned. A number of restaurants already have separate sections for smokers. Also, individual restaurants can decide their own smoking policy.
　　訳　レストランでの喫煙は禁止されるべきではない。多くのレストランではすでに喫煙者のための隔てられたスペースがある。また、個々のレストランは独自の喫煙方針を決めるべきだ。

例　I do not think that recycling should be required by law. Recycling is a complicated issue, and often it is difficult to know which items are recyclable.
　　訳　リサイクルは法によって強制されるべきではないと思う。リサイクルは複雑な問題であり、どの製品がリサイクルできるかを知るのが難しいことも多い。

例　I agree that online learning is just as effective as face-to-face learning. In fact, it has many advantages, such as customizable pacing and time-saving benefits.
　　訳　オンライン学習は対面型の学習と同じくらい効果があるという意見に賛成だ。実際、人それぞれにペースを決められる、時間の節約になるといったメリットなど、多くの利点がある。

　理由を先に述べたうえで、自分の立場を表明することもできます。その場合は、間にThus, Therefore（したがって）、For these reasons（そのようなわけで）といった語句をはさむとよいでしょう。

例 Humans have been using animals for entertainment for thousands of years. In fact, some animals only continue to exist because they are used by humans. Thus, I believe animals should still be used for entertainment.
> 訳 人間は何千年もの間、動物をショーに使ってきた。実際、動物の中には人間に使われるからこそ存続しているものもいる。したがって、動物はショーに使ってもよいと思う。

前置きとして一般論について一言触れたうえで、テーマの文を続けるパターンもあります。

例 Although workers should be paid fair salaries, this does not mean that legal minimum wages should be raised. Low wages are appropriate for many simple jobs, and forcing higher wages would harm businesses and the economy.
> 訳 労働者には適正な給与が支払われるべきだが、このことは法的最低賃金が引き上げられるべきだということを意味しない。低賃金がふさわしい単純労働はたくさんあるし、より高い賃金を強制すれば企業や経済に悪影響を与えるだろう。

まず自分の立場と反対の意見を一般論として挙げておいて、それを否定するという形もあります。この形を取ると、一般的な議論を踏まえたうえでオリジナルの議論を展開しているという印象を与えることができます。

例 Most would agree that the Internet is a useful tool. However, it also causes some problems such as increased communication between criminals and popularity of dangerous trends.
> 訳 たいていの人はインターネットが便利なツールであることに同意するだろう。しかしながら、それはまた犯罪者同士のコミュニケーションや、危険な流行の人気を増大させるといった問題も引き起こす。

7 本論の形式

第2パラグラフから第4パラグラフの三つのパラグラフが本論（body）となります。ここで、なぜあなたが導入で表明した立場を取るのか、その理由を説明します。前述のように、ここで説得力のある議論を展開できるかが、答案全体の成否を決めます。

具体的にどんな内容を書いたらいいかについては、Chapter 2の「分野別コンテンツブロック212」で見るので、ここでは形式的な側面について見ておきましょう。

本論の構成は、「トピックセンテンス」（1文）→「具体的な説明［事例］」（1文か2文）→「まとめ」（1文）が基本的な形です。

例 First, ①online learning allows students to progress at their own pace. ②Traditional classes move too quickly for some students and too slowly for others. This limits learning for the majority of students. ③With online courses, though, students can use the exact amount of time that they need to understand new information.

訳 第一に、オンライン学習では、生徒は自分のペースで進んでいくことができる。従来の授業では、ある生徒たちにとっては進むペースが速すぎ、また別の生徒たちにとっては遅すぎる。このことは大多数の生徒の学習を制限してしまう。しかし、オンラインコースでは、生徒は新しい情報を理解するのに必要とするちょうどよい時間をかけることができる。

上のブロックでは、①がこのパラグラフ全体を要約するトピックセンテンス、②が具体的な説明、③がまとめとなります。

● **本論の構成**

トピックセンテンス
∨
具体的な説明・事例
∨
まとめ

三つのトピックを挙げる際、冒頭にFirst（第一に）、Second（第二に）、Third（第三に）と置くのが一番わかりやすく、かつ議論の流れを明快に示す方法です。

ただし、それ以外の始め方も知っておいたほうが書き方にバリエーションを持たせることができるでしょう。第2、第3のbodyを始めるときには、Furthermore（さらに）、Moreover（さらに）、Additionally（それに加えて）、In addition（それに加えて）、Yet another ...（さらに別の…もある）といった表現を使うことができます。第2bodyにはNext（次に）を、第3bodyにはFinallyやLast（最後に）を使うこともできます。

> 例 In addition, online learning eliminates some negative aspects of face-to-face learning. With traditional classes, it costs students time and money to commute to lessons. Also, group classes are full of distractions. One-on-one, face-to-face lessons do not have these distractions, but they are too expensive for most students. All of these problems disappear with online learning.
>
> 訳 それから、オンライン学習は対面型の学習のいくつかの悪い面を取り除く。従来の授業では、生徒には授業に通うのに時間とお金がかかる。それに、グループでの授業には気が散ることがたくさんある。マンツーマンの対面型の授業では、このような気を散らすものはないが、ほとんどの生徒にとって高すぎる。オンライン学習ではこうした問題のすべてがなくなるのだ。

> 例 Yet another benefit of mixed-sex schools is that students are able to learn about their peers' varying experiences and views of the world.
>
> 訳 共学校のメリットの中には、生徒たちが同級生の多様な経験や世界観を知ることができるというものもある。

8　結論のまとめかた

第5パラグラフの結論では、第1パラグラフの導入で表明した立場を繰り返します。できれば表現を多少変えましょう。そして語数に余裕があれば、本論で述べた理由を簡潔にまとめます。第4パラグラフまでに使った語数を見て調整しましょう。

結論は In conclusion（結論として、要するに）で始めるのが一番オーソドックスなパターンです。そのほかに、In summary（要約すると）、For the reasons listed（上に挙げた理由によって）、For the reasons mentioned above（上述の理由によって）、Considering the points mentioned above（上述の諸点を考慮すると）、Based on the points mentioned above（上述の諸点に基づき）、In light of the points mentioned above（上述の諸点に照らして考えると）といった表現もあります。

例 In conclusion, I disagree with the view that the drinking age should be lowered.

訳 結論として、飲酒年齢は引き下げられるべきであるという考えに私は反対だ。

例 In conclusion, the benefits of a minimum wage do not outweigh the drawbacks. Fair wages should occur naturally in a healthy economy.

訳 結論として、最低賃金のメリットはデメリットを上回ることはない。健全な経済においては、適正な賃金はおのずから決まる。

例 For the reasons mentioned above, I believe that online learning is just as effective as—if not more effective than—face-to-face learning.

訳 上述の理由から、オンライン学習は対面型の学習と同じくらい──対面型の学習以上にとは言わないまでも──効果があると私は思う。

9 パラフレージング（言い換え）

英作文の試験では、同じ語句を何度も繰り返し使って単調な文章になると減点の対象になる可能性があります。特に文中でよく使われる因果関係や変化、程度を表す語句などは、いくつかの言い換えのパターンを頭に入れておき、表現に変化を持たせるようにしましょう。

- cause / result in / lead to / give rise to / bring about / provoke / promote（〜を引き起こす）

  例 Refusing to establish reasonable trade agreements could cause [result in / lead to / give rise to / bring about / provoke / promote] animosity from other developed nations.

  訳 理にかなった貿易協定を結ぶのを拒否すれば、他の先進国の敵対心を引き起こす可能性がある。

＊cause と result in が最も因果関係が直接的で、provoke と promote はほかのものに比べて因果関係が希薄。

- fuel / contribute to / promote（〜を刺激する、促進する）

  例 An increase in consumption will fuel [contribute to / promote] the economy.

  訳 消費の増加は経済を促進する。

＊promote が一番因果関係が強い。

- come from / be a result of（〜の結果生じる）

  例 Countless health problems come from [are a result of] a lack of diet and exercise.

  訳 食事と運動の不足の結果、無数の健康問題が生じる。

- huge / major / significant / immeasurable / catastrophic / immense
  ((被害などが) 大きい)
  > 例 Import taxes can cause huge [major / significant / immeasurable / catastrophic / immense] damage to domestic businesses and industries.
  > 訳 輸入税は国内の企業と産業に大きなダメージを引き起こす可能性がある。

- drastically / significantly / considerably (著しく、劇的に)
  > 例 The genetic diversity of the planet may change drastically [significantly / considerably] in the near future.
  > 訳 地球における遺伝子の多様性は近い将来劇的に変化するかもしれない。

- harmful / damaging / detrimental (有害な)
  > 例 The use of fossil fuels is harmful [damaging / detrimental] to the planet.
  > 訳 化石燃料の使用は、地球にとって有害だ。

＊detrimentalはほかの二つよりも意味が強い。

- shift / transition (移行する)
  > 例 Shifting [Transitioning] to a new form of government is extremely difficult, controversial, and time-consuming.
  > 訳 新体制の政府への移行は、極めて困難で賛否両論があり、時間がかかるだろう。

- decrease / reduce / lessen / lower (〜を減らす、〜の程度を下げる)
  > 例 Doctors are still struggling to decrease [reduce / lessen / lower] the negative side effects of cancer treatments.
  > 訳 医師たちは、がん治療のマイナスの副作用を軽減するべく今なお努力を続けている。

10 説得力のある文を書くためのテクニック

CHAPTER_1

　ここでは、説得力のある文を書くためのいくつかのテクニックを見ておきましょう。ここに挙げたテクニックを使わなければ答案を書くことができないというわけではありませんが、知っていれば一歩上の答案を目指すことができます。

具体的な例を挙げる

　説得力のある文を書くときの最大のコツは具体例を挙げることです。知らないことは書けませんが、抽象論に終始せず、少しでも具体的な話をすることで議論にリアリティーを出すことができます。

例 For example, entire cities can be powered by hydroelectricity, solar power, and wind energy, just to name a few.

　訳 例えば、いくつか例を挙げてみるだけでも、すべての都市の電力を水力発電、太陽光、風力によってまかなうことができる。

＊上の文のjust to name a fewは「いくつか例を挙げてみるだけでも」という意味で、省略することもできます。また上の文はJust to give a few examples, entire cities can be powered by hydroelectricity, solar power, and wind energy. のように言い換えることもできます。

具体的な数字を入れる

　説明文中に具体的な数字を入れると、説得力が増します。もちろん解答中にデータを調べることはできないので、ポイントになるいくつかの数字を覚えておかなければなりませんが、うまく使えるととても効果的です。普段からニュースなどに触れ、新しい情報を身につけておくことも大切です。

例 Prisons do not stop criminal activity. In fact, in the U.S. almost two-thirds of criminals are arrested again within three years of being released from prison. This suggests that prisons do not prevent future crimes. Society needs to find more effective methods for rehabilitating criminals.

　訳 刑務所が犯罪行為をなくすことはない。実際、米国では犯罪者の約3分の2が刑務所から釈放されて3年以内に再逮捕される。このことは、刑務所が将来の犯罪を防止できていないことを示唆している。社会は犯罪者を社会復帰させるためのより効果的な方法を見出す必要がある。

挿入節・挿入句の使いかた

以下の例のような挿入節や挿入句を使うと、表現に変化を持たせることができます。やや高度なテクニックですが、覚えておくと便利な表現手段です。挿入部分を削っても文としては完全に成立します。

例 If the Earth's temperature continues to increase—and many scientists believe that it will—it is likely to result in food shortages around the world.

> **訳** 地球の気温が上昇し続けると――そして多くの科学者はそうなると考えているが――世界中の食糧不足につながる可能性がある。

例 In countries where this is true—for example, in Japan and South Korea—it leads to other problems as well.

> **訳** このことが当てはまる国々では――例えば日本や韓国では――それは別の問題も引き起こす。

修辞疑問による強調

次の文中にある How many ～? のような修辞疑問を使うと、文が生き生きとします。

例 Due to our dependence on technology, many traditional skills and crafts are disappearing. How many people today know how to sew their own clothes? How many people know how to hunt or fish? Surely there are fewer people with these skills than there used to be.

> **訳** 技術に依存しているせいで、多くの伝統技術や伝統工芸が姿を消しつつある。今日、自分の服の縫い方をどのくらいの人が知っているだろうか。狩りや釣りの仕方をどのくらいの人が知っているだろうか。こうした技術を持つ人は以前より確実に少なくなっている。

決まり文句を使う

次のような、ネイティブであれば誰でも知っている決まり文句がさりげなく使えるときれいに決まります。

例 Better safe than sorry.

> **訳** 用心するに越したことはない。(転ばぬ先の杖。／備えあれば憂いなし。)

Easier said than done.

> **訳** 言うは易し、行うは難し。

Better late than never.

> **訳** 遅れてもやらないよりはまし。

分野別
コンテンツブロック
212

CHAPTER 2

このChapterでは、
答案のbodyを構成するコンテンツブロック212を、
12の分野別に収録した。
解答でそのまま使えるものばかりなので、
頭に入れてしまおう。
各分野の出題傾向やキーワードもまとめたので
併せて覚えておこう。

1 現代日本社会

CHAPTER_2

少子高齢社会

　15歳以下の年少人口の割合が低く、65歳以上の老年人口の割合が高い社会を少子高齢社会という。日本をはじめ、多くの先進国に見られる。医療の発達などによる寿命の伸長および出生率の低下によって生じる。若年労働力が不足し、高齢者の医療費が増加するといった問題がある。少子化については、産休・育休制度の整備や児童手当、保育所の待機児童解消などの施策がとられているが、根本的な解決には至っていない。

　過去にも高齢化社会や低出生率に関する出題があり、現代日本社会の問題の中でも取り上げられやすいテーマの一つと言える。
（→11 医療・生命倫理「医療」）

現代人のモラル

　漠然としたテーマのように見えるが、2009年に現代社会を生きる人々の**倫理観**（moral value）について出題されたことがある。核家族化や一人親世帯の増加といった家族形態の変化に加え、インターネットやSNSの普及による対人関係の変化が進んでいる点も、ポイントになるだろう。また、経済優先主義や現代における宗教の意味について触れる方向もある。さらに、公共のマナーなどに関して、具体例を挙げて論じることもできるだろう。
（→10 テクノロジー「インターネット」、→12 経済・ビジネス）

都市化

　人口が都市に集中し、近郊の農村地帯が住宅地や工業用地へと変わって住民の生活が変化する現象をいう。インフラが整備され生活が便利になり、経済活動が活発になる一方で、排ガスによる大気汚染、水質汚濁といった環境汚染、地価高騰、住宅不足、通勤ラッシュや交通渋滞、農村における伝統的な農業や文化の消滅といった問題も生じる。
（→8 環境保護、→9 教育・文化・スポーツ「伝統文化」）

🔍 キーワード

●少子高齢社会

☐ 高齢化社会	aging society
☐ 医療の発達	advancement of medicine
☐ 医療制度	healthcare system
☐ 労働力不足	labor shortage
☐ 労働人口の減少	a decline in the working-age population
☐ 税収の減少	a decline in tax revenue
☐ 年金制度の崩壊	pension system collapse
☐ 福祉の危機	welfare crisis
☐ 景気の悪化	economic deterioration
☐ 予防医学	preventive medicine
☐ 高齢者の雇用	employment of senior citizens
☐ 持続可能な社会	sustainable society
☐ 失業率の低下	fall in the unemployment rate
☐ 生活の質	quality of life

●現代人のモラル

☐ 道徳教育	moral education
☐ 利他的な行動	altruistic behavior
☐ 物質主義	materialism
☐ 倫理観の喪失	loss of moral values
☐ 核家族化	the growing trend of nuclear families
☐ 世俗主義の一般化	the growing popularity of secularism
☐ デリケートな問題	sensitive issue

●都市化

☐ 都市化	urbanization（＜urbanize 都市化する）
☐ 人口が集中する	have a high concentration of population
☐ 都市部の人口過剰	overpopulation in urban areas
☐ インフラの発達	development of infrastructure
☐ 通勤者	commuter
☐ 自然破壊	destruction of nature
☐ 人と自然とのつながり	man's connection with nature

低出生率社会

Content Block 1 高齢者と医療費　MP3 001

A consequence of an aging population is that more people need medical care. However, countries like Japan with aging populations are not equipped to deal with an increased demand for costly healthcare. This is a huge problem because there are not enough medical staff and not enough funds to hire them.

Content Block 2 若者の負担　MP3 002

When the population of young workers is less than that of the elderly, this means the smallest group of people carries the heaviest economic responsibility. The younger working population must do all the work to support the older generation, who receive pensions and expensive medical care. The government cannot support the elderly without forcing young people to work unreasonable hours.

Content Block 3 子どもの養育費　MP3 003

Taking care of children is expensive in developed countries because parents need to pay for education, healthcare, and bigger houses. Families with fewer children spend less money. As a result, they are more capable of purchasing goods and services, which improves their quality of life.

Content Block 4 食糧問題の軽減　MP3 004

Countries with lower populations may have an advantage in the future because they will need less food. Experts predict that there will be major worldwide food shortages only a few decades from now. This is especially frightening for countries like Japan that do not produce enough food to feed their citizens. Decreased population will alleviate this problem.

訳 1 人口の高齢化の結果、医療を必要とする人が増える。しかし日本のような国民の高齢化が進む国は高額医療の需要の増加に対処する備えができていない。医療従事者の数が足りず、彼らを雇用する資金も足りないので、これは非常に大きな問題だ。

Vocabulary

□ be equipped to *do* 〜する備えができている

訳 2 若い労働者の人口が高齢者よりも少なくなると、最も数が少ない集団に属する人々が最も重い経済的責任を負うことになる。年金を受給し、高額な医療を受ける上の世代を支えるためのあらゆる仕事を、若い労働者人口が引き受けなければならない。政府は、若者に法外な長時間労働を強いることなしに高齢者を支えることができない。

Vocabulary

□ pension 年金

訳 3 子どもの面倒をみることは、先進国では高くつく。親は教育、医療、より広い住居にお金をかける必要があるからだ。子どもが少ない家庭では出費が少ない。その結果、より多くの製品やサービスを購入できるようになり、生活の質が向上する。

Vocabulary

□ be capable of *doing* 〜することができる

訳 4 人口の少ない国は必要となる食糧も少ないので将来有利になるかもしれない。専門家はほんの数十年先には深刻な食糧不足が世界的に起こると予測している。これは自給率の低い日本のような国にとっては特に脅威である。人口の減少はこの問題を軽減する。

Vocabulary

□ frightening 恐ろしい　□ alleviate 〜を緩和する

モラル

1-5 Content Block 家族関係の変化

As society changes, people are spending less time with their families. More and more young people are moving to big cities for jobs. Also, even when they are at home, they can spend all of their time looking at their smartphones. Since they talk to their older family members less often, they have fewer opportunities to learn important moral lessons.

1-6 Content Block 物質主義とモラル

Increased materialism is leading to a drop in moral values. Society is teaching people that nothing is more important than money. This results in a situation where people are willing to do horrible things just to make money. Unless society can find some way to decrease its focus on money, moral values will continue to fade away.

1-7 Content Block 公共のマナー

Changes to public manners are putting more distance between people. Not long ago, starting a conversation with a stranger in your neighborhood was a polite thing to do. In a large city, though, this behavior is not common anymore. Some people even think that this type of behavior is rude.

1-8 Content Block 宗教と倫理観

Although religion is decreasing around the world, this does not mean that moral values are disappearing. Studies have shown that non-religious people still have healthy moral beliefs. In fact, history has shown that highly religious people are the ones with questionable morals. The latest example of this is terrorism, but it is true of almost every major religion.

訳 15 社会の変化に伴って、人々が家族と過ごす時間は減っている。仕事を求めて大都市に移ってくる若者は増え続けている。また、若者たちは家にいるときも、ずっとスマートフォンを見て過ごすことができる。年上の家族と話す頻度が減り、道徳に関する重要な学びを得る機会が少なくなっている。

Vocabulary

☐ moral lesson 道徳的な教訓

訳 16 物質主義の高まりは、倫理観の低下につながっている。社会は人々に対し、お金よりも重要なものはないと教えている。このことは、お金を稼ぐためになら恐ろしいことをするのもいとわない状況をもたらす。社会が金銭を今ほど重要視しなくなるような何らかの方法を見出さない限り、倫理観はこれからも薄れていくだろう。

Vocabulary

☐ moral value 倫理観　　☐ fade away 次第に衰える

訳 17 公共のマナーの変化は、人と人との間の距離を広げている。つい最近まで、近所で知らない人と言葉を交わすことは礼儀だった。しかし、大都市では、こうした行為はもはや一般的ではなくなっている。このような行いを無礼だと考える人さえいる。

Vocabulary

☐ rude 失礼な

訳 18 世界中で宗教は衰退しているが、だからと言って倫理観が消えつつあるわけではない。研究によると、無宗教の人々でも健全な道徳的信条を持っているということが示されている。むしろ、歴史は信仰心の強い人が疑わしい倫理観を持っていることを示している。この最近の例はテロ行為だが、このことはほとんどすべての主要な宗教に当てはまる。

Vocabulary

☐ questionable 不審な、疑問に思われる

都市化

1 Content Block 利便性

9 Urbanization makes daily life more convenient. Urban areas have better public transportation, and people in urban areas have access to shops such as convenience stores, supermarkets, and restaurants. Because daily life is more convenient, people have more time to focus on important things like work and time with loved ones.

1 Content Block 経済効果

10 Urbanization improves economies. Large cities tend to attract a lot of skilled workers. With so many people in a small area, more types of businesses can be established. Also, people get exposed to more ideas and can make more useful connections. Plus, the area becomes an attractive destination for businesses visiting from abroad.

1 Content Block 都市化と環境

11 The environment has been negatively impacted by rapid urbanization. Growing numbers of urban centers and factories have polluted the air, destroyed natural ecosystems, and harmed wildlife. Furthermore, people living in urban areas have no connection with nature, so they tend to have less respect for the environment in general.

1 Content Block 伝統文化の喪失

12 Urbanization can result in the loss of traditional culture and practices. Small, family-run businesses are less common in highly populated urban areas, which leads to a decrease in traditional products. Traditional activities like festivals are also less common. Plus, traditional architecture is replaced by large buildings and skyscrapers.

訳 1-9 都市化は日常生活をより便利にする。都市部では、公共交通機関がより充実していて、都市住民はコンビニエンスストアやスーパー、レストランのような店を利用しやすい。日常生活が便利なので、人々は仕事や大切な人たちと過ごす時間など、重要なことにより多くの時間を割くことができる。

Vocabulary
☐ urbanization 都市化

訳 1-10 都市化は経済を上向かせる。大都市は多くの熟練労働者を引きつける傾向がある。狭い地域に非常に多くの人がいるので、より多くの業種の企業が設立できる。また、人々はより多くの考え方に触れ、より多くの人との有益なつながりを築くことができる。加えて、都市部は海外から来る企業にとっても魅力的な場所となる。

Vocabulary
☐ skilled worker 熟練労働者 ☐ destination 目的地

訳 1-11 急速な都市化により、環境は悪影響を受けている。都会の密集地や工場が増加の一途をたどる結果、大気を汚染し、自然の生態系を破壊し、野生生物に害を与えてきた。さらに、都市住民は自然とのつながりがないため、概して環境に対する関心が低い傾向にある。

Vocabulary
☐ negatively 否定的に、マイナスに

訳 1-12 都市化は、伝統的な文化や慣習の消滅につながる可能性がある。家族経営の小規模事業は、人口が多い都市部では少なくなってきており、伝統的な製品の減少につながっている。祭りなどの伝統的な慣習も衰退してきている。さらに、伝統的な建築物は、大きな建物や超高層ビルに取って代わられている。

Vocabulary
☐ highly populated 人口の多い ☐ skyscraper 超高層ビル

2 人権

基本的人権

人が生まれながらにして持つと考えられている社会的権利で、自由権、社会権、平等権、参政権などに分けられる。日本国憲法第11条は、これを永久・不可侵の権利であるとし、全国民に認めている。このほか、憲法では直接保障されていないものの、最近では環境権や知る権利といった「新しい人権」が主張されるようになっている。過去の問題では、刑務所やマスメディアに関するテーマのPOINTとして「**人権**」（Human rights）が挙げられている。
（→3 犯罪「刑務所」、→8 環境保護）

プライバシー

私生活をみだりに公開されない権利のこと。マスメディアによる私生活についての報道が増えたため、その侵害に対し、侵害行為の差し止めや慰謝料の請求を認めるべきだとする意見が出てきた。また社会のデジタル化に伴い、公開された自らに関する個人情報の訂正や削除を求める積極的プライバシー権についても議論されている。プライバシーの権利は、報道の自由や知る権利、さらに警察などによるアクセスと抵触するという問題をはらんでいる。
（→12 経済・ビジネス「マスメディアと広告」）

言論の自由

自由権の一種で、検閲を受けることなく自身の思想を表明する自由を指す。日本国憲法で保障される表現の自由の根幹をなすもので、世界人権宣言においても規定されている。ただし、虚偽広告やヘイトスピーチなど、言論の自由が無制限で認められるべきかについては議論がある。

女性の権利

世界的・歴史的に、女性はさまざまな場面で性別による差別を受けてきた。そして日本でも、女性は就職や結婚において差別を受けてきた。夫婦同姓も一種の女性差別と考えることができる。しかし1985年に男女雇用機会均等法（1999年には改正男女雇用機会均等法）が制定、施行され、男女の平等を理念とする社会環境は徐々に整備されつつある。

キーワード

▶プライバシー

□ 基本的人権	**basic [fundamental] human rights**
□ 人のプライバシーを侵害する	**invade [violate]** *someone's* **privacy**
□ 人命保護	**human life protection**
□ 国家権力による監視	**regulation by state powers**

▶言論の自由

□ 言論の自由	**freedom of speech**
□ (合衆国憲法)修正第1条	**the First Amendment**
□ 抗議活動の制限	**regulation of protests**
□ 政府による弾圧	**suppression by the government**
□ ヘイトスピーチ	**hate speech**
□ 検閲	**censorship**

▶女性の権利

□ 男女の平等	**gender equality**
□ ガラスの天井	**the glass ceiling**
□ 女性差別	**discrimination against women**
□ セクハラ	**sexual harassment**
□ 多様性	**diversity**
□ 役割分担	**division of roles**
□ 夫婦別姓	**dual surnames** / **two surnames**
□ (既婚女性の)旧姓	**maiden name**
□ 優秀な人材	**excellent human resources**
□ キャリアの中断	**a break in** *one's* **career**
□ 競争の激化	**intensified competition**
□ 女性管理職の割合	**ratio of female managers**

プライバシーと公衆の安全

Content Block 2-1 人命の重要性　MP3 013

Although protecting personal privacy is vital, it is not as valuable as maintaining public safety. If human lives can be saved by violating the privacy of one or more people, then it is acceptable to do so. Governments and police only access private personal information in order to protect people.

Content Block 2-2 犯罪者とプライバシー　MP3 014

Limiting the amount of private information that governments and police can access aids criminals and terrorists. For example, when prepaid cellphones were introduced, they quickly became popular among drug dealers, because they are difficult to track. If everyone has more privacy, then criminals and terrorists will have more privacy, too.

Content Block 2-3 プライバシーの重要性　MP3 015

The primary reason privacy must be respected is that humans need privacy to live happy, healthy lives. Privacy is a fundamental human right recognized in the Universal Declaration of Human Rights. When privacy rights are violated, people feel vulnerable, insecure, and afraid. Protecting the mental health of people is just as crucial as maintaining public safety.

Content Block 2-4 プライバシー保護を解除する危険性　MP3 016

Removing privacy protections does not necessarily lead to increased public safety. For example, recently many government agencies have demanded that large tech companies create methods for breaking into devices such as smartphones. Decreasing the security features of devices like this would make it easier to conduct investigations, but it would also make it easier for criminals to steal information from private citizens.

訳 2-1 個人のプライバシーを保護することは不可欠だが、公衆の安全を維持することに比べれば重要度は低い。もし、個人のプライバシーを侵すことで人命が守られるならば、そうすることは許容できる。政府と警察が個人情報にアクセスするのは、あくまで人々を保護するためなのだ。

Vocabulary
□ vital 必須の、不可欠の

訳 2-2 政府と警察がアクセスできる個人情報の量を限定すれば、犯罪者やテロリストを利することになる。例えば、プリペイド携帯電話が導入されたとき、プリペイド携帯電話は追跡が難しいため、すぐに麻薬ディーラーの間で広まった。すべての人々にもっとプライバシーが認められれば、犯罪者やテロリストにもより多くのプライバシーが認められることになる。

Vocabulary
□ aid 〜を助ける

訳 2-3 プライバシーが尊重されなければならない第一の理由は、人間が幸福で健康的な生活を送るためにはプライバシーが必要だからだ。プライバシーは、世界人権宣言で認められた基本的人権である。プライバシーが侵害されると、人は弱さと危険と恐れを感じる。人々の精神衛生を守ることは、公衆の安全を維持するのとまったく同等に重要だ。

Vocabulary
□ fundamental 根本的な、基本的な　□ vulnerable 脆弱な　□ crucial 重大な、必須の

訳 2-4 プライバシーの保護を取り払っても、必ずしも公衆の安全を高めることにはならない。例えば、最近、多くの政府機関がスマートフォンなどの機器のロックを解除する方法を開発するよう大手テクノロジー企業に要求している。このように機器のセキュリティー機能を低下させることは、捜査をしやすくするだろうが、犯罪者が市民の情報を盗むことも容易にするだろう。

Vocabulary
□ conduct 〜を行う　□ investigation 捜査

言論の自由

2-5 Content Block 言葉の暴力 　MP3 017

There should be laws against speech that directly harms other people. These laws already exist in many countries. In these places, it is illegal to falsely accuse someone of a crime or to harm their public reputation by lying. Officials have established laws like these because words can sometimes be just as harmful as violence.

2-6 Content Block 虚偽広告 　MP3 018

Lies to the public such as false advertising should be banned. For example, companies should not be allowed to lie about the benefits of their products or services. This type of speech can trick customers into purchasing things that they do not actually want, which is a type of stealing.

2-7 Content Block 言論の自由の規制の難しさ 　MP3 019

The main reason that freedom of speech should not be restricted is that people cannot agree on what type of speech is unacceptable. The large number of debates surrounding this topic is evidence of this. Even if people have strange or offensive ideas, they should be able to express them freely.

2-8 Content Block 言論の自由と思想の自由 　MP3 020

The world needs controversial—and sometimes offensive—art, ideas, and politics. For example, hundreds of famous books that are now used in literature classes were once banned by governments. The reason that governments usually restrict these books is because they want to control the ideas and principles of society in general, which is unacceptable. Freedom of speech supports freedom of thought.

訳 2 5 他者に直接的な被害を与える言論を取り締まる法律を設けるべきである。このような法律はすでに多くの国に存在している。こうした国々では、虚偽の告発をすることや、虚偽によって人の世評を傷つけることは違法とされている。当局がこのような法律を制定しているのは、言葉が暴力とまったく同じくらいの被害をもたらす場合がありうるからだ。

Vocabulary

□ falsely 不当に、偽って　□ accuse 〜を告発する、非難する

訳 2 6 虚偽広告のような一般市民への嘘は禁止されるべきだ。例えば、企業に、自社の製品やサービスの長所について嘘をつくことを許すべきではない。このような言論は、顧客をだまして本当は必要のないものを買わせる可能性があるが、これは一種の盗みである。

Vocabulary

□ trick A into *doing* Aをだまして〜させる

訳 2 7 言論の自由が規制されるべきではない主な理由は、どのような言論が受け入れられないのかについて、人々が合意を形成することはできないということだ。このテーマをめぐって議論が百出していることがその証拠だ。たとえ誰かが、奇妙で不快な考えを持っていたとしても、自由にそれを表現できるようにすべきである。

Vocabulary

□ unacceptable 受け入れられない、容認できない　□ offensive 不快な

訳 2 8 世界には異論の多い――そして時には不快な――芸術や考え、政治信条が必要だ。例えば、今日の文学の授業で使われている何百という著名な書籍は、かつては政府が発禁としていたものだ。政府がこうした本を規制する理由はたいてい、社会全体の考えや信条をコントロールしたいからであり、これは受け入れがたいことだ。言論の自由は思想の自由を支える。

Vocabulary

□ controversial 異論の多い、物議をかもす

女性の権利

日本企業の女性管理職

The number of women in executive positions at companies is embarrassingly low in Japan compared to other developed nations. According to a recent study, only about 10% of management positions at Japanese companies were held by women, and only 1% of senior, executive-level positions.

政界の女性

Japan has one of the worst levels of political gender equality among developed countries. According to one survey, the percentage of female lower house members in Japan was less than that of over 100 other countries, including both China and North Korea. Discriminatory policies are not likely to change unless women have more representation in politics.

他国との比較

Although women in Japan do not yet have as many opportunities as men, they are not victims of any human rights violations. In countries that are extremely prejudiced against women, females are treated as second-class citizens that cannot attend schools or acquire valuable skills. But in Japan women receive the same world-class education as men.

女性により公平なシステム

Japan does need to work to improve the opportunities for women in society, but this change is already taking place. Specifically, women need more chances to obtain respectable, high-paying jobs and leadership positions, especially after having children. The majority of both men and women in Japan appear to agree on this issue. Accordingly, policymakers are already working to create a fairer system for women.

訳 2-9 日本の企業では、女性の重役の数が、他の先進国に比べてあきれるほど少ない。最近の調査によると、日本企業の女性管理職の割合はわずか10％ほどで、シニアレベル、エグゼクティブレベルに至ってはわずか1％ほどに過ぎない。

Vocabulary
□ embarrassingly 当惑するほどに

訳 2-10 日本は、政治におけるジェンダーの公平性が先進国の中で最低レベルの国の一つだ。ある調査によれば、日本の衆議院議員の女性の割合は中国や北朝鮮を含む100以上の諸外国よりも低かった。差別的な政策は、政界にもっと女性が進出しない限り、変わりそうにない。

Vocabulary
□ lower house 衆議院　□ discriminatory 差別的な

訳 2-11 日本の女性はまだ男性並みには機会を持っていないが、人権侵害の犠牲者になっているわけではない。女性に対する偏見の激しい国々では、女性は学校にも通えず、有用なスキルを身につけることもできない二流の市民として扱われている。しかし日本では、女性は男性と同じ世界レベルの教育を受けている。

Vocabulary
□ prejudiced 偏見のある

訳 2-12 日本が社会における女性の機会改善のために努力しなければならないのは確かだが、こうした変化はすでに起こっている。具体的に言うと、女性は、とりわけ出産後、きちんとした高給の仕事と指導的な地位を得るためのより多くの機会が与えられるべきだ。日本の大半の男性と女性の両方がこの問題について意見が一致していると思われる。そしてそれを受けて、政策立案者たちはすでに、女性により公平なシステムを作ることに取り組んでいる。

Vocabulary
□ policymaker 政策立案者

少数者の権利

2 Content Block 在日中国人・朝鮮人への差別　MP3 025

13　In recent years, officials from the UN have repeatedly declared that racism is a serious, countrywide problem in Japan. In particular, the discrimination against Chinese and Korean residents in Japan is seen to be a major problem. Of course, not all Japanese citizens discriminate against these minorities, but the government still needs to do more to protect and support them.

2 Content Block 性的少数者への理解　MP3 026

14　In recent years, Japan has become much more supportive of members of the LGBT community. In some areas of Tokyo, same-sex partnerships are also permitted. Also, many non-Japanese gay residents in Japan say that they feel less physically threatened than in their home countries. These gradual changes show that minority groups are beginning to receive more respect and equal rights.

2 Content Block 性的少数者への無理解　MP3 027

15　Japan is a very unwelcoming place for members of the LGBT community. The vast majority of gay people are unable to reveal their sexuality to family members due to fear of rejection. Recently, some cities have started allowing same-sex partnerships, but government leaders openly looked for ways to ban them. Also, homosexual partners cannot obtain a spouse visa in Japan.

2 Content Block ヘイトスピーチ　MP3 028

16　Japan's treatment of minorities is steadily improving. For example, there are frequently complaints that right-wing groups in Japan hold racist demonstrations targeting Korean residents in the country. But the views of these small groups do not reflect the opinions of Japanese people in general. That is why the government recently passed a law banning hate speech.

訳 2 13 近年、国連の関係者は、日本で人種差別が全国的に深刻な問題になっていると繰り返し言明している。特に、日本在住の中国人と韓国人に対する差別は大きな問題であると見なされている。もちろん、日本人全員がこうしたマイノリティを差別しているわけではないが、それでも政府は、マイノリティを保護し支援する取り組みにもっと力を入れるべきだ。

Vocabulary
- racism 人種差別主義、レイシズム

訳 2 14 近年、日本はLGBTの人々に対して、以前よりもずっと協力的になってきている。東京では、同性のパートナーシップが認められている地域もある。また、日本に住む外国人の同性愛者の多くが、母国よりも身体的な脅威を感じることが少ないと話している。こうした漸進的な変化は、マイノリティの人々が尊重され、平等な権利を受けられるようになってきていることを示している。

Vocabulary
- LGBT 性的少数者(lesbian, gay, bisexual, and transgenderの略) □ threaten ～を脅かす

訳 2 15 日本はLGBTの人々にとって非常に居心地の悪い場所だ。同性愛者の大多数が、拒絶されることを恐れて家族に自分のセクシャリティを明かすことができない。最近では、同性のパートナーシップを認めるようになった都市もあるが、政府のトップは、こうしたパートナーシップを禁止する方策を公然と探っている。また、同性愛者のパートナーは日本で配偶者ビザを取得することができない。

Vocabulary
- unwelcoming 〈場所が〉居心地の悪い、魅力のない □ spouse visa 配偶者ビザ

訳 2 16 日本のマイノリティに対する扱いは、着実に改善している。例えば、日本の右翼団体が在日朝鮮人を標的にした人種差別的なデモを実施しているという苦言がよく聞かれる。しかし、こうした少数の人々の考え方は、日本人全体の意見を反映したものではない。だからこそ、政府は最近、ヘイトスピーチを禁止する法律を可決した。

Vocabulary
- right-wing 右翼の

3 | 犯罪

CHAPTER_2

犯罪

　法律によって禁じられ、刑罰を科せられるべき行為。一般的に、法律に規定がない行為（違法性のない行為）は犯罪とは見なされない。犯行主体から見た場合、少年犯罪、外国人犯罪、組織犯罪などに分類され、手段や背景で見た場合は、都市型犯罪、サイバー犯罪、企業犯罪、国際犯罪などに分類される。

　犯罪に関しては、過去の問題では、凶悪犯罪に対する社会の対応や未成年犯罪に対する刑罰、刑務所の持つ意味などのテーマが出題されている。

少年法

　1949年に施行された20歳未満の未成年者が犯した罪を審判する法律。その根底には、少年は人格的に発展途上であり、その未熟性、柔軟性ゆえに、適切な教育、処遇によって更生することができるという考えがある。しかし、少年犯罪の凶悪化により、2000年に刑事罰の対象年齢が16歳から14歳に引き下げられるなど、厳格化する方向にある。
（→9 教育・文化・スポーツ）

刑務所

　法に違反し、裁判において懲役（強制労働に服させる刑）や禁錮（身体的自由を制限する刑）などの刑を言い渡された者を拘禁し刑を執行する刑事施設。更生、社会復帰を目的とした施設であるという考えがある一方で、人権侵害の観点から廃止すべきだという意見もある。
（→2 人権「基本的人権」）

著作権と違法ダウンロード

　著作権とは、文芸、学術、音楽、美術、写真、コンピュータープログラムなどの著作物の作者や管理者が持つ権利であり、それを保護するための法律が著作権法。ネットワーク化やコンテンツのデジタル化により、著作物が違法に大量複写、配信されるようになったため、2010年に著作権法が改正され、違法なインターネット配信による音楽・映像を違法と知りながらダウンロード（複製）することは著作権法違反と規定された。

🔍 キーワード

●犯罪

□	刑事事件	criminal case
□	少年犯罪	juvenile crime
□	凶悪犯罪の増加	increase of atrocious crimes
□	反社会的行動	anti-social behavior
□	犯罪組織	criminal organization
□	犯罪率の低下	decrease in crime rates
□	捜査	investigation（< investigate ～を捜査する）
□	有力な証拠	compelling evidence
□	疑わしきは罰せず	innocent until proven guilty
□	判断能力	judgment ability
□	犯罪被害者	crime victim / victim of a crime
□	被害者感情	emotion of victims

●刑務所

□	更正の可能性	possibility of correction
□	社会復帰	social rehabilitation
□	犯罪抑止	crime prevention
□	重罰の効果	effect of heavy punishment
□	再犯者	repeat offender
□	再犯率	rate of repeated crime
□	囚人の増加	increase of prison population
□	囚人間の暴力	violence among prisoners
□	仮釈放	parole
□	脱獄	prison break

●違法ダウンロード

□	著作権の侵害	copyright infringement
□	動画共有サイト	torrent site
□	違法なファイル共有	illegal file sharing
□	著作権法	copyright law
□	海賊行為をする	pirate
□	いたちごっこ	cat and mouse game

犯罪

Content Block 凶悪犯罪とメディア

1 In order to prevent violent crime, society needs to restrict access to violent media. For years, psychologists have been researching the connection between violence and the media. Children are particularly vulnerable to influence. Accordingly, children who spend many hours watching violent television tend to be more aggressive in their teenage years.

Content Block 犯罪と貧困

2 We should focus on increasing income for people without money, not reducing crime. Traditionally, society tries to prevent crime by punishing people and sending them to prison. But this does not solve the problem, as many people return to crime after prison. Instead, we should attempt to provide more income opportunities for poor households.

Content Block 武器と犯罪

3 Society has dealt with the problem of violent crime by banning weapons. In Japan, it is more difficult to purchase a gun than in other developed countries. Japan banned the ownership of firearms and swords in 1958. Removing these weapons from society is one reason that Japan has the second lowest murder rate in the world.

Content Block 監視カメラによる抑止

4 In order to deter violence, more surveillance cameras should be installed. Studies suggest that crime decreases in areas that have prominently displayed surveillance cameras. While some may argue that this violence is then displaced to areas with less supervision, video evidence is a powerful way to discourage violence and other criminal acts.

訳 3-1 凶悪犯罪を防ぐために、社会は暴力的なメディアへのアクセスを制限する必要がある。何年にもわたり、心理学者たちは暴力とメディアの関連を調査している。子どもは特に影響を受けやすい。したがって、暴力的なテレビ番組を長い時間見て過ごす子どもは、10代になると攻撃的になる傾向がある。

Vocabulary
☐ restrict 〜を制限する　☐ vulnerable（攻撃などを）受けやすい

訳 3-2 私たちは、犯罪を減らすことにではなく、お金のない人々の収入を増やすことに注意を向けるべきだ。社会は従来、人を処罰し、刑務所に送ることで犯罪を防ごうとする。しかしこれでは問題の解決にならず、多くの人が出所後に再び罪を犯す。むしろ、私たちは貧しい家庭の人々により多くの収入の機会を提供するよう努力するべきだ。

Vocabulary
☐ punish 〜を罰する　☐ household 家庭、世帯

訳 3-3 社会は武器を禁止することで凶悪犯罪の問題に対処してきた。日本はほかの先進国よりも銃を購入するのが難しい。日本は1958年に銃器や刀剣の所有を禁止した。これらの武器を社会から排除していることは、日本の殺人率が世界でも二番目に低い理由の一つだ。

Vocabulary
☐ firearm 銃器　☐ sword 刀剣

訳 3-4 暴力を抑止するために、もっと多くの監視カメラを設置するべきだ。研究によれば、目につくところに監視カメラが設置された区域では犯罪は減少する。この暴力はより監視の少ない区域に移るだけだという人もいるかもしれないが、ビデオの証拠は暴力やその他の犯罪行為を阻止する強力な手段だ。

Vocabulary
☐ surveillance camera 監視カメラ　☐ prominently 目立って　☐ displace 〜を移す、ずらす
☐ supervision 監視、管理

3 | Content Block 監視カメラの問題　MP3 033

5 Some people argue that police should use more surveillance cameras to stop crime, but this invades the privacy of good citizens. Also, there is not substantial evidence that surveillance cameras reduce crime. Money and resources should not be invested in any crime prevention techniques unless they are proven to be effective.

未成年者の罰則

3 | Content Block 犯罪者の意図と刑罰　MP3 034

6 When deciding punishments for crimes, criminals' intentions are important. For example, according to the law, people rarely receive life imprisonment for accidentally killing another person. But when a crime is intentional, then life imprisonment is sometimes justified. Likewise, heavy penalties should be imposed on minors if they understood the results of their actions.

3 | Content Block 未成年者と成人の線引き　MP3 035

7 The details of some crimes show that minors can be capable of making adult decisions. Countries have specific age numbers to divide children from adults, but in reality these numbers should vary for each person. Some children develop more quickly than others. This means that sometimes a 16-year-old "child" has the mental capacity of a 20-year-old "adult."

3 | Content Block 発達途上の脳　MP3 036

8 Young people's brains have not finished developing. Research has shown that the decision-making part of the brain continues to develop until an individual's mid-20's. So young people's brains are not as quick at making good decisions. This must be taken into account when considering punishments for minors.

訳 3-5 犯罪を防ぐために警察はもっと監視カメラを使うべきだと主張する人もいるが、これは善良な市民のプライバシーを侵害する。また、監視カメラが犯罪を減少させるという十分な証拠もない。効果があると証明されない限り、資金とリソースは犯罪防止のためのどのような技術にも投入するべきではない。

Vocabulary

☐ substantial かなりの、十分な

訳 3-6 犯罪に対して刑罰を決める際には、犯罪者の意図が重要だ。例えば、法によれば、人は故意ではなく他人を殺してしまった場合、終身刑を受けることはまれだ。しかし、犯罪が意図されたものである場合は、終身刑が正当とされることがある。同じように、自分の行為の結果が理解できている場合には、未成年者にも重罰を科すべきだ。

Vocabulary

☐ intentional 意図的な、故意の　☐ heavy penalty 重罰　☐ minor 未成年者

訳 3-7 いくつかの犯罪を詳細に見ると、未成年者が成人と同じ判断力を備えている例もあることがわかる。各国は未成年と成人を区分する具体的な年齢を定めているが、現実にはこの年齢は人によって異なるはずだ。ほかの人々よりも発達が早い子どももいる。これはつまり、16歳の「子ども」が20歳の「大人」の思考力を持つこともあるということだ。

Vocabulary

☐ specific 特定の、具体的な

訳 3-8 若い人々の脳は発達を終えていない。意思決定に関わる脳の部位は20代半ばまで発達し続けることが、調査で示されている。つまり、若者の脳は、（大人ほど）素早く適切な判断を下すことができない。このことは、未成年者の刑罰を考える際に考慮されなければならない。

Vocabulary

☐ decision making 意思決定

3 Content Block 更生の可能性 〔MP3 037〕

9 There is a high chance that minors who commit crimes can be rehabilitated. Young people's behavior can change drastically if they receive proper guidance. Rather than spending millions of dollars keeping minors in prisons, governments should invest in better support and education systems for these young people.

刑務所

3 Content Block 刑務所の目的 〔MP3 038〕

10 Reforming criminal behavior is one of the main goals of prisons. While there are many ways prisons can do better at rehabilitating criminals, that does not mean that prisons are completely ineffective. Society should focus on improving the current prison system. Creating a new system to replace prisons would be too costly and possibly ineffective.

3 Content Block 刑務所の意味 〔MP3 039〕

11 Prisons are a good way to stop crimes from happening. For example, when somebody thinks about the bad living conditions in prisons, they will often refrain from committing a crime. Nobody wants to lose their freedom, so the threat of prison is a powerful way to prevent illegal activities.

3 Content Block 犯罪を減らすには 〔MP3 040〕

12 Some argue that removing criminals from society is good for public safety. However, punishing criminals does not reduce crime. To reduce crime, we should help former criminals to become good members of society. This can be done by helping them to obtain useful skills, find jobs, and pursue opportunities that do not involve crime.

訳 3-9 罪を犯した未成年者が更生できる可能性は高い。若者の行動は、適切な指導を受ければ大幅に変わりうる。未成年者を刑務所に入れておくのに何百万ドルも費やすより、政府は、こうした若者をより手厚くサポートし、教育する制度にお金を使うべきだ。

Vocabulary

□ rehabilitate 〜を更生させる、社会復帰させる

訳 3-10 犯罪行動を矯正することは、刑務所の主要な目的の一つだ。刑務所が犯罪者を更生させるよりよい方法はたくさんあるが、だからと言って刑務所の効果がまったくないというわけではない。社会は現在の刑務所制度を改善することに重点を置くべきだ。刑務所に代わる新しい制度を作っても、費用がかかりすぎて効果がない可能性がある。

Vocabulary

□ reform 〜を矯正する、改心させる

訳 3-11 刑務所は犯罪が起こらないようにするためのよい手段だ。例えば、刑務所での劣悪な生活環境を考えれば、犯罪を起こすのを踏みとどまることが多いだろう。自由を失いたい人はいないので、刑務所という脅威は違法行為を防止する強力な手段である。

Vocabulary

□ refrain from 〜 〜を差し控える　□ threat 脅威、脅し

訳 3-12 犯罪者を社会から排除することは、公共の安全のためによいことだと主張する人もいる。しかし、犯罪者を罰しても犯罪は減少しない。犯罪を減らすには、私たちは犯罪経験者が社会の善良な一員になれるよう手助けするべきだ。これは、役に立つ技能を身につけ、仕事を見つけ、犯罪と関わりのない仕事を続けられるよう支援することによって達成できる。

Vocabulary

□ former かつての　□ involve 〜に関わる

違法ダウンロード

3 | Content Block | 無許可ダウンロードの犯罪性   MP3 041

13　People need to realize that downloading copyrighted music and movies without purchasing them is a crime. Stealing digital products online is the same as stealing physical products from a store. Society will fall apart if people are allowed to break the law. So it makes sense to punish people for stealing this type of content.

3 | Content Block | 音楽業界と映画業界のダメージ   MP3 042

14　Illegal downloading is a threat to the music and film industries. For example, in the last twenty years the number of singles purchased in the U.K. has decreased significantly. This is partly due to illegal downloading. This crime causes damage to artists and companies working hard to produce entertainment products.

3 | Content Block | 処罰の非現実性   MP3 043

15　It is not possible to punish everyone that downloads music and movies illegally. Millions of people in hundreds of countries download music and movies without permission. The costs of capturing and fining all of them would be astronomical. Also, it is unfair to only fine or imprison a small percentage of these people.

3 | Content Block | 違法ダウンロードの有害性に対する疑問   MP3 044

16　There is not enough evidence to prove that pirating is harmful. A recent study in Europe has shown that pirating actually has very little influence on legal music downloads. According to this study, the majority of people who listen to illegal downloads would not have purchased the music even if they could not obtain it illegally. Plus, illegal downloads increase the popularity of music, which leads to higher revenue.

訳 3 13　著作権のある音楽や映画を購入することなくダウンロードすることは犯罪であるということを、人々は認識する必要がある。電子版の製品をオンラインで盗むことは、物的な製品を店舗で盗むのと同じだ。人々が法律を破ることを許されれば、社会は崩壊するだろう。ゆえに、この種のコンテンツを盗む人を罰することには意味がある。

Vocabulary

□ fall apart バラバラになる、崩壊する

訳 3 14　違法ダウンロードは音楽業界と映画業界への脅威だ。例えば、イギリスでは過去20年間で、購入されるシングルCDの枚数が著しく減っている。これは違法ダウンロードに一因がある。この犯罪は、エンターテイメント製品を作るために懸命に努力しているアーティストや企業にダメージを与えている。

Vocabulary

□ illegal downloading 違法ダウンロード

訳 3 15　音楽や映画を違法にダウンロードするすべての人を罰することは不可能だ。何百という国の何百万人もの人々が、許可なく音楽や映画をダウンロードしている。そのような人々全員を捕まえて罰金を支払わせるコストは、天文学的な数字になるだろう。また、このうちのごくわずかな割合の人々にだけ罰金を科したり投獄したりするのは不公平だ。

Vocabulary

□ capture 〜を捕まえる　□ fine 〜に罰金を科す　□ astronomical 天文学的な、けた外れに多い
□ imprison 〜を投獄する

訳 3 16　違法コピーが有害だということを証明する十分な証拠がない。ヨーロッパで実施された最近の研究で、違法コピーは実は、合法的な音楽ダウンロードにほとんど影響を与えていないことが示されている。この研究によると、違法ダウンロードされた音楽を聞いている人々の大多数は、仮にそれらを違法に入手できなかったとしてもその音楽を買ってはいなかったという。加えて、違法ダウンロードは音楽の人気を高めており、収益を上げることにつながっている。

Vocabulary

□ pirate 海賊行為をする、著作権を侵害する

4 | 世界の問題

CHAPTER_2

世界の貧困

貧困とは、栄養、保健、医療、教育などが不足、欠乏した状態。1日あたりの購買力が1.25ドル以下の貧困層は世界で10億人に上る。地域紛争、自然破壊、教育の欠如、感染症のまん延、モノカルチャー経済、人種差別など、原因は多岐にわたる。またグローバリゼーションは、富裕国と貧困国の格差を増大させている。貧困はテロの要因の一つともいわれる。

過去の問題では、世界の貧困の撲滅がテーマとして出題されている。
(→5 戦争・核兵器・テロリズム、→9 教育・文化・スポーツ)

世界の飢餓

飢餓とは、身体を成長・維持させるのに必要な水や栄養が欠乏し、体調維持が困難な状態をいう。世界的な飢餓や食糧不足の問題に取り組む国連機関、国連世界食糧計画（略称WFP（World Food Programme））の発表によれば、2015年時点で、世界で飢餓の状態にある人々は約8億人近くおり、これは世界の9人に1人にあたる（ただし、この25年間で飢餓人口は2億人以上減少している）。一方で、世界の食糧の総生産は100億人を養うことができるという試算があり、真の問題は食糧不足ではなく、食糧が行き渡ることを阻む諸問題であるといわれる。これには流通の問題や紛争などが含まれる。また、世界の食糧総生産重量の約3分の1が廃棄されていると言われている。

過去の問題では、世界の飢餓や世界の食糧供給のテーマも出題されている。
(→5 戦争・核兵器・テロリズム、→6 世界経済)

水問題

日本は水資源が豊富なためにあまり意識に上らないかもしれないが、世界的に見ると水資源の問題も深刻なテーマである。2015年時点において、世界で6億人以上の人が適切な飲用水を確保できていないと言われる。また河川や地下水から過剰な量の水を汲み上げたために水資源の枯渇を招き、農業の維持も危機的な状況にある場所がある。過去の問題でも、2012年に水需要に関するテーマが出題されている。
(→8 環境保護)

🔍 キーワード

●世界の貧困

□ 発展途上国	developing country
□ 急激な人口増加	rapid population growth
□ 人口のコントロール	population control
□ 避妊具の不足	lack of contraceptives
□ 経済格差	economic disparity
□ 感染症のまん延	spread of infections
□ 貧困対策	fight against poverty
□ 極度の貧困を根絶する	eradicate extreme poverty
□ フェアトレード	fair trade
□ 農業技術	farming [agricultural] technique
□ 技術革新	innovation
□ 教育機会	opportunities for education
□ 遺伝子組み換え技術	genetic modification technology
□ 環境破壊	environmental destruction

●世界の飢餓・水問題

□ 食糧不足	food shortage
□ 食糧不安、食糧不足	food insecurity
□ 食糧供給	food supply
□ 飢饉	famine
□ 日照り、干ばつ	drought
□ 栄養失調	malnourishment / malnutrition
□ 子どもの発育不全	stunted growth of children
□ 食糧安全保障	food security
□ 食糧自給率を改善する	improve food self-sufficiency (rate)
□ 食糧廃棄	food waste [loss]
□ 水資源の枯渇	depletion of water supply
□ ハイテクの灌漑システム	high-tech irrigation system
□ 脱塩施設	desalination plant

| 社会的不平等

Content Block 4-1 人口増加と不平等の拡大　MP3 045

The human population will continue to expand in the future, causing the depletion of resources. The world population is expected to be around 10 billion by 2050. Experts predict that there will also be major food shortages around this time. These problems are likely to get worse, worsening equality.

Content Block 4-2 貧困の是正と不平等　MP3 046

Fixing poverty does not fix inequality. Thanks to technological developments, it is theoretically possible that poverty can be eliminated eventually. However, this does not mean that inequality will disappear. The world will always have extremely rich people with much more money than the average person. In fact, wealth inequality is at record highs in countries like the U.S.

Content Block 4-3 テクノロジーによる不平等の解決　MP3 047

Developments in technology will lead to less work for all people. For example, experts estimate that in the near future, robots will be able to perform nearly half of all jobs. This low-cost productivity will boost the economy, and the extra money can be spent to improve the lives of the poor. As a result, inequality will decrease.

Content Block 4-4 教育と不平等　MP3 048

Education will become accessible to everyone. The main reason that poor people stay in poverty is that they do not know how to improve their lives. They have never received professional training related to saving and investing money, acquiring valuable skills, and so on. Eventually, all of this information will be available for free on the Internet.

訳 4-1 将来人口は増加を続け、資源の枯渇を引き起こす。世界の人口は2050年までに約100億人になると予想されている。このころには大規模な食糧不足も起こると専門家たちは予測している。こうした問題はさらに悪化する見込みで、その結果、不平等は拡大する。

Vocabulary
□ depletion〈資源などの〉枯渇　□ worsen 〜を悪化させる

訳 4-2 貧困の是正は不平等の是正にはならない。技術の発達のおかげで、理論的には、いずれは貧困を根絶することが可能とされる。しかし、これは不平等がなくなることを意味するわけではない。世界には、平均的な人よりもはるかに多くのお金を持つ極端に裕福な人々が今後も常にいるだろう。実際、アメリカなどでは富の不平等は記録的なものになっている。

Vocabulary
□ wealth inequality 富の不平等

訳 4-3 技術の発展は、すべての人にとって労働を減らすことにつながる。例えば、専門家たちは近い将来、ロボットがすべての仕事のうちの半分近くを行えるようになるだろうと推定している。このコストの低い生産力は、経済を上向かせ、余剰の資金は貧しい人々の生活を改善するのに使うことができる。その結果、不平等は縮小するだろう。

Vocabulary
□ boost〈景気など〉を回復させる

訳 4-4 誰もが教育を受けられるようになるだろう。貧しい人々が貧困状態から抜け出せない主な理由は、どうすれば生活を改善できるのかを知らないことだ。貧しい人たちは貯蓄や投資、役に立つスキルの獲得などに関する専門的な訓練を受けたことがない。いずれは、こうした情報のすべてがインターネットで無料で得られるようになるだろう。

Vocabulary
□ related to 〜 〜に関して

貧困・飢餓

4 Content Block　世界の飢餓の真の原因　MP3 049

5　The real cause of world hunger is not scarcity of food, as research has shown that humans already produce enough food to feed 10 billion people. Rather, the problem is making this food available and affordable to those living in poverty. Since there is already sufficient food, world hunger should decrease as transportation and production costs go down.

4 Content Block　技術による生産・輸送コストの削減　MP3 050

6　One key to combating world hunger is lowering production and transportation costs. Technology is improving the likelihood of this. The development of automated farming tools has the potential to save billions of dollars annually, and this technology is improving rapidly. With more efficient transportation also emerging, it will not be long before cheap food can reach the world's poor individuals.

4 Content Block　世界の人口増加　MP3 051

7　The human population is currently growing at an alarming and unsustainable rate. Experts estimate that the ideal population for humans on earth is under 2 billion people, but there are already over 7 billion people on the planet, and that number is likely to reach about 10 billion by 2050. Our planet cannot sustain such a great number of people.

4 Content Block　資源の枯渇　MP3 052

8　As the world's population grows, the earth's resources are also disappearing. According to scientific calculations, humans are already using more resources than the earth can continue to produce. With our current consumption patterns, we are likely to deplete the world's supply of fossil fuels, wildlife areas, and, in turn, food supply.

訳 4-5　世界の飢餓の真の原因は食糧不足ではない。研究では、人類はすでに100億人を養うのに十分な食糧を生産していることが示されている。むしろ問題は、その食糧を貧しい暮らしをしている人々のもとに行き渡らせ、無理なく買える価格にすることである。すでに十分な食糧があるのだから、輸送コストと生産コストが減少するにつれて、世界の飢餓は軽減されるはずだ。

Vocabulary

□ scarcity 不足、欠乏

訳 4-6　世界の飢餓と闘ううえで鍵となる点の一つは、生産コストと輸送コストを下げることだ。技術によりその可能性は高まっている。自動化された農器具の開発により、年間何十億ドルというコストを節減できると見込まれており、この技術は急速に進歩している。より効率的な輸送方法も現れつつあり、世界の貧しい人々が安価な食糧を手にするようになるのに、そう長くはかからないだろう。

Vocabulary

□ likelihood 可能性

訳 4-7　人口は現在、驚異的かつ持続不可能なペースで増加している。専門家は、地球の理想的な人口は20億人以下だと推定しているが、すでに地球上には70億人以上の人々がおり、その数は2050年までに100億人近くに達すると見込まれる。地球はこれほど多くの人々を支えることはできない。

Vocabulary

□ unsustainable 持続不可能な

訳 4-8　世界の人口が増加するにつれて、地球上の資源もまた消えつつある。科学的な試算によると、人類はすでに地球が継続して生産できる量を上回る資源を使っているという。私たちの現在の消費パターンでは、世界の化石燃料供給量を使い尽くし、野生生物の生息域を激減させ、その結果、食糧供給を枯渇させるだろう。

Vocabulary

□ deplete ～を使い果たす

Content Block　テクノロジーの発達

9 Technology will be a major reason for the elimination of poverty. In particular, developments in robotics and agricultural technology will lead to a world where we have more food, but people need to work less. In other words, we will have the technology to provide food and shelter for the world's poorest people.

Content Block　人口増加

10 Poverty cannot be eliminated because there will be too many people in the future. It is expected that there will be around 10 billion people by 2050. Meanwhile, the world's supply of fossil fuels, rainforests, and other natural resources is decreasing. This scarcity will lead to increased inequality.

Content Block　教育と認知

11 Quality of life and education are improving constantly. Not only are people becoming more educated, but more people are also becoming aware of those in poverty all over the world. As awareness and education increase, more fortunate people will use their knowledge and skills to improve the lives of those who are less fortunate.

Content Block　グローバリゼーションと他者への関心

12 Globalization will inevitably lead to decreases in poverty. As globalization increases, the world becomes more connected. As a result, wealthy people become more aware of the poor conditions that many people are living in, and they are more likely to help. Poverty will become a problem that is impossible to ignore.

訳 4-9 技術は、貧困の根絶の主たる要因となるだろう。特にロボット工学と農業技術の発達は、今より多くの食糧がありながら、人々が今よりも働かなくて済む世界をもたらすだろう。言い換えれば、技術を利用して、世界の最貧層の人々に食糧と住居を提供できるようになるだろう。

Vocabulary

□ robotics ロボット工学　□ shelter 住居、住まい

訳 4-10 将来人口が過剰になるため、貧困は根絶できない。2050年までに人口は約100億人になるだろうと予想される。一方、世界の化石燃料、熱帯雨林、その他の天然資源の供給量は減っている。資源の不足はますます不平等を拡大することになるだろう。

Vocabulary

□ scarcity 不足、欠乏

訳 4-11 生活の質と教育は継続的に向上している。人々の教育が進んでいるだけではなく、世界中の貧困状態にある人々のことを意識する人が増えている。関心が高まり、教育が広がれば、より多くの恵まれた人々が、恵まれない人々の生活を改善するために知識や技術を活用するようになるだろう。

Vocabulary

□ awareness 意識、認知

訳 4-12 グローバリゼーションは必然的に貧困を減らすことになる。グローバリゼーションが進むにつれて、世界はいっそう密接なつながりを持つようになる。その結果、裕福な人々が、多くの人々が置かれている貧困状態に今よりも関心を持つようになり、支援を行う可能性が高まる。貧困は看過できない問題になるだろう。

Vocabulary

□ inevitably 不可避的に、必然的に

4 Content Block　グローバリゼーションと市場競争　MP3 057

13 Globalization will not solve poverty. As the world becomes more connected, all markets become more competitive. People with less access to education will be forced to compete with large companies and skilled businesspeople in more developed countries. In turn, a large number of people will be unable to escape poverty.

4 Content Block　政治腐敗　MP3 058

14 As long as political corruption exists, world poverty cannot be eliminated. Sadly, though, it is unlikely that the world will ever be free of political corruption. Humans are greedy by nature, and politicians have too many opportunities to misuse their power. This leads to a world where the poor get left behind.

4 Content Block　自立支援　MP3 059

15 To improve living conditions in developing countries, individuals must have opportunities to advance their own economic position. For example, giving farmers access to biotechnology is more beneficial than providing financial aid because they can use this new information to sell their own crops and stimulate the local economy. Simply providing more funding or "support" is meaningless.

水需要

4 Content Block　農業における水利用　MP3 060

16 Better technology and education are helping farmers to conserve more water. This is important because a significant percentage of the world's water is used for agriculture. Historically, a lot of this water has been wasted. Nowadays, though, farmers are using various techniques to conserve water, such as drip irrigation and organic farming.

訳 4 13 グローバリゼーションは貧困を解消しない。世界がいっそう密接につながるにつれて、あらゆる市場で競争が激化する。教育をあまり受けられない人々は、自国よりも発展した国々の大企業や能力のあるビジネスパーソンと競争することを余儀なくされる。それによって、今度は、非常に多くの人々が貧困から抜け出せなくなる。

Vocabulary

□ competitive 競争的な

訳 4 14 政治腐敗が存在する限り、世界の貧困は根絶できない。しかし悲しいことに、政治腐敗が世界からなくなることはなさそうだ。人間は生来、貪欲であり、政治家には権力を濫用する機会があまりに多い。このことは、貧しい人々が置き去りにされる世界につながっている。

Vocabulary

□ be free of ～ ～がない　□ greedy 貪欲な、欲深い　□ misuse ～を悪用する、濫用する

訳 4 15 発展途上国の生活状況を改善するために、各人には自分の経済状態を向上させる機会がなければならない。例えば、農業従事者がバイオテクノロジーを利用できるようにすることは、金銭的な支援をするよりも役に立つ。彼らはこれらの新しい情報を、自分の作物を販売し、地域経済を刺激するために活用することができるからだ。与える資金や「支援」を増やすだけでは意味がない。

Vocabulary

□ stimulate ～を刺激する

訳 4 16 技術と教育の向上により、農業従事者はより多くの水を節約するようになっている。世界の水のかなりの割合が農業に使われていることを考えれば、これは重要なことだ。歴史的に、この水の多くが無駄にされてきた。しかし最近では、農業従事者は節水のために、細流灌漑や有機農法など、さまざまな技術を活用している。

Vocabulary

□ drip irrigation 細流灌漑

Content Block 4 — 気候変動と水

17 Climate change will give rise to severe water shortages. Although global warming is linked to heavier rainfall, it does not result in more drinking water. Instead, it causes things like floods, which make water flush into the seas more quickly. Also, climate change will lead to serious droughts in some areas.

Content Block 4 — 個人の水消費

18 One of the keys to meeting global water demand in the future will be educating people about water conservation. Once people realize that water is a scarce resource—and as it becomes more expensive—they will become more careful about how they use it. For example, this happened recently in California, where residents decreased their water use by about 30%.

Content Block 4 — 水のインフラ整備

19 With regards to water, distribution is a bigger problem than supply. Storage and transport of water need to improve. Fortunately, economic development should solve this problem naturally. People will continue to demand cheap access to drinkable water. This means governments and companies will be motivated to improve infrastructure.

Content Block 4 — 脱塩

20 The world has plenty of water. The only problem is that most of it is not drinkable. Approximately 98% of the Earth's water is salty. As technology improves—for example, with the development of desalination facilities—we will be able to use more of this water for humans. This means that we will have plenty of water for the foreseeable future.

訳 4-17　気候変動は深刻な水不足をもたらすだろう。地球温暖化は降雨量の増大につながるが、飲み水が増えることにはならない。代わりに、洪水など、水がすぐに海に流れ込んでしまう事態をもたらす。また、気候変動が深刻な干ばつをもたらす地域もある。

Vocabulary
□ flush 〈水が〉どっと流れる　□ drought 干ばつ

訳 4-18　将来の世界の水需要を満たす鍵の一つは、人々に水の保全について学んでもらうことだ。水が乏しい資源であることに気づけば——そして水がより高価なものになるにつれて——人々は水の使いかたにもっと気をつけるようになるだろう。最近のカリフォルニアの例では、住民は水の使用を約30％削減している。

Vocabulary
□ conservation 保全、保護　□ scarce 乏しい

訳 4-19　水に関しては、供給よりも配水のほうが大きな問題だ。水の貯留と輸送を改善する必要がある。幸い、経済発展によってこの問題はおのずと解決しそうだ。人々は飲料水が安価に入手できることを絶えず求めるだろう。これは、政府と企業がインフラを改善する契機になるということを意味する。

Vocabulary
□ with regard to 〜　〜に関して　□ storage 貯蔵　□ drinkable 飲むのに適した

訳 4-20　世界には大量の水がある。唯一の問題は、そのほとんどが飲用できないということだ。地球の水の約98％が塩水である。技術が向上するにつれ——例えば、脱塩施設の開発などによって——もっと多くの海水を人間が使えるようになるだろう。これはつまり、近い将来、私たちが利用できる水が豊富になるということだ。

Vocabulary
□ desalination 脱塩　□ foreseeable 予測できる

5 戦争・核兵器・テロリズム

CHAPTER_2

戦争と紛争

戦争とは、国家間の対立によって生じる軍事力を使った戦闘行為をいい、紛争はより広く、対立する者同士が争うことを指す。したがって、戦争も紛争の一種だが、普通は比較的小規模な武力衝突を紛争と呼ぶ。戦争や紛争のない状態が平和である。

過去には、平和が実現可能な目標であるかを問う問題が出題されているが、それは裏返せば、戦争をなくすことができるかというテーマだと考えることができる。

核兵器

戦争で使われる兵器のうち、核エネルギーを利用した兵器を核兵器と呼ぶ。核分裂を利用するのが原子爆弾で、核融合を利用するのが水素爆弾。核戦争が起きれば人類は滅亡の危機に陥るため、その拡散を防ぐための国際条約である核拡散防止条約（あるいは核不拡散条約）が1968年に成立した。軍拡競争のピークだった1980年代以降、核軍縮が進んでいるが、それでも世界にある核兵器の数はまだ約10,000を数え、その9割以上を米ロ2か国が保有している。「核なき世界」の実現への道のりは遠い。

過去の問題では、日本の世界における役割に関するテーマで「核軍縮」がPOINTとして挙げられたことがある。

テロリズム

テロリズムとは、政治目的のために、一般市民に恐怖心を呼び起こす、無差別の暴力などの行為。交通機関への攻撃、無差別殺傷、実行犯が自爆する自爆テロ、核兵器または核物質を使用する核テロリズム、病原菌を使うバイオテロ、コンピューターネットワークを攻撃するサイバーテロなどに分類される。背景には貧困や医療整備の不備などがあり、戦闘行為でテロを撲滅することは困難だと認識されつつある。

過去の問題では、国際テロ撲滅が可能かどうかを問うテーマが出題されている。また世界における日本の役割に関するテーマで「テロリズム」がPOINTとして挙げられたこともある。

（→4 世界の問題）

🔍 キーワード

● 戦争と紛争

□	全面戦争	**all-out war**
□	大量破壊兵器	**weapons of mass destruction**（略：**WMD**）
□	核兵器	**nuclear weapon**
□	生物兵器	**biological weapon**
□	化学兵器	**chemical weapon**
□	ミサイル防衛	**missile defense**
□	先制攻撃	**preemptive strike**
□	宗教対立	**religious conflict**
□	報復の連鎖	**a vicious cycle of violence [revenge]**
□	空爆	**air bombing**
□	誤爆	**accidental bombing**
□	サイバー戦争	**cyber war(fare)**

● 核兵器

□	水爆	**hydrogen bomb**
□	核の拡散	**proliferation of nuclear weapons**
□	抑止力	**deterrent**
□	核なき世界	**a world without nuclear weapons**
□	核拡散防止条約	**Treaty on the Non-Proliferation of Nuclear Weapons**
□	相互確証破壊	**mutual assured destruction**
□	秘密裏の開発	**secret development**
□	制御不能で	**out of control**
□	技術の発展	**development of technology**

● テロリズム

□	テロ網	**terror networks**
□	テロや戦争の増加	**increase of terrorism or war**
□	テロ抑止	**prevention of terrorism**
□	テロ支援国家	**state sponsor of terrorism**
□	テロとの闘い	**War Against Terrorism** / **War on Terror**

国際テロ

5-1 「対テロ戦争」の矛盾　MP3 065

International terrorism cannot be destroyed, because governments and the media unintentionally give power to terrorists. The goal of a terrorist is to cause widespread fear in a population. This cannot be done through terrorist attacks alone. Terrorists need governments and the media to publicize the attacks. From this perspective, the "War Against Terrorism" is terrorism's greatest supporter.

5-2 グローバリゼーションの影響　MP3 066

Globalization will continue to make terrorism one of the most effective forms of warfare. Thanks to advances in technology, people around the world can share news and information in seconds. This means that a small terrorist attack can instantly be shared with millions—even billions—of people. As globalization continues, it will become even easier for terrorists to get media coverage.

5-3 テロ行為阻止の技術　MP3 067

One reason that terrorism is likely to disappear is that governments are becoming highly skilled at stopping terrorism. In recent years, governments have been able to prevent dozens of terrorist attacks. As government technology advances, it will become increasingly difficult for terrorists to organize attacks without being noticed.

5-4 生活の質の向上　MP3 068

Improved international equality will lead to the disappearance of terrorism. Better living conditions and political policies are resulting in less discrimination and more opportunities for minority groups. If more people feel that they are being treated fairly, then fewer of them will become terrorists.

訳 5-1　国際テロは撲滅できない。政府とメディアが意図せずしてテロリストに力を与えているからだ。テロリストの目的は、人々に広く恐怖を与えることだ。このことはテロ攻撃だけでは不可能だ。テロリストは、政府とメディアを使って、その攻撃を公に知らしめる必要がある。この観点からすると「対テロ戦争」はテロ行為を助長する最大の原因である。

Vocabulary

☐ unintentionally 意図せずに　☐ publicize 〜を公にする、公表する

訳 5-2　グローバリゼーションにより、テロ行為は最も有効な戦争行為の一形態であり続けるだろう。技術の発達のおかげで、世界中の人々は、ニュースや情報を瞬時に共有できる。これはつまり、小さなテロ攻撃を一瞬にして何百万人——何十億人さえ——もが知るということだ。グローバリゼーションが進むにつれ、テロリストはますますメディアで取り上げられやすくなっていくだろう。

Vocabulary

☐ warfare 戦争、戦争行為　☐ get media coverage メディアで報道される

訳 5-3　テロ行為がなくなるだろうと思われる一つの理由は、各国政府がテロ行為を阻止する高度な技術を獲得しつつあることだ。近年では、政府は何十件ものテロ攻撃を防ぐことができた。政府の技術の向上に伴い、テロリストが秘密裏に攻撃を企てることはますます難しくなるだろう。

Vocabulary

☐ dozens of 〜 数十の〜

訳 5-4　世界の平等が改善されることはテロの消滅につながるだろう。生活環境と政策の向上により、少数派に対する差別は減り、少数派に与えられるチャンスは増大している。もし、公平な待遇を受けていると感じる人が増えれば、テロリストになる人は少なくなる。

Vocabulary

☐ discrimination 差別　☐ be treated fairly 公平に扱われる

核兵器

Content Block 核兵器使用の危険　MP3 069

5 The main reason that nuclear weapons should be banned is that they threaten all life on the planet. If two nations used nuclear weapons against each other, it would lead to catastrophic climate change. Smoke from fires would block out the sun for months, causing widespread famine and possibly billions of deaths.

Content Block 開発・維持の危険性　MP3 070

6 Nuclear weapons are dangerous to develop and maintain. Although a nuclear weapon has never been detonated accidentally, the possibility does exist. One mistake could result in the loss of thousands of lives. This is particularly true in less developed nations, which have limited access to professional equipment and trained professionals.

Content Block 抑止力　MP3 071

7 Nuclear weapons are one of the few weapons in the world that actually prevent wars. There has not been a large-scale violent conflict between two major nations since the first nuclear bombs were dropped in Hiroshima and Nagasaki. This is because world leaders know that a nuclear war would be catastrophic.

Content Block 違法化の非現実性　MP3 072

8 Outlawing nuclear weapons worldwide is unrealistic. The two nations with the most nuclear weapons—Russia and the United States—are unlikely to get rid of them in the near future, because it would decrease their level of security. Instead, they are more likely to improve defenses and make it clear that they can deal with nuclear attacks if necessary.

訳 5 5　核兵器を禁止するべき主な理由は、地球上のすべての生命を危険にさらすからだ。もし、二つの国家が互いに核兵器を使用すれば、壊滅的な気候変動につながるだろう。火災から出る煙は何か月も太陽を覆い隠し、飢饉が広がって、何十億人もの人々が死亡するかもしれない。

Vocabulary

□ threaten ～を脅かす　□ catastrophic 破壊的な、大惨事の

訳 5 6　核兵器を開発、維持するのは危険である。これまで核兵器が誤って爆発させられたことはないが、その可能性は確実に存在する。一つの間違いが数千の人命の喪失につながってしまう。このことは途上国においてはとりわけ切実だ。こうした国では専門的な機器と訓練された専門家が不足している。

Vocabulary

□ detonate〈爆弾など〉を爆発させる

訳 5 7　核兵器は実際に戦争を防ぐ世界で数少ない兵器の一つだ。初の核爆弾が広島と長崎に投下されて以来、二つの主要国間での大規模な武力衝突は起きていない。これは、世界の指導者たちが、核戦争は破滅をもたらすだろうということを知っているからだ。

Vocabulary

□ violent conflict 武力衝突　□ catastrophic 破滅的な

訳 5 8　世界中で核兵器を禁止することは非現実的だ。最も多くの核兵器を保有する2か国——ロシアとアメリカ——が近い将来核兵器を廃絶する可能性はないだろう。核兵器を廃絶すれば、安全保障レベルが下がるからだ。核兵器を廃絶するのではなく、両国は防衛能力を高め、必要があれば核攻撃に対処できるということを明確にする可能性のほうが高い。

Vocabulary

□ outlaw ～を不法とする

軍事力の行使

5 | Content Block | 自衛のための武力行使 — MP3 073

9 In some situations, military force is necessary for self-defense. For example, if it is clear that another country is likely to attack in the near future, then a preemptive strike can be justified. Everyone has a right to safety and security, and everyone also has a right to fight for safety and security. There are almost no leaders in the world against using a military for self-defense.

5 | Content Block | 弱者保護のための武力行使 — MP3 074

10 There are times when military force is needed to protect people who are weak and in danger. In other words, the militaries of developed countries should act as the police of the world. One example where military force should have been used is in Rwanda in 1994. Powerful militaries did not intervene in the conflict, and as a result over 1 million people were brutally murdered.

5 | Content Block | 民間人の犠牲 — MP3 075

11 The main reason that military force is not justifiable is that it always results in the deaths of innocent people. It is terrible for soldiers to kill one another. However, it is even worse when average people suffer due to war, and innocent people are always harmed as a result of military force.

5 | Content Block | グローバリゼーション時代の戦争 — MP3 076

12 Due to advances in technology and globalization, the primary "wars" between developed nations are now economic and digital. For example, leaders in both China and the U.S. understand that going to war would be a disaster. Therefore, they choose to "fight" using economic policies and various forms of cyber warfare.

訳 5-9　軍事力は自衛のために必要な場合がある。例えば、もし近い将来に他国が攻撃してくることが明らかであれば、先制攻撃は正当化されうる。すべての人々には、安全と安心を確保する権利があり、また安全と安心のために戦う権利がある。自衛のために軍隊を使うことに反対する指導者は、世界で皆無に等しい。

Vocabulary

□ self-defense 自衛　□ preemptive strike 先制攻撃

訳 5-10　軍事力は、弱い人々や危険にさらされた人々を守るために必要な場合がある。言い換えれば、先進国の軍隊は世界の警察の役割を務めるべきである。軍事力が行使されるべきだった一例は、1994年のルワンダでのことだ。強力な軍隊が紛争に介入しなかったために、結果として100万人以上の人々が虐殺された。

Vocabulary

□ intervene 介入する　□ brutally 残忍に、残酷に

訳 5-11　軍事力を正当化できない主な理由は、軍事力は常に罪なき人々の死という結果を招くからだ。兵士が殺し合うことは悲惨である。しかし、普通の人々が戦争のために苦しむのはさらに悲惨で、軍事力を行使すれば必ず罪のない人々に被害が及ぶのである。

Vocabulary

□ justifiable 正当化できる

訳 5-12　技術の発展とグローバリゼーションによって、先進国間の主な「戦争」は今や経済上のものとデジタルなものになった。例えば、中国とアメリカの首脳はどちらも、戦争に突入すれば壊滅的な結果となることを理解している。そこで、両国は経済政策やさまざまな形態のサイバー戦争で「戦う」ことを選んでいる。

Vocabulary

□ cyber warfare サイバー戦争

軍事費

Content Block 5 　資金の使い道　MP3 077

13　Military spending should be decreased in developed nations so that more can be spent on more important things like education and infrastructure. Spending money to make our children more intelligent and knowledgeable is the greatest investment we can make. Also, improved infrastructure will lead to many economic benefits.

Content Block 5 　強い軍事力を持たない事例　MP3 078

14　Military spending should be decreased because there are many developed nations without powerful militaries. For example, countries like Iceland, Ireland, and Mexico have extremely low military spending. Although they do not have strong militaries, they do not get invaded by other countries, so they can focus on economic growth instead.

Content Block 5 　高まる懸念　MP3 079

15　Military spending should not be decreased because the future is unpredictable. Due to the rapidly increasing world population, along with deforestation and climate change, it is possible that there will be extremely serious, worldwide crises sometime in the near future. If this does happen, military action may be needed to secure resources. As they say, "Better safe than sorry."

Content Block 5 　新技術の促進　MP3 080

16　Military spending actually improves the education and technology of society in general. Members of the military are able to acquire special skills, which they can use for the rest of their lives. Also, developments in military technology often lead to a variety of benefits for average people. For example, computers, microwaves, and GPS all started as military technology.

訳 5 13 先進国では、教育やインフラといったもっと重要なことにより多くの資金を使えるように、軍事費を減らすべきだ。子どもたちの知性を育て、知識を豊富にするために資金を使うことは、私たちにできる最も素晴らしい投資だ。また、インフラの改善は、多くの経済的な恩恵をもたらすだろう。

Vocabulary

□ knowledgeable 知識の豊富な、詳しい

訳 5 14 軍事費は減らすべきだ。強い軍隊を持たない先進国も多くあるからだ。例えば、アイスランドやアイルランド、メキシコのような国々は、軍事費が極めて少ない。これらの国々は強い軍隊を持たないが、他国から侵略されることはなく、その分、経済成長に力を注ぐことができている。

Vocabulary

□ invade 〜に侵入する、侵略する

訳 5 15 軍事費は減らすべきではない。未来は予測不可能だからだ。世界人口が急速に増加しているため、また、森林破壊と気候変動とも相まって、近い将来、世界中で極めて深刻な危機が起こるかもしれない。本当にそうなれば、資源を確保するために軍事行動が必要となるかもしれない。よく言われるように、「備えあれば憂いなし」だ。

Vocabulary

□ unpredictable 予測できない　□ Better safe than sorry. 備えあれば憂いなし

訳 5 16 軍事費は実際には、社会全般の教育と技術を向上させている。軍人は特殊なスキルを身につけることができ、退役後もそれを生かすことができる。また、軍事技術の発達は、一般の人々にもさまざまな恩恵をもたらすことが多い。例えば、コンピューター、電子レンジ、GPSシステムはすべて、軍事用に開発された技術だ。

Vocabulary

□ microwave 電子レンジ

6 | 世界経済

CHAPTER_2

貿易と関税

　貿易とは、各国間で行われる商品の取引のこと。加工貿易、中継貿易、仲介貿易など、さまざまな形態がある。輸入した商品にかけられる税を関税（または輸入税）といい、国内産業を保護するために関税を高く設定する貿易を保護貿易、逆に関税などの制限や規制をかけない貿易を自由貿易という。関税の税率は本来自国で決められるが、実際にはWTO（世界貿易機関）や2国間の条約によって取り決められる税率が優先的に適用される。

世界経済のボーダーレス化

　世界貿易機関（WTO）とは世界貿易の自由化とルールの策定を行う機関で、150以上の国が加盟し、「○○ラウンド」と呼ばれる一連の多角的貿易交渉を行っている。しかしドーハ・ラウンドが行き詰まって以降、世界貿易の軸は自由貿易協定（FTA）や経済連携協定（EPA）といった地域協力・地域主義に移りつつある。

　自由貿易協定とは、特定の国や地域が貿易を活発化するために関税を低減・撤廃したり、互いの制度を調整したりする取り決めのことで、代表的なものには欧州連合（EU）、東南アジア諸国連合（ASEAN）、北米自由貿易協定（NAFTA）などがある。

　また、自由貿易協定に加え、人、資本、知的財産の円滑な移動など、幅広い分野での連携強化を目指す協定を経済連携協定という。環太平洋経済連携協定（TPP）や環大西洋貿易投資パートナーシップ（TTIP）などがその例である。

　過去の問題では、自由貿易のメリットとデメリットを比較するテーマが出題されており、また、企業レベルではあるが、多国籍企業が現代の世界において建設的な役割を果たしているかを問う問題も出題されている。

🔍 キーワード

●貿易と関税

□ 保護(貿易)主義	protectionism
□ 輸入関税	tariff / import tariff / import tax
□ 関税率	tariff rate
□ 関税障壁	tariff barriers
□ 輸入禁止	import ban
□ 輸入制限	import restriction
□ 輸出規制	export restriction
□ 禁輸、通商禁止	embargo
□ 産業の保護	protection of an industry
□ 価格の安定	stabilization of prices
□ 価格の下落	fall in price
□ 貿易収支	trade balance
□ 貿易摩擦	trade friction
□ 貿易不均衡	trade imbalance
□ 貿易赤字	trade deficit
□ 貿易黒字国	surplus trader

●世界経済のボーダーレス化

□ 自由貿易	free trade
□ 市場開放	market liberalization
□ 関税撤廃	tariff elimination
□ 関税と貿易に関する一般規定	General Agreement on Tariffs and Trade（略：GATT）
□ 世界貿易機関	World Trade Organization（略：WTO）
□ ドーハ開発ラウンド	Doha Development Round
□ 多角的貿易自由化	multilateral trade liberalization
□ 多国間貿易交渉	multilateral trade negotiation
□ 自由貿易協定	free trade agreement（略：FTA）
□ 2国間自由貿易協定	bilateral free trade agreement
□ 環太平洋戦略的経済連携協定	Trans-Pacific Partnership（略：TPP）
□ 経済連携協定	economic partnership agreement（略：EPA）
□ 通商圏	trading bloc

自由貿易

Content Block 6-1 国際関係　MP3 081

Free trade is good for international relations. For two countries to have good relations, they need to treat each other's citizens and businesses fairly. One way to do this is by removing barriers to trading with one another. Free trade agreements lead to healthy relationships, which are necessary for long-term prosperity.

Content Block 6-2 経済効果　MP3 082

Free trade is good for economic growth. It is common for domestic workers to complain about losing their jobs to foreign workers, but several studies have shown that free trade actually improves the job market overall. This is because society wastes less money when competition increases and prices decrease. In other words, the economy runs more smoothly.

Content Block 6-3 製品・サービスの向上　MP3 083

The main benefit of free trade is that companies are forced to provide better products and services. When domestic companies are protected by import taxes, they feel less pressure to improve their products, services, and prices. This is not good for the economy. If a domestic company cannot compete with an international company, then it deserves to go out of business.

Content Block 6-4 消費者にとっての利点　MP3 084

Free trade is good for consumers because they always benefit when businesses compete. Competition leads to both higher quality products and lower prices. With lower prices, consumers also have more money to spend. This extra money is spent on other products and services, and new jobs are created as a result.

訳 6-1 自由貿易は国際関係にとってよいことだ。二つの国が良好な関係を築くためには、双方の国の国民と企業を公平に待遇する必要がある。そうするための一つの方法が、相互の貿易の障壁を取り払うことだ。自由貿易協定は健全な関係につながり、健全な関係は長期的な繁栄に必要だ。

Vocabulary
□ free trade agreement 自由貿易協定　□ prosperity 繁栄

訳 6-2 自由貿易は経済成長にとってよいことだ。よく国内労働者が外国人労働者に仕事が奪われると不平を言っているが、複数の研究により、自由貿易は実際には労働市場全体を改善することが示されている。これは、競争が増えて価格が下がれば、社会で無駄になるお金が減るためだ。つまり、経済がより円滑に回るのである。

Vocabulary
□ job market 労働市場

訳 6-3 自由貿易の主な利点は、企業がよりよい製品やサービスを提供しなければならなくなることだ。国内企業が輸入税で保護されていると、製品やサービス、価格を改善しなければという圧力を感じることが少ない。これは経済にとってよいことではない。もし、国内企業が国際企業と競合できなければ、倒産してもしかたがない。

Vocabulary
□ deserve to do 〜するに値する　□ go out of business 倒産する、廃業する

訳 6-4 企業間に競合があると消費者には必ず利益があるので、自由貿易は消費者にとってよいことだ。競争は、製品の品質の向上と価格の低下につながる。価格が下がれば、消費者はお金をもっと多く使うこともできる。この余剰のお金はほかの製品やサービスに使われるので、その結果、新たな雇用が創出される。

Vocabulary
□ extra 余剰の

Content Block 5 　地域経済への打撃　MP3 085

A major problem with free trade is that it harms local economies. A lot of domestic companies cannot compete with the low prices of foreign companies. As a result, many businesses have to close. This means that citizens lose jobs, and sometimes local economies are completely destroyed.

Content Block 6 　伝統と文化　MP3 086

Free trade can lead to the disappearance of traditional businesses and culture. Some countries with highly powerful corporations can dominate industries globally. This can result in an extremely high number of their products appearing in many countries. Local businesses cannot compete with these major corporations, and their unique products often disappear as a result.

輸入税

Content Block 7 　地元企業の保護　MP3 087

One of the primary benefits of import taxes is that they protect local jobs and companies. Some foreign countries have extremely low labor costs. As a result, their companies can sell products at lower prices than domestic competitors. This can cause local companies to go out of business, which would cause citizens to lose their jobs.

Content Block 8 　重要な産業の強化　MP3 088

A positive aspect of import tariffs is that they can strengthen vital industries. This is important for national security. It is impossible to predict what will happen in the future. It is theoretically possible that trade with many countries will stop due to war or natural disasters. If this happens, nations need to be able to produce the products that their citizens require.

訳 6 5 自由貿易の大きな問題は、地域経済にダメージを与えることだ。多くの国内企業は、海外企業の低価格に太刀打ちできない。その結果、たくさんの企業が閉業しなければならない。これはつまり、国民が職を失うということであり、場合によっては地域経済が完全に破壊されることにもなる。

Vocabulary

☐ domestic 国内の

訳 6 6 自由貿易は、従来型のビジネスと文化の消滅につながる可能性がある。強大な企業を抱えた一部の国が、世界中で諸産業を支配することができる。このことは、それらの国々のおびただしい数の製品が多くの国々に出現することにつながる可能性がある。地元の企業は、こうした大企業と競合することができず、その結果、個性豊かな製品が姿を消すケースが少なくない。

Vocabulary

☐ dominate 〜を支配する

訳 6 7 輸入税の主な利点の一つは、地元の雇用と企業を保護することだ。海外には、労働コストが極めて低い国もある。その結果、そうした国々の企業は国内の競合他社よりも安い値段で製品を販売することができる。これが原因で、地元企業が倒産する可能性もあり、それによって国民が仕事を失うことになるかもしれない。

Vocabulary

☐ go out of business 倒産する、廃業する

訳 6 8 輸入関税のよい側面の一つは、重要な産業を強化できることだ。これは、国内の安全保障にとって重要だ。将来、何が起こるか予測するのは不可能だ。多くの国々との貿易が戦争や自然災害で止まることも、理論上はあり得る。もしこのようなことが起こった場合、国は国民が必要とする製品を生産できなければならない。

Vocabulary

☐ tariff 関税 ☐ theoretically 理論上は

6 Content Block　輸入税と失業率　MP3 089

9　The main disadvantage of import taxes is that they harm employment rates. Proponents of import taxes say they are needed so that local companies do not go out of business and raise unemployment. But tariffs actually increase unemployment rates. This is because import taxes cause prices to rise, and the market stagnates.

6 Content Block　非効率な企業の助長　MP3 090

10　Tariffs promote the emergence and growth of ineffective companies. When companies are protected by a tariff, they have less competition from foreign businesses. Thus, they have less incentive to create higher quality products at lower prices. Ultimately, this creates a market where domestic consumers overpay for inferior products from companies that cannot compete internationally.

6 Content Block　事業へのダメージ　MP3 091

11　Tariffs actually hurt the majority of businesses. For example, if there is a tariff on raw materials like steel and rubber, then domestic producers of those goods can control the market and raise prices. This causes major problems for companies that need to obtain these materials at competitive rates to produce their own products cheaply.

6 Content Block　税全体への影響　MP3 092

12　Import taxes generate valuable tax revenue for governments. A common complaint of citizens is that taxes are too high. By using tariffs, governments can slightly shift this tax burden to foreign companies. This is a good thing for local people and companies that want lower taxes.

訳 6 9 輸入税の主な欠点は、雇用率を低下させることだ。輸入税に賛成する人々は、地元の企業が倒産して失業率が上がることがないようにするために、輸入税が必要だと言っている。しかし実際には、関税は失業率を上げている。それは、輸入税は物価を上げ、市場を低迷させるからだ。

Vocabulary

□ proponent 支持者（＝people in favor）　□ stagnate 停滞する、不活発になる

訳 6 10 関税は無能な企業の出現と成長を助長する。企業が関税で守られると、海外の企業との競争が少なくなる。そのため、そうした企業には、より低価格で、より高品質な製品を製造する意欲が生まれにくい。これは最終的に、国内の消費者が、国際的な競争力を持たない企業から質の悪い製品を高すぎる金額で購入する市場を生み出してしまう。

Vocabulary

□ overpay 払いすぎる

訳 6 11 関税は、実は大多数の事業にダメージを与えている。例えば、スチールやゴムのような原材料に関税をかければ、それらの製品を製造している国内のメーカーは、市場をコントロールして価格を上げることができる。このことは、自社製品を安く製造するために、安い価格でこうした原材料を入手する必要のある企業に、大きな問題をもたらしている。

Vocabulary

□ competitive 競争力のある、安い

訳 6 12 輸入税は、政府に貴重な税収をもたらす。国民からよく聞かれる不満の一つは、税金が高すぎることだ。関税を活用することで、政府は外国の企業にこの税負担を少し移行させることができる。これは、減税を望む地元の人々と企業にとってよいことだ。

Vocabulary

□ tax burden 税負担

7 世界の中の日本

CHAPTER_2

日本の役割

　過去の問題では、国際問題において日本が果たすべき役割を問うテーマが出題されている。日本が世界において求められる役割とは、裏を返せば世界が抱えている問題にどう関わるかということである。世界の貧困、飢餓、水不足。多くの途上国が抱えるそうした問題に対して、資金援助や技術援助など、日本が行えることを考えていくとトピックの手がかりが見えてくるはずだ。

　発展途上国の経済・社会の発展や福祉向上を目的とした政府開発援助（ODA）の取り組みについて簡単に調べておくといいだろう。
（→4 世界の問題）

自衛隊

　日本の平和と独立を守り、外国からの侵略に対して防衛するものとして設置された武装部隊。自衛隊の海外派遣は憲法によって制約されてきたが、1991年の湾岸戦争時にペルシャ湾へ掃海部隊が派遣されて以降、武力行使を目的としないで、紛争に巻き込まれる可能性の低い地域において活動を行うようになっている。国連平和維持活動（PKO）以外にも、特措法に基づく後方支援や大規模災害の復興支援、難民救援などの活動を行っている。
（→5 戦争・核兵器・テロリズム）

難民・移民の受け入れ

　難民（refugee）とは「人種、宗教、国籍、政治的意見などの理由で、自国にいると迫害を受けるか、あるいは迫害を受ける恐れがあるために他国に逃れた人」。難民認定をすると国際法で保障された保護を与える責任が国に生じ、受け入れた国の政府が相応のコストを負担することになる。一方、**移民**（immigrant）とは「仕事や教育、よりよい生活環境などを求め、異国の地に定住する人」。受け入れ国はその国の法律に基づいた処遇をすることが認められている。

　2014年、日本では約5000人の難民申請があり、認定されたのはそれ以前に申請した人を含めて11人。一方労働力確保のため、政府は年間20万人の移民受け入れを計画している。

🔍 キーワード

●世界の問題

☐ 発展途上国	developing country
☐ 貧困国	impoverished country
☐ 開発援助	development aid
☐ 経済援助	economic aid
☐ 食糧援助	food aid
☐ 人道支援	humanitarian support
☐ 国際貢献	international contribution
☐ 国際的地位	international status

●自衛隊

☐ 日米同盟	U.S.-Japan alliance
☐ 人命の犠牲	loss of life
☐ 国際紛争	international conflict
☐ 憲法違反	breach of the Constitution
☐ 国民感情	popular sentiment
☐ 国民の保護	protection of the people
☐ 正当防衛	self-defense

●難民・移民の受け入れ

☐ 違法難民	illegal refugee
☐ 難民流入	refugee influx
☐ 移民政策	immigration policy
☐ 移民流入	migrant influx
☐ 入国審査	immigration screening
☐ 本国送還	repatriation
☐ 文化の違い	cultural differences
☐ 税収の増加	increase of tax revenue
☐ 労働力の維持	maintenance of a workforce
☐ 経済の安定	economic stabilization
☐ 治安の悪化	deterioration of public order
☐ 差別	discrimination

移民政策

7-1 Content Block　労働力不足の解消　MP3 093

Due to Japan's aging population, the younger generation will eventually need to support the older generation. The government will have a difficult time providing financial support for its citizens without forcing young people to work longer hours. However, Japan could get more workers by accepting more immigrants into the country.

7-2 Content Block　有能な労働者の流入　MP3 094

If Japan has more lenient immigration policies, it will attract skilled workers from abroad. There are millions of highly talented, hard-working people in the world that would love to live and work in Japan. If they were allowed into the country, they could contribute to Japanese society in many ways.

7-3 Content Block　労働者の賃金低下　MP3 095

Research shows that increases in migrant workers lead to decreased wages for the poorest workers. This means that natural born citizens are forced to work for lower salaries in order to compete with migrant workers. Companies have no reason to pay higher salaries when foreign workers are willing to work for lower wages.

7-4 Content Block　不法入国者の増加　MP3 096

Lenient immigration policies would lead to higher taxes because there would be more illegal immigrants. Even illegal immigrants benefit from public services like emergency medical care, high-quality roads, and law enforcement. However, they do not pay enough taxes to fund these. Instead, legal citizens are forced to pay higher taxes.

訳 7-1 日本では、人口の高齢化のため、若い世代がいずれ上の世代を支えなければならなくなる。若者に長時間労働を強いることなく、政府が国民を経済的に支援するのは困難になる。しかし、国内にもっと多くの移民を受け入れれば、日本は労働者を増やすことができるだろう。

Vocabulary

□ immigrant 移民

訳 7-2 もし日本が寛容な移民政策をとれば、海外から技能を備えた労働者が集まるだろう。世界には日本に住んで働きたいと思っている有能で勤勉な人が何百万人もいる。もし彼らが入国を許されれば、彼らはさまざまな形で日本社会に貢献することだろう。

Vocabulary

□ lenient 寛容な　□ contribute to ～ ～に貢献する

訳 7-3 調査によれば、移民労働者の増加は、最貧層の労働者の賃金低下につながるという。これは、自国民が移民労働者と競争力を保つために、さらに低い賃金で働かざるをえないということを意味する。外国人労働者が低賃金で働くのをいとわないのであれば、企業が高い賃金を払う理由はない。

Vocabulary

□ migrant 移住の　□ compete with ～ ～と競う

訳 7-4 寛容な移民政策をとると、不法入国者が増えるために税の引き上げを招くだろう。不法入国者も救急医療や質の高い道路、警察などの公共サービスを受ける。しかし彼らはこうしたサービスをまかなうのに十分な税を支払わない。代わりに合法的な在住者がより高い税金を支払わなければならなくなる。

Vocabulary

□ emergency medical care 救急医療　□ law enforcement 法の執行、警察による取り締まり

Content Block 7-5 日本人の国際化 MP3 097

If more people from other countries join the workforce in Japan, Japanese people can learn more about other cultures, and their foreign language abilities are likely to improve as well. Language barriers are one of Japan's biggest disadvantages in the global economy. Improving language ability will make Japan a more attractive place to do business and visit for vacations.

国際紛争への関与

Content Block 7-6 平和国としての立場 MP3 098

Ignoring international conflicts does not help to solve them, but participating with maturity does. Japan is a peaceful nation. But part of being a peaceful nation is actively trying to stop international conflicts from escalating. It is not enough to simply ignore conflicts, which is what causes them to get out of control.

Content Block 7-7 サイバー攻撃への備え MP3 099

The most threatening dangers for most developed countries are online. The U.S. Director of National Intelligence ranks cybercrime as the greatest national security threat, ahead of terrorism and weapons of mass destruction. The Japanese government should dedicate more resources to improving defenses against cyber-attacks.

Content Block 7-8 優先されるべき防衛強化 MP3 100

Japan needs to focus more on building its defenses than on joining conflicts abroad. The future of the country has very little connection to most conflicts that are occurring in other countries. However, it is important to be prepared for local threats. One example is nearby North Korea, as Japan could be a possible target when its nuclear weapons improve.

訳 7 5　日本の労働力に外国人がもっと加われば、日本人は他国の文化についてより多くのことを学べ、外国語の能力も向上するだろう。言葉の壁は世界経済において日本の最大の不利な点の一つだ。言語能力が向上すれば、ビジネスをしたり休暇で訪れたりするのに日本はいっそう魅力的な場所になるだろう。

Vocabulary

□ workforce 労働力　□ language barrier 言葉の壁

訳 7 6　国際紛争を無視することはその解決の助けにはならないが、分別を持って関与することは解決の助けになる。日本は平和な国だ。しかし、平和な国であるならば、国際紛争がエスカレートするのを積極的に止めようとする必要がある。単に関与しないのでは十分でない。それでは国際紛争を制御不可能にしてしまう。

Vocabulary

□ with maturity 分別を持って　□ escalate エスカレートする

訳 7 7　ほとんどの先進国にとって最も恐ろしい危険はオンライン上にある。アメリカの国家情報長官は、サイバー犯罪をテロ行為や大量破壊兵器よりも上に置き、国家の安全保障上最大の脅威と位置づけている。日本政府は、サイバー攻撃への備えの改善にもっと多くの資金を投入するべきだ。

Vocabulary

□ rank ～を順位づけする　□ dedicate ～をささげる

訳 7 8　日本は海外の紛争に関与するよりも自国の防衛の確立にもっと力を注ぐ必要がある。日本の将来は他国で起きている大部分の紛争とはほとんど関係がない。一方、近隣の脅威に備えることは重要だ。一例は隣国の北朝鮮で、北朝鮮の核兵器が改良されれば日本が標的になる可能性があるからだ。

Vocabulary

□ threat 脅威

8 環境保護

化石燃料と再生可能エネルギー

　化石燃料（fossil fuel）とは、具体的には石油、石炭、天然ガスを指す。その大量消費は**二酸化炭素**（carbon dioxide）やメタンなどの**温室効果ガス**（greenhouse gases）を発生させ、**地球温暖化**（global warming）を引き起こしている。これに対し、風力、太陽光、地熱、潮力、波力、バイオマスなど自然の力を利用したエネルギーを、**再生可能エネルギー**（renewable energy）と呼ぶ。二酸化炭素をほとんど排出しないため、温暖化対策として有効とされるが、風の有無や日照時間など自然状況に左右されるため電力が安定しない問題があるとされる。

　過去の問題では、化石燃料が主要なエネルギー源であり続けるかというテーマが出題されている。また地球温暖化や**気候変動**（climate change）といった語はPOINTとして繰り返し登場している。

原子力発電

　エネルギーでもう一つ忘れていけないのは原子力エネルギーである。**原子力発電**（nuclear power generation）とは、ウランやプルトニウムなどの核物質を核分裂させたときに出る熱エネルギーを利用する発電法。コストが安く、発電時に二酸化炭素を排出しないことから地球温暖化対策に有効とされる。一方で、放射性物質の危険性や放射性廃棄物の処理などの問題も大きい。

　過去の問題では、福島原発事故に先立つ2008年に原子力の利用について出題されたことがあるが、今後も出題される可能性は十分にある。

森林破壊

　自然の回復力を超える**森林伐採**（deforestation）や焼畑などによって、森林が減少し、失われること。森林の保水力が失われる結果、洪水や土砂崩れを引き起こし、動植物や昆虫の生息地・生育地を奪うことで生態系に甚大な影響を与えている。また地球規模で見ると、砂漠化や地球温暖化を進行させる要因にもなっている。

　過去の問題でも、**自然が残る地域**（wilderness area）を保護する取り組みについて出題されており、生物多様性や絶滅危惧種といった語もPOINTとして登場している。

🔍 キーワード

● 化石燃料と再生可能エネルギー

☐	火力発電	thermal power generation
☐	天然資源の枯渇	exhaustion of natural resources
☐	低エネルギー社会	low-energy society
☐	経済活動の低下	lower economic activity
☐	クリーンエネルギー	clean energy
☐	バイオ燃料の開発	development of biofuel
☐	燃料電池	fuel cell
☐	代替エネルギーの開発	development of alternative energy
☐	省エネルギー	energy conservation
☐	リサイクルの有効性への疑問	doubt(s) about the effectiveness of recycling

● 原子力発電

☐	原子力発電所	nuclear power plant
☐	電力の安定供給	reliable supply of electricity
☐	原子力のリスク	risks of nuclear power
☐	核物質	nuclear material
☐	使用済み核燃料	spent nuclear fuel
☐	放射性廃棄物	radioactive waste
☐	炉心溶融	nuclear meltdown
☐	放射能漏れ	radiation leakage
☐	軍事利用	military utilization

● 森林破壊

☐	環境保護	protection of the environment
☐	酸性雨	acid rain
☐	生物多様性	biological diversity / biodiversity
☐	砂漠化	desertification
☐	環境アセスメント	environmental assessment
☐	世界自然遺産	world natural heritage
☐	エコツーリズム	ecotourism
☐	カーボンオフセット	carbon offset
☐	二酸化炭素排出量、カーボンフットプリント	carbon footprint

93

化石燃料

8-1 代替エネルギー MP3 101

The world is already capable of replacing fossil fuels. Scientists have presented detailed plans showing how the entire world could theoretically be powered by wind, solar, and water sources. The technology already exists. The only problem that remains is getting it adopted by the general public.

8-2 再生可能エネルギーの費用効率 MP3 102

Thanks to developments in technology, sustainable energy sources are becoming more cost effective. For example, recently in Australia it was found that producing wind energy was cheaper than using coal or natural gas. Also, solar panels become cheaper every year. Eventually, renewable energy sources will be so cheap that everyone starts using them.

8-3 エネルギーの移行を阻む諸事情 MP3 103

Society in general is not motivated to quit using fossil fuels. Scientists have shown that it is possible, in theory, to replace fossil fuels with renewable energy. But the implementation of such theories would require trillions of dollars in investment, extensive public education, and support from both governments and individuals. Organizing all of these is not likely in the near future.

8-4 化石燃料への過剰な依存 MP3 104

Society is still too dependent on fossil fuels. Even respected environmentalists have acknowledged that the world will continue relying on natural gas for many years. Additionally, technology is making it easier to drill for oil, which is increasing supply and making it cheaper. As long as there is an affordable supply, dependence will not decrease.

訳 8-1　世界にはすでに化石燃料を別のものに置き換える能力がある。科学者たちは、風力、太陽光、水力によって理論上いかにして世界全体に電力を供給できるかを示す詳細な計画を提示してきた。この技術はすでに存在する。残る唯一の課題は、一般市民に受け入れられることだ。

Vocabulary

□ fossil fuel 化石燃料　□ theoretically 理論上　□ power ～に電力を供給する

訳 8-2　技術の発展のおかげで、持続可能なエネルギー源の費用効率は高まってきている。例えばオーストラリアでは最近、風力エネルギーを生み出すことは石炭や天然ガスを使うよりも安いことがわかった。また、太陽光パネルも年々安くなっている。いずれ、再生可能エネルギーは非常に安くなり、誰もが使い始めるだろう。

Vocabulary

□ sustainable energy 持続可能エネルギー　□ renewable energy 再生可能エネルギー

訳 8-3　社会は全体として、化石燃料の使用をやめる動機づけがない。科学者は、化石燃料を再生可能エネルギーに置き換えることは、理論上可能だと示している。しかし、このような理論を適用するには何兆ドルという投資と、広範な市民教育、政府と個人両方からの支援が必要となる。これらすべてを準備することは、近い将来に実現しそうにない。

Vocabulary

□ implementation 実現、実行

訳 8-4　社会は化石燃料に頼りすぎている。尊敬を集める環境保護活動家でさえも、世界は今後何年もの間、天然ガスに頼り続けるだろうと認めている。それに加え、石油の採掘は以前よりも技術的に容易になっており、その結果石油の供給は増え、価格は下がっている。手ごろな価格の供給がある限り、依存が減ることはないだろう。

Vocabulary

□ affordable 手ごろな[手の届く]価格の

Content Block 8-5 化石燃料廃止にかかる時間　MP3 105

Removing fossil fuels will be a lengthy, complex process. Back in the 19th century, for example, it took over 50 years for coal to replace wood as the main source of energy. Replacing gas and oil may take much longer because such a large number of machines use these resources.

Content Block 8-6 環境への影響　MP3 106

The world cannot handle the environmental impact of fossil fuels any longer. Many scientists have predicted that there will be huge problems in the near future due to global warming. As these problems worsen, more people will start to avoid using fossil fuels. People are already starting to realize that the protection of our planet is at stake.

Content Block 8-7 エネルギーの自給と国際関係　MP3 107

Countries will work to develop more renewable power sources so that they can be more independent. Some countries have very limited supplies of fossil fuels, which means that they need to import them from foreign countries. In order to increase security and put more money into the local economy, these countries will quickly switch to renewable power.

Content Block 8-8 民意　MP3 108

The public is starting to demand renewable energy options. More and more people are buying electric cars, putting solar panels on their homes, and so on. This is especially true in developed countries, where people are highly educated about the extensive damage we are causing to this planet.

訳 8 5　化石燃料をなくすことは時間のかかる複雑なプロセスになるだろう。例えば、19世紀にさかのぼると、主要なエネルギー源が木材から石炭に代わるのに50年以上かかった。ガスと石油の代替化は、これらの資源を使用する機械がこれほど多数ある以上、はるかに長い時間がかかるだろう。

Vocabulary
□ lengthy 長い時間のかかる

訳 8 6　世界は、化石燃料による環境への影響にこれ以上対処することができない。多くの科学者たちが、近い将来、地球温暖化が原因で深刻な問題が起こると予測している。こうした問題が悪化するにつれ、化石燃料の使用を控えるようになる人が増えるだろう。地球の保全が危機的状況にあることを、人々はすでに認識し始めている。

Vocabulary
□ be at stake 危機に瀕して

訳 8 7　各国は、自立性を高められるように、より多くの再生可能エネルギーの開発に取り組んでいくだろう。化石燃料の供給量が極めて限られている国もあり、そうした国では外国から化石燃料を輸入する必要がある。安全保障を強化し、地域経済にもっと資金を投じるために、こうした国々は速やかに再生可能エネルギーに切り替えるだろう。

Vocabulary
□ switch to ～ ～に切り替える

訳 8 8　一般市民は、再生可能エネルギーという選択肢を求め始めている。電気自動車を買ったり、ソーラーパネルを自宅に取りつけたりする人が増えている。これはとりわけ先進国で言えることだが、先進国では、私たちが地球に与えている広範なダメージについて知識水準が高い。

Vocabulary
□ highly educated 教育水準の高い　□ extensive 広範な

8 Content Block 入手可能性　MP3 109

9　Although there is a limited supply of fossil fuels in the world, we do have enough to last for several more decades. Also, while our reliance on renewable energy sources will probably increase in the near future, transitioning will be a slow process. This is particularly true for developing countries with less money.

8 Content Block エネルギー会社の圧力　MP3 110

10　Energy companies make a lot of money on fossil fuels, so they will continue to promote their use for many years. Major oil companies have an amazing amount of power. Aside from dominating the energy industry, they can also affect government policies. This means that governments will not fully support the switch to renewable energy sources.

リサイクル

8 Content Block リサイクルされないプラスチック　MP3 111

11　A lack of recycling worldwide is a gigantic problem. The vast majority of plastic, for example, is not recycled. A large percentage of plastic products are thrown away after being used only once. Unfortunately, significant amounts of plastic end up in the oceans. Scientists estimate that there are over 5 trillion pieces of plastic debris in the ocean today.

8 Content Block リサイクルの難しさ　MP3 112

12　The general consensus is that more recycling is always good, but the truth is more complicated. For example, producing aluminum and paper from recycled materials saves money and decreases greenhouse emissions. However, there may be no long-term economic or environmental benefits to recycling plastic and glass because the process of recycling them uses too much energy and is not cost-effective.

訳 8 9　世界の化石燃料の供給量は限られているが、それでもあと数十年は十分にまかなえる量がある。また近い将来、再生可能エネルギー源への依存度は高まるだろうが、その移行はゆっくりとしたプロセスになるだろう。このことは、資金の少ない発展途上国に特に当てはまる。

Vocabulary

□ transitioning 移行、推移

訳 8 10　エネルギー会社は化石燃料でたくさん儲けているので、当分は引き続き化石燃料の使用を推進するだろう。大手石油企業は驚くほどの権力を持っている。エネルギー産業を牛耳っているだけでなく、政府の政策にも影響を与えている。このことは、政府が再生可能エネルギー源への切り替えを完全に支持するようにはならないだろうということを意味する。

Vocabulary

□ dominate ～を支配する

訳 8 11　世界中でリサイクル率が不十分であることは極めて大きな問題だ。例えば、プラスチックの大部分はリサイクルされていない。プラスチック製品の大部分は、1度使っただけで捨てられる。残念ながら、かなりの量のプラスチックが、最終的に海にたどりつく。科学者たちは、海には現在、5兆以上のプラスチックの破片があると推定している。

Vocabulary

□ gigantic 非常に大きな　□ debris 破片、がれき

訳 8 12　一般的に同意されているのは、リサイクルを増やすことは常にいいことだというものだが、事実はもっと複雑だ。例えば、再生材でアルミや紙を製造するのは費用の節約になり、温室効果ガスの排出を減らす。しかし、プラスチックやガラスのリサイクルは、長期的に見て、経済的利点や環境的利点はないかもしれない。というのも、それらのリサイクルはエネルギーを使いすぎ、費用効率が悪いからだ。

Vocabulary

□ consensus 一致した意見、総意　□ greenhouse emission 温室効果ガスの排出

自然の残る地域

Content Block　始まった植林　MP3 113

13　Governments, large corporations, and individual volunteers have begun to invest a significant amount of time and money into planting trees around the world. Recently, there was an event in Ecuador where over half a million trees were planted in a single day. Activities like this show that great efforts are being made to preserve nature.

Content Block　各国の施策　MP3 114

14　Nations around the world are doing more to protect their forests. For example, Brazil, which contains a large percentage of the Amazon rainforest, has managed to decrease deforestation significantly in recent years. In addition, the United Nations Forum on Forests now meets regularly to plan and promote the sustainable management and protection of forests all over the world.

Content Block　人口と消費レベル　MP3 115

15　The human population continues to increase, and consumption levels are too high in developed countries. Thus, people are required to exploit an unsustainable amount of the planet's resources, and forests all over the world are destroyed. We need to find a sustainable solution for managing this rapid growth and high consumption as soon as possible.

Content Block　変化のスピードの不十分さ　MP3 116

16　Although many nations have begun to adopt environmental conservation policies, and the rate of deforestation is slowing, positive change is not happening quickly enough. Until humans are consistently consuming less resources than the planet can sustain, then environmental efforts should be considered a failure overall. Consequently, all people should come together to reverse these problems.

訳 8 13 政府、大企業、個人のボランティアは、世界中で木を植えることにかなりの時間と資金を投じ始めた。最近では、エクアドルで50万本以上の木を1日で植えるイベントがあった。このような活動は、自然を守るために多大な努力がなされていることを示している。

Vocabulary

☐ significant かなりの、大幅な

訳 8 14 世界中の国々が、森林を保護するためにいっそうの取り組みを行っている。例えば、アマゾンの熱帯雨林の大部分が国内にあるブラジルは、近年、森林破壊を著しく減らすことができた。加えて、国連森林フォーラムは現在、世界中の森林の持続可能な管理と保護の計画を策定し促進するために、定期的に会合を開いている。

Vocabulary

☐ deforestation 森林伐採、森林破壊

訳 8 15 人口は増加を続け、また先進国における消費レベルは高すぎる。このため、人々は持続不可能な量の地球の資源を使わざるを得ず、世界中の森林は破壊されている。私たちは、この急速な（人口の）増加と大量消費に対処できる持続可能な解決策をできるだけ早く見出す必要がある。

Vocabulary

☐ consumption 消費　☐ exploit〈資源など〉を開発する

訳 8 16 多くの国々は環境保護政策をとり始め、森林破壊のスピードは鈍化しつつあるが、好ましい変化の速さは十分ではない。人類が一貫して、資源の消費を地球が持続できる量に抑えるようにならなければ、環境保護の取り組みは、概して失敗と見なすべきだ。したがって、すべての人々がこの問題を一転させるために協力すべきだ。

Vocabulary

☐ environmental conservation policy 環境保護政策　☐ sustain 〜を維持する

Content Block 生物多様性　MP3 117

17 To ensure biodiversity, we must do more to protect the world's wilderness areas. This is important for sustaining the earth's ecosystem. Failing to do so would mean the mass extinctions of several species, which would then adversely affect the availability of food and medicine. In fact, research has shown that drops in biodiversity also negatively impact human health.

Content Block 先住民の生活　MP3 118

18 The livelihood of many indigenous peoples greatly depends on wilderness areas. These habitats are a source of food, medicine, spirituality, and culture for them. Thus, by protecting these natural environments, we are also protecting their ability to grow crops, obtain herbs to treat illnesses, and preserve their cultural and spiritual heritage.

Content Block 開発の必要性　MP3 119

19 The necessity of economic development to support the growing world population is more important than protecting wilderness areas. Not only do we have to build more residential areas and schools to accommodate future generations, but we also have to expand our economic infrastructure so that children will have many career options when they grow up.

原発

Content Block 原発の危険性　MP3 120

20 Nuclear power plants are too vulnerable to disasters and attacks. The nuclear catastrophe that occurred in Fukushima in 2011 shows the danger of these facilities. They may be a target for attacks by terrorists and other governments. In fact, cyber-attacks have already taken place at nuclear facilities in Korea and Iran.

訳 8-17　生物多様性を保つため、私たちは世界の自然が残された地域を守るさらなる取り組みをしなければならない。これは地球の生態系を維持するために重要だ。それができなければ、かなりの種の大量絶滅につながり、その結果、食料や医薬品の供給に悪影響を与えかねない。実際、生物多様性の減少は人間の健康にもマイナスの影響を与えることが研究で示されている。

Vocabulary
□ biodiversity 生物多様性　□ mass extinction 大量絶滅　□ availability 入手できること

訳 8-18　多くの先住民の暮らしは、自然が残された地域に大きく依存している。こうした生活域は彼らにとって、食料、医薬品、スピリチュアリティ、文化の源だ。したがって、私たちがこうした自然環境を守ることは、先住民が作物を育て、病気を治療する薬草を入手し、文化的・精神的な遺産を保持する力を守ることにもなっている。

Vocabulary
□ indigenous 先住の、土着の

訳 8-19　増加を続ける世界人口を支える経済発展の必要性は、自然の残された地域を守ることよりも重要だ。将来の世代が住まう住宅地域や学ぶ学校をもっとたくさん建設する必要があるだけでなく、子どもたちが成長したときに多くの仕事の選択肢を持てるように経済的なインフラを拡充しなければならない。

Vocabulary
□ accommodate ～に場所を提供する

訳 8-20　原発は災害や攻撃に対してあまりにも脆弱だ。2011年に福島で起きた原発の大事故はこれらの施設の危険性を示している。それらはテロリストや他の政府の攻撃対象になるかもしれない。実際、韓国やイランの原子力施設ではサイバー攻撃が起きている。

Vocabulary
□ vulnerable 脆弱な、(攻撃・被害を)受けやすい　□ catastrophe 大惨事

8 Content Block 放射性廃棄物の問題 MP3 121

21 Disposing of radioactive waste is a major problem. Nuclear fuel remains highly radioactive for thousands of years after it is no longer useful. There is no way to know what might happen in the next few thousand years. Because of this, it is impossible for governments to design a reliable process for disposing of this waste.

8 Content Block 原発の安定性 MP3 122

22 Nuclear power is more reliable than other power sources. Renewable energy sources such as solar and wind energy are dependent on weather conditions, which can change at any time. But nuclear power plants can generate energy consistently over long periods of time. Moreover, the fuel to run these power plants will last much longer than fossil fuels.

8 Content Block 新タイプの原発 MP3 123

23 Nuclear power research is very promising. Nuclear power plants currently use nuclear fission to generate power. But scientists are working to generate power using nuclear fusion, which is a process that occurs naturally in stars. If scientists succeed in doing this, the world will finally have an unlimited source of clean, renewable energy.

8 Content Block 原発と温室効果ガス MP3 124

24 While proponents of nuclear power argue that it contributes much less to global warming than fossil fuels, the truth is far from this. Although nuclear power does emit far less greenhouse gases than fossil fuels, nuclear power also generates far more heat than fossil fuels. This means that nuclear power significantly increases the global warming problem.

訳 8-21 放射性廃棄物の処理は大きな問題だ。核燃料は使用できなくなってから何千年もの間、高い放射性を保持する。今後数千年の間に何が起こるかを知るすべはない。このため、政府が放射性廃棄物の信頼できる処理プロセスを策定するのは不可能だ。

Vocabulary

□ dispose of ～ ～を処分する

訳 8-22 原子力は他のエネルギー源よりも安定している。太陽光や風力のような再生可能エネルギー源は天候に左右されるが、天候は不安定なものだ。しかし、原子力発電所は長期間一定して発電できる。さらに、これらの発電所を稼働するための燃料は、化石燃料よりもずっと長く使える。

Vocabulary

□ consistently 一貫して　□ run ～を動かす

訳 8-23 原子力発電の研究はとても有望だ。原子力発電所は現在、発電に核分裂を使っている。しかし、科学者たちは恒星で自然に起こっているのと同じプロセスである核融合を使っての発電に取り組んでいる。もし、科学者たちがこれに成功すれば、世界はついに、クリーンで再生可能な無限のエネルギー源を手にすることとなるだろう。

Vocabulary

□ nuclear fission 核分裂　□ nuclear fusion 核融合

訳 8-24 原発推進派は、原発は化石燃料よりも温室効果がはるかに少ないと主張するが、事実はこれとかけ離れている。確かに原発は、化石燃料よりも温室効果ガスの排出量がずっと少ないが、原発は化石燃料よりもはるかに多くの熱も発生させている。このことは、原発が地球温暖化の問題を著しく悪化させていることを意味している。

Vocabulary

□ proponent 支持者、推進者

9 | 教育・文化・スポーツ

CHAPTER_2

教育

過去の問題では、大学教育が万人に必要かを問うテーマが出題されているが、そのほかにも、**義務教育**（compulsory education）や男女共学、小学校英語の是非、高等教育の無償化の問題、習熟度別の授業の必要性、オンライン教育（あるいはeラーニング・デジタル教科書）のメリット／デメリットなど、テーマになる可能性のあるものは少なくない。

また、過去の問題では世界の貧困や未成年犯罪のテーマでも「教育」がPOINTとして挙げられている。教育の目標をどうとらえるかで上述の諸問題に対するスタンスは変わってくるので、それを軸に考えたい。

伝統文化

伝統文化は基本的に近代化、テクノロジーなどによって破壊され、忘れ去られるものとして考えられる。過去の問題では伝統文化そのものがテーマになってはいないが、テクノロジーへの依存や自由貿易、都市化などのテーマが出題された際に「伝統文化」がPOINTとして挙げられている。単に古いものとしてではなく、それが長い間果たしてきた役割を考えて初めてそれを活かしたトピックを考えることができるだろう。
（→10 テクノロジー、→6 世界経済「貿易と関税」、→1 現代日本社会「都市化」）

スポーツイベント

スポーツそのものをネガティブに論じることは考えづらいので、スポーツそのものがテーマとして出題されたことはないが、国際スポーツイベントを開催するメリットに関する出題はあった。2020年には東京オリンピックもあり、関連する話題が出題される可能性はあるだろう。特にスポーツ振興が国民の健康増進につながり、医療費の軽減につながる可能性があるという論点は押さえておいてよい。

🔍 キーワード

●教育

☐ 入学金	entrance fee
☐ 授業料	tuition (fee)
☐ 奨学金	scholarship
☐ 大学の単位	college credit
☐ 大学の学位	college degree
☐ 大学院	graduate school
☐ カリキュラム	curriculum
☐ 必修科目	required [mandatory] course
☐ 通信教育	distance [correspondence] education
☐ 対面教育	face-to-face education
☐ 学力、学業成績	academic performance [achievement]
☐ 創造的思考	creative thinking
☐ 高等教育	higher education
☐ 初等教育	elementary [primary] education
☐ 早期教育	early education
☐ 職業体験	work experience
☐ インターンシップ	internship

●伝統文化

☐ 文化遺産	cultural heritage
☐ 歴史的建造物	historic structure
☐ 史跡	historic site
☐ 伝統行事	traditional event
☐ 伝統文化	traditional culture

●スポーツイベント

☐ 雇用創出	creation of jobs
☐ 一時的な経済効果	temporary economic effect
☐ 国際交流の促進	promotion of international exchange
☐ 競技場の維持費	stadium maintenance costs
☐ 国家予算	national budget

大学教育とオンライン教育

Content Block 9-1 大学教育のコスト

Traditional universities have several high costs. Tuition fees have risen consistently over the years. Additionally, students' time and money are required for commuting to campuses. For students that want to avoid spending too much and going into debt, this makes online alternatives very attractive.

Content Block 9-2 キャリアへの影響の低下

A university degree is no longer a requirement for a successful career. Companies are starting to realize that many high quality workers come from online schools, and they are likely to hire more of these people in the future. Moreover, many students are able to start freelance businesses using skills that they acquire online.

Content Block 9-3 人脈の形成

Attending a college campus allows students to meet new people every day. In university, students make friends they will know until they are old, which is very valuable. Moreover, knowing many people is helpful for getting a good job after graduation, so the conventional college experience is good for both personal and professional reasons.

Content Block 9-4 学費の低下

Policies that support lowering education costs are becoming more popular, especially in European countries. For example, Germany has completely removed higher education costs. As a result, students will be able to enjoy the benefits of a college experience while keeping fees as low as an online education.

訳 9 1　従来の大学にはいくつもの高い費用がかかる。学費は年々上がってきている。加えて、学生にはキャンパスに通学する時間とお金も必要だ。多額の出費をしたり借金を抱えたりしたくない学生にとって、このことは、オンラインによる代替手段をとても魅力的なものにしている。

Vocabulary
□ go into debt 借金に陥る

訳 9 2　大学の学位はもはや仕事で成功するための必須要件ではない。企業は、オンラインスクールが質の高い労働者を多数輩出していることに気づき始め、将来はこうした人々をもっと多く雇用するようになるだろう。そのうえ、多くの学生はオンラインで身につけた技能を活用して、フリーランスで仕事を始めることもできる。

Vocabulary
□ requirement 必須条件

訳 9 3　大学のキャンパスに通うことで、学生は毎日新しい人々と出会うことができる。大学で、学生は、年を取るまで関係の続く友人ができる。これはとても価値のあることだ。また、多くの人と知り合いであることは、卒業後によい仕事に就くのに役立つので、従来の大学での経験は、個人としても、仕事の面でもよいことだ。

Vocabulary
□ conventional 従来の、伝統的な

訳 9 4　教育費の低減を促す政策が、特にヨーロッパ諸国で一般的になってきている。例えば、ドイツは高等教育の学費を完全に撤廃した。その結果、学生はオンライン教育と同程度の安い学費で、大学での経験のメリットにあずかることができるだろう。

Vocabulary
□ enjoy ～を享受する

Content Block 9-5 オンライン化によるコストの低下　MP3 129

Education is becoming cheaper and more accessible. For example, it is now possible to learn skills like web design, programming, and marketing for free online. All that is needed is an Internet connection. In developing countries, the number of people with Internet access is increasing rapidly. This means everyone in the world will have more opportunities.

道徳教育

Content Block 9-6 道徳教育　MP3 130

The current education system does not teach moral values enough. Schools are overly focused on testing students' knowledge. Testing is certainly necessary and effective in some cases, but it is very difficult to give tests about moral issues. There is often no single correct solution for moral matters. As a result, schools avoid teaching morals and ethics.

教育の質の低下

Content Block 9-7 終身雇用制の現在　MP3 131

The ultimate goal of Japanese education—lifetime employment at a prestigious company—is no longer valid. The basic idea in Japan is that if you study hard and do well on exams, you will be able to enter a good university. Theoretically, this should lead to a secure position at a good company for life. But lifetime employment is no longer a realistic goal.

Content Block 9-8 日本の教育の長所　MP3 132

In international rankings, Japan always scores extremely high in reading, science, and math. This ongoing high performance led to the creation of innovative companies like Toyota, Sony, and Canon. Also, it is not uncommon for Japanese scientists to win Nobel prizes, especially in Physics and Chemistry.

訳 9-5 教育はより安く、受けやすくなってきている。例えば、今ではオンラインで、ウェブデザイン、プログラミング、マーケティングなどのスキルを無料で学ぶことができる。必要なのはインターネット接続だけだ。発展途上国では、インターネットに接続できる人の数が急速に増えている。これは、世界中の誰もがより多くの機会を手にするということだ。

Vocabulary
□ accessible 利用しやすい、入手しやすい

訳 9-6 現在の教育システムは道徳倫理を十分に教えていない。学校は、生徒の知識を測ることに焦点を当てすぎている。試験が必要かつ有効な場合があるのは確かだが、道徳の問題についてテストをするのは極めて困難だ。道徳の問題には唯一の正しい解答がないことが多い。その結果、学校は道徳や倫理を教えることを避けている。

Vocabulary
□ ethics 倫理(学)

訳 9-7 日本の教育の最終目標——有名企業での終身雇用——は、もはや通用しない。日本の基本的な考えは、一生懸命勉強して試験でいい成績を取れば、いい大学に入ることができるというものだ。このことは理屈のうえでは、いい会社で生涯安定して働けることにつながるはずだ。しかし、終身雇用はもはや現実的な目標ではなくなっている。

Vocabulary
□ ultimate 最終的な、究極の　□ lifetime employment 終身雇用

訳 9-8 世界のランキングで、日本は常に読解、科学、数学で極めて高い水準の成績を収めている。こうして好成績が続くことは、トヨタやソニー、キヤノンのような革新的な企業の創出につながった。また、日本人の科学者が、特に物理学と化学でノーベル賞を受賞することは珍しいことではない。

Vocabulary
□ score 得点する、成功する

Content Block 9 — 日本の教育の機能不全　MP3 133

9. Japan's current education system is clearly not working. If it were working, Japan's economy would be improving, but the country has suffered problems continuously the last two decades. Students are not willing to take risks, and language education is largely unsuccessful. As a result, Japan is having difficulty competing with international companies.

Content Block 9 — 日本の教育制度の問題点　MP3 134

10. The Japanese education system needs to put more emphasis on creativity, unconventional thinking, and social skills. Students in Japanese schools study an incredible amount, but all of that studying is for standardized tests, which are unable to measure things like creative problem-solving, communication, and so on. These are skills which are absolutely necessary in modern companies, especially for international businesses.

子どものスマートフォン

Content Block 9 — 生活を守るスマートフォン　MP3 135

11. Children are safer when they have smartphones. For example, there are now apps that allow parents to track the location of their children at all times using GPS. Also, there are apps for storing important health information in phones, such as a child's allergies or medical conditions. With tools like these, smartphones could save children's lives.

Content Block 9 — 人間関係を築くツール　MP3 136

12. Smartphones are a great tool for interacting with friends and building strong relationships. Using smartphones, children can chat, play games, and even help each other with homework. Also, there is a chance that a child without a smartphone will be left out of social activities and possibly even bullied.

訳 9 9 日本の現在の教育制度は、明らかにうまく機能していない。もしうまく機能していれば、日本の経済はよくなっているはずだが、日本はこの20年間継続的に問題を抱えている。学生はリスクを冒そうとせず、言語教育はおおむね成功していない。その結果、日本は国際企業と競合するのが難しくなっている。

Vocabulary
□ continuously 継続的に

訳 9 10 日本の教育制度は、創造性、型にはまらない思考、そして社会的スキルにもっと重点を置く必要がある。日本の学校の生徒は信じられないほどたくさん勉強するが、その勉強はすべて標準テストのためのものであり、標準テストではクリエイティブな問題解決やコミュニケーション能力といったものは測ることができない。こうした能力は、現代の企業、特に国際的企業においては絶対に必要なものだ。

Vocabulary
□ unconventional 型にはまらない、慣習にとらわれない

訳 9 11 子どもはスマートフォンを持っているほうが安全だ。例えば、今は、GPSを使って親が常時子どものいる場所をたどることができるアプリがある。また、子どものアレルギーや病状といった重要な健康上の情報を電話に保存するアプリもある。こうしたツールによって、スマートフォンは子どもの命を守ることができる。

Vocabulary
□ track ～の跡をたどる

訳 9 12 スマートフォンは友だちと交流し、堅固な人間関係を築く優れたツールだ。子どもたちはスマートフォンを使っておしゃべりをし、ゲームで遊び、宿題でお互いに助け合うことさえできる。また、スマートフォンを持っていない子どもが仲間はずれにされたり、場合によってはいじめられたりする可能性もある。

Vocabulary
□ bully ～をいじめる

Content Block　インターネットにアクセスする危険　MP3 137

13　Children should not be given access to the Internet by themselves, because it is too dangerous. Aside from the large number of websites with adult material that is not appropriate for children, it is also risky for children to interact with new people online. They could be deceived into meeting with a kidnapper or a child molester.

Content Block　スマートフォン依存　MP3 138

14　Studies have revealed that smartphone use can be addictive for some people. A lot of people are unable to maintain a normal lifestyle without access to their smartphones because they have become so dependent on them. This can often harm interpersonal relationships. Surely we should not give our children any devices that cause obsession and addiction.

伝統文化

Content Block　伝統文化の衰退　MP3 139

15　Due to changes in the global economy, more and more people are leaving rural areas and moving to cities. Also, young people are less likely to work at family businesses, especially in small, rural towns. Consequently, many traditional practices are being lost. For example, many forms of traditional kimono making are disappearing in Japan.

Content Block　都市化と伝統文化　MP3 140

16　Traditional culture is disappearing fast in quickly developing countries. For example, since 2000, a huge number of Chinese villages have disappeared. Part of the reason for this is that the government forces urbanization. But most of traditional Chinese culture is rural-based. This means that countless valuable traditions are being destroyed.

訳 9 13　子どもは自分でインターネットにアクセスする手段を与えられるべきではない。それはあまりにも危険だからだ。子どもにふさわしくない成人向けの内容のウェブサイトがたくさんあるだけでなく、知らない人とオンラインでやり取りをするのも危険だ。子どもがだまされて誘拐犯や児童性的虐待者に会ってしまうことにもなりかねない。

Vocabulary

□ kidnapper 誘拐犯　　□ molester 痴漢

訳 9 14　人によっては、スマートフォンは中毒になりうるということが、研究で明らかになってきた。スマートフォンに過剰に依存し、それなしには普通の生活が送れない人が数多くいる。このことは人間関係に害を及ぼす可能性がある。子どもたちに強迫観念と中毒を引き起こすような機器を与えるべきではないのは明らかだ。

Vocabulary

□ addictive 中毒性の、病みつきになる　　□ obsession 強迫観念、とりつかれること

訳 9 15　世界経済の変化により、ますます多くの人が地方を離れて都市部へ移動している。また若者は家族経営の仕事をしようとせず、とりわけ小さな田舎の町ではその傾向が強い。その結果、多くの伝統的な慣習が失われつつある。例えば、日本では多くの種類の伝統的な和服の製造法が失われている。

Vocabulary

□ rural 田舎の、地方の

訳 9 16　急激に発展を遂げている国々では、伝統文化が急速に失われつつある。例えば2000年以降、中国では膨大な数の村が姿を消した。これは、政府が都市化を推し進めていることに一因がある。しかし、中国の伝統文化のほとんどは、地方に根ざしたものだ。これはつまり、無数の貴重な伝統が破壊されつつあることを意味する。

Vocabulary

□ countless 無数の

スポーツイベントの開催

雇用の創出

17 Hosting an international sporting event leads to the creation of new jobs. These events require investment in building stadiums and hotels. This creates more jobs for the local community. Although not all of these jobs are permanent, some of them last for multiple years, and the local people are able to acquire new skills and save money.

インフラの整備

18 Investment in infrastructure benefits local people significantly. For example, improvements to public transportation are usually required before hosting a major sporting event. After the event is over, this improved infrastructure makes people's lives easier. Also, it makes the area a more attractive place to do business.

開催費用

19 The costs of preparing for a major event are astronomical. In addition to building hotels and stadiums, most areas also need to improve their transportation systems and infrastructure. This can cost billions of dollars. Because of this, many countries lose a significant amount of money by hosting major sporting events.

安全保障の強化

20 Improving security for major events is costly and problematic. Due to the increased danger of terrorism, security must be strengthened significantly. For large events, several thousand security guards need to be hired. This is extremely expensive. Also, it is difficult to manage security because many security guards are not well-trained. So the safety of the local people also goes down.

訳 9 17 国際スポーツイベントを開催することは、新しい雇用の創出につながる。こうしたイベントには、スタジアムやホテルの建設への投資が必要だ。これにより、地域社会により多くの働き口が創出される。こうした仕事のすべてが永続的であるわけではないが、数年は続くものもあり、地元の人々は新たなスキルを身につけ、お金を貯めることができる。

Vocabulary

□ permanent 永続的な、恒久的な

訳 9 18 インフラへの投資は、地元の人々に多大な恩恵を与える。例えば、大きなスポーツイベントを開催する前には、通例、公共交通機関の改善が必要となる。イベントが終わったあと、この改善されたインフラは人々の暮らしを楽にする。また、事業を行うにもより魅力的な場所になる。

Vocabulary

□ infrastructure インフラ、社会基盤

訳 9 19 大きなイベントの準備にかかる費用は莫大だ。ホテルやスタジアムの建設に加え、ほとんどの地域は交通網とインフラを改善する必要がある。これには何十億ドルもかかるかもしれない。このため、多くの国が、大きなスポーツイベントの開催により、多額の資金を失っている。

Vocabulary

□ astronomical 天文学的な、けた外れに多い

訳 9 20 大きなイベントに向けた安全対策の強化には費用がかさみ、問題をはらむ。テロの危険性が高まっているので、安全対策は大幅に強化されなければならない。大きなイベントでは、数千人の警備員を雇う必要がある。これには極めて高額な費用がかかる。また、警備員の多くは十分な訓練を受けていないため、安全を確保することも難しい。そのため、地域住民の安全性もまた低下する。

Vocabulary

□ problematic 問題のある

Content Block 21 — 観光業への寄与 [MP3 145]

International sporting events attract a great amount of attention to local communities. This results in more tourism. Some people argue that this boost in publicity does not compensate for the high costs of hosting these events, but it is important to consider the long-term effects. Some international tourists might visit a local area several years later.

Content Block 22 — 地元企業への悪影響 [MP3 146]

Although a major sporting event might help some businesses related to tourism, it also causes problems for many local businesses. For example, increased traffic and security regulations make it hard for companies with delivery trucks. Also, increased prices at various shops and hotels are a problem for people that regularly visit to do business.

ギャンブル

Content Block 23 — ギャンブルと犯罪 [MP3 147]

When people cannot stop gambling, they lose a lot of money. They are forced into debt and often commit crimes in order to pay it back. Some statistics suggest that a high percentage of serious gamblers have committed crimes like stealing to pay for their gambling habit. If gambling is banned, then crime can be reduced.

Content Block 24 — ギャンブルと家族関係 [MP3 148]

Families are negatively affected by gambling. The most common problem is the loss of money or belongings that were sold to pay for a gambling habit. Family members feel confused and hurt by the gambler's actions, often leading to divorce. Furthermore, family violence increases in families with money problems. These issues can be solved by outlawing gambling.

訳 9-21 国際スポーツイベントは、地域に多大な関心を集める。このことは観光事業の増大につながる。こうして知名度が高まってもそれはイベントの開催にかかる高いコストに見合うものではないと主張する人もいるが、長期的な効果を考えることが重要だ。数年たってからその地域を訪れる外国人観光客もいるだろう。

Vocabulary
- publicity 知名度、評判　□ compensate for ～ ～を埋め合わせる

訳 9-22 大きなスポーツイベントは、一部の観光関連の企業には利益をもたらすだろうが、地元の多くの企業に問題も引き起こす。例えば、交通量の増加やセキュリティー上の規制により、企業は配送トラックを利用しにくくなる。また、さまざまな店やホテルの値段が上がることは、普段から仕事で訪れる人々にとって問題だ。

Vocabulary
- regulation 規制

訳 9-23 ギャンブルをやめられないと、人はたくさんのお金を失う。借金せざるを得なくなり、その返済のために犯罪を起こすことも多い。重度のギャンブラーは高い割合で、常習的なギャンブルに使うお金のために窃盗などの罪を犯していることを示す統計もある。ギャンブルを禁止すれば、犯罪を減らすことができる。

Vocabulary
- statistics 統計（学）

訳 9-24 家庭はギャンブルによって悪影響を受ける。最もよくある問題は、お金がなくなったり、常習的なギャンブルに使うために所有物を売り払ってしまったりすることだ。ギャンブラーの行動に家族は困惑し、傷つき、離婚に至ることも多い。さらに、金銭的な問題がある家庭では、家庭内暴力が増える。これらの問題はギャンブルを法律で禁止すれば解決できる。

Vocabulary
- outlaw ～を違法とする

10 | テクノロジー

CHAPTER_2

テクノロジー

　テクノロジー（科学技術）は、辞書的には「実用的な目的のために科学的な知識を応用すること、その手法、およびそれによって作り出された機械や道具」のことで、具体的には、スプーン、振り子時計、薬品、スマートフォン、宇宙ステーションなど、すべてテクノロジーである。

　1級英作文では最も重要なコンセプトの一つで、かつて、現代社会がテクノロジーに依存しすぎているかを問われたことがある。また貧困や飢餓、エネルギー問題などのテーマにおいてPOINTとしても出題されている。テクノロジーとは何かを考えていると議論が進まなくなるので、先進技術くらいの意味合いでとらえておこう。

インターネット

　インターネットは「全世界のコンピューターネットワークを接続してできた地球規模の情報通信網」であり、現代のテクノロジーの中でも代表的なものの一つである。このネットワークにより、膨大な情報が瞬時に地球規模で共有できるようになり、また一般市民が情報を世界に向けて発信できるようになった一方で、匿名性を悪用した犯罪が増え、一度流出した情報を回収することも困難である。

　これまでインターネットを直接のテーマにした出題はないが、そのメリット／デメリットを問われる可能性は十分にあるだろう。

宇宙開発

　回数は少ないが、宇宙開発を継続すべきかを問うテーマが出題されたことがある。宇宙開発には、天体観測・気象観測・測地・航海援助・通信などを目的とした実用衛星による技術開発も含まれる。宇宙開発は、宇宙そのものの解明につながるだけでなく、そのための技術開発が日常生活に役立つ場合もあるが、危険であるうえ、莫大な費用もかかるため、その意義を疑問視する考え方もある。

🔍 キーワード

●テクノロジー

□ 技術革新	technological innovation
□ 情報技術	information technology（略：IT）
□ エレクトロニクス産業	electronics industry
□ 人工知能	artificial intelligence（略：AI）
□ スマート家電	smart appliances
□ テクノロジー利用の子どもへの影響	the impact of technology usage on children

●インターネット

□ アクセシビリティ	accessibility
□ 閲覧履歴	browsing history
□ 画像検索	image search
□ 検索エンジン	search engine
□ スマートフォン中毒	smartphone addiction
□ インターネットの出現	the emergence of the Internet
□ 信ぴょう性の要求	a demand for authenticity
□ アフィリエイトマーケティング	affiliate marketing
□ サイバー犯罪	cybercrime
□ ハッキング攻撃	hacking (attack) / cyber attack

●宇宙開発

□ 宇宙飛行士	astronaut
□ 商用衛星	commercial satellite
□ 生物が生存可能な惑星	habitable planet
□ 有人探査	human exploration
□ 無重力環境	zero-gravity environment
□ 国際宇宙ステーション	International Space Station（略：ISS）
□ 宇宙食	space food
□ 宇宙開発競争	the space race
□ 宇宙関連技術への投資の実用性	the practicality of investment in space-related technology
□ 技術の限界	the limits of technology
□ リソースの配分	allocation of resources

技術の進歩

10-1 Content Block 情報へのアクセスの飛躍的な進歩 　MP3 149

Technology now allows people to learn a great deal of things by themselves. The average person with a smartphone today has access to more information than the President of the United States had only 15 years ago. As the amount of information available increases, people have more opportunities to learn.

10-2 Content Block 医療的な進歩 　MP3 150

Thanks to technology, people are healthier than ever before. Since 1900 the global average life expectancy has more than doubled. Also, women are far less likely to die from childbirth than before, and new babies are far more likely to survive. All of these improvements are due to technology.

10-3 Content Block 自然の抑制からの逸脱 　MP3 151

The human population is expected to be around 10 billion by 2050. Unfortunately, the Earth cannot support so many people. Living organisms tend to expand and consume resources as much as possible. Usually nature prevents them from getting out of control. Because of technology, however, humans have not been stopped by nature, and the outcome may be disastrous.

10-4 Content Block 伝統的慣行の破壊 　MP3 152

Developments in technology are destroying many of the world's traditional practices. For example, most people in modern, developed countries do not know how to farm or raise livestock anymore. As a result, many people get unhealthy, GMO-packed food from giant agricultural companies. This also decreases people's appreciation for nature and the animals and plants that provide food.

訳 10-1 科学技術は現在、人々がさまざまなことを一人で学べるようにしている。スマートフォンを持っている今日の平均的な人は、わずか15年前のアメリカの大統領よりも多くの情報にアクセスすることができる。情報量が増えるにつれて、人は学ぶ機会が多くなる。

Vocabulary
- have access to ～〈もの・情報など〉を入手できる

訳 10-2 科学技術のおかげで、人は以前よりも健康になった。1900年以降、世界の平均寿命は2倍以上になった。また、女性が出産で死亡する確率は以前よりもずっと少なくなり、新生児の生存率ははるかに高まった。これらの改善はみな科学技術のおかげだ。

Vocabulary
- expectancy 見込み、余命

訳 10-3 人口は2050年までに100億人近くに達すると予想されている。残念ながら、地球はこれほど多くの人々を支えることができない。生物は可能な限り拡大し、資源を消費できるだけ消費する傾向がある。通常なら、自然は生物が抑制不可能にならないようにしている。しかし、科学技術があるために、人類には自然による抑制がきかず、結果は破滅的になるかもしれない。

Vocabulary
- living organism 生物、生体　□ disastrous 破滅的な

訳 10-4 科学技術の発達は、世界の伝統的な慣行の多くを破壊してきた。例えば、現代的な先進国のほとんどの人々が、今では作物や家畜の育てかたを知らない。その結果、多くの人は大手農業企業がつくった遺伝子組み換え原料が詰まった不健康な食品を買うようになった。これにより、自然や、食べ物を与えてくれる動植物に対する人間の感謝の気持ちも減っている。

Vocabulary
- practice 実践、習わし　□ livestock 家畜　□ GMO（＝genetically modified organism）遺伝子組み換え生物（作物）

科学技術への依存

環境破壊

Perhaps the greatest problem with technology is its negative impact on the planet. It is estimated that human civilizations are responsible for the destruction of nearly 50% of the world's trees. It took millions of years for the world's forests to develop, but with technology we are destroying them in mere decades. This will lead to serious problems in the future.

コミュニケーションの向上

Interpersonal communication has improved because of technology. It is now possible to stay in touch with friends and family members from almost anywhere in the world. Also, digital communication is not a replacement for face-to-face communication. Instead, it is a supplement to in-person meetings.

伝統技術の伝承

A common belief about the development of technology is that it is causing people to forget traditional skills and crafts. But this is not true. For example, thanks to online courses, people all over the world can learn traditional skills like woodworking, farming, and using medical herbs. Without technology, it would only be possible to learn traditional skills from people living nearby.

体力の低下

Our dependence on technology has led to a decrease in healthy hobbies and leisure activities. Children and teenagers spend their time watching television and playing video games when they should be outside playing sports and enjoying nature. According to recent research, children are becoming weaker, less muscular, and unable to do physical tasks that previous generations found simple.

訳 10 5 科学技術に関する最大の問題は、恐らく、地球に与える悪影響だろう。人類の文明のせいで、世界の森林の 50％近くが破壊されたと推定されている。世界の森林が成長するのには何百万年もかかるが、私たちは科学技術によって、ほんの数十年間で森林を破壊している。これは将来、深刻な問題につながるだろう。

Vocabulary

□ mere ほんの、単なる

訳 10 6 人と人とのコミュニケーションは、科学技術のおかげで向上した。今や世界中のほとんどどこにいても、友人や家族と連絡を取り合うことが可能になった。また、デジタルなコミュニケーションは、面と向かってのコミュニケーションに置き換わるものではない。そうではなく、直接会うことを補完するものなのだ。

Vocabulary

□ supplement 補うもの、補完　□ in-person 直接会う、対面の

訳 10 7 科学技術の発達のせいで伝統技術や伝統工芸が忘れられているというのが、科学技術の発達についての通念になっている。しかしこれは真実ではない。例えば、オンラインコースのおかげで、世界中の人々が木工、農業、薬草の使いかたなどの昔ながらの技術を学ぶことができる。科学技術がなければ、伝統技術は近くに住む人たちから学ぶことしかできないだろう。

Vocabulary

□ woodworking 木工

訳 10 8 科学技術に依存する結果、健康的な趣味やレジャー活動が減っている。子どもや十代の若者は、本来は外でスポーツをしたり自然を楽しんだりするべきなのに、テレビを見たりテレビゲームをしたりして過ごしている。最近の調査によると、子どもは身体が弱くなり、筋力が低下し、上の世代には簡単だった肉体的な作業ができなくなっているという。

Vocabulary

□ muscular 筋肉の (発達した)　□ physical task 肉体作業

仕事の効率

Technological developments lead to improvements in workplace efficiency. Thanks to the Internet, it is possible to communicate with several employees, companies, and clients simultaneously. As a result, less time is wasted talking on the phone and traveling for business meetings. Less time is also spent on simple, repetitive tasks, which are a waste of employees' skills.

インターネット

連絡手段としてのインターネット

The Internet supports interpersonal communication. One common complaint is that online communication is not as healthy as face-to-face communication. However, online communication does not replace face-to-face meetings. Instead, it is a supplement to in-person communication, and it increases the overall volume of interaction. This additional method for staying in touch is especially valuable for friends and family members that live far apart.

教育のツール

The Internet is an important tool for worldwide education. Thanks to the Internet, individuals in developing countries with limited access to education can obtain high quality information and skills from experts in other countries. More education for a larger number of people will raise the number of individuals able to perform skilled jobs, which results in more innovation and improves the global economy.

直接のやり取りとオンライン上の交流

Recent studies show that the majority of business executives prefer face-to-face interaction, arguing that it builds stronger and more meaningful relationships. Creating a positive emotional environment is a result of in-person communication, which benefits both personal and professional relationships. This cannot be replaced by online interaction.

訳 10 9 科学技術の発展は、職場の効率の向上につながる。インターネットのおかげで、複数の従業員や企業やクライアントと同時にコミュニケーションをすることが可能になった。その結果、電話で話すことや、仕事の打ち合わせのために移動することで無駄になる時間が減る。単純な繰り返しの作業に費やされる時間も減る。こうした作業は、従業員の能力を無駄に費やすものである。

Vocabulary
□ simultaneously 同時に　□ repetitive 繰り返しの

訳 10 10 インターネットは、人と人とのコミュニケーションをサポートする。よく聞かれる不満に、オンラインでのコミュニケーションは面と向かってのコミュニケーションに比べて健全でないというものがある。しかし、オンラインでのコミュニケーションは、直接会ってのコミュニケーションに置き換わるものではない。むしろ、対面のコミュニケーションを補助するものであり、交流の全体量を増加させるのだ。連絡を取り合うためのこの追加的な手段は、特に、遠く離れて暮らす友人や家族にとって利用価値が高い。

Vocabulary
□ interpersonal 対人の、個人間の　□ supplement 補足、補完

訳 10 11 インターネットは、世界の教育にとって重要なツールである。インターネットのおかげで、教育の機会が限られている発展途上国の人々は、他国にいる専門家から、質の高い情報とスキルを得ることができる。より多くの人々により多くの教育の機会が与えられれば、スキルの必要な仕事ができる人の数が増え、その結果、イノベーションが増して世界経済は向上する。

Vocabulary
□ worldwide 世界的な　□ obtain 〜を得る

訳 10 12 最近の研究によると、企業の重役の大多数が面と向かってのやり取りを好み、そのほうが強固で有意義な関係が築かれると主張しているという。望ましい感情的環境ができることは、直接のコミュニケーションの成果であり、個人間および仕事上の関係の両方でよい影響をもたらす。これにオンラインでの交流が置き換わることはできない。

Vocabulary
□ face-to-face interaction 対面の交流

Content Block サイバー犯罪

13. Personal information posted online is often stolen. As Internet usage increases, more and more people feel comfortable purchasing products and entering private information online. As a result, the frequency of identity theft and credit card fraud is increasing. Experts estimate that the annual global cost of cybercrime is enormous.

Content Block 倫理観の低下

14. The Internet is leading to a decrease in moral values. Most importantly, it is causing people to forget about the importance of their local community. When young people spend all of their time looking at social media, they are less likely to interact with the people around them. This drop in face-to-face communication leads to a lack of empathy for other people.

Content Block 倫理観の向上

15. The Internet is leading to improvements in moral values. Thanks to the Internet, it is possible to interact with people all over the world. This results in a more sophisticated exchange of new ideas. By understanding more about different people around the world, it is natural to become more sympathetic about their situation. Moral values improve as a result.

人工知能

Content Block 人工知能の危険性

16. Though artificial intelligence has many potential benefits, the risk is too great. If a computer program or a robot became more intelligent than all of the people on the planet, then stopping it would be virtually impossible. Such a program may decide to limit the freedom of humans. In the worst case, it may decide to kill all of the humans on the planet.

訳 10-13 インターネット上に投稿された個人情報が頻繁に盗まれている。インターネット利用が増えるにつれて、ますます多くの人が、インターネットで商品を購入し、個人情報を入力することに違和感を覚えなくなっている。その結果、個人情報詐取とクレジットカード詐欺の数が増している。専門家は、サイバー犯罪による世界の年間被害額は巨額だと推定している。

Vocabulary

□ cybercrime サイバー犯罪、ネット犯罪　□ fraud 詐欺

訳 10-14 インターネットは倫理観の低下につながっている。とりわけ重要なのは、インターネットは人々に、地域社会の重要性を忘れさせていることだ。若者は四六時中ソーシャルメディアを眺めて過ごしていて、まわりの人々と交流することが少なくなっている。こうした面と向かってのコミュニケーションの減少は、他者に対する共感の欠如につながる。

Vocabulary

□ moral value 倫理観　□ empathy 共感、感情移入

訳 10-15 インターネットは倫理観の向上につながっている。インターネットのおかげで、世界中の人々とやり取りすることができるようになった。その結果、新しい考えをより見識をもってやり取りできるようになる。世界中のさまざまな人々についてより多くのことを理解すれば、そうした人々の置かれている状況に共感が増すのは自然なことだ。その結果、倫理観は向上する。

Vocabulary

□ sympathetic 共感する

訳 10-16 人工知能には数多くの潜在的な利点があるが、リスクも大きすぎる。コンピュータープログラムやロボットが地球上の人間の誰よりも賢くなったら、それを止めることは事実上不可能になるだろう。そうしたプログラムは、人間の自由を制限すると決めるかもしれない。最悪の場合、地球上のすべての人間を殺すという決定を下すかもしれない。

Vocabulary

□ artificial intelligence 人工知能（略：AI）　□ virtually 実質的に、事実上

10 Content Block 人工知能の軍事利用　MP3 165

17 Even if humans are able to control intelligent programs and robots, they would still be extremely dangerous. Many governments are already developing AI for a variety of military purposes. Any type of robot that can be programmed to kill humans is too risky. It might be used by terrorists or corrupt governments to kill innocent people.

10 Content Block 人工知能のメリット　MP3 166

18 Developments in artificial intelligence will make life better for all of the people on the planet. For example, companies are already developing self-driving cars. These will decrease traffic jams, save time, and lower the number of accidents from drinking and driving. As AI programs get better, we will be able to automate all kinds of dangerous and tedious tasks.

10 Content Block 人工知能と医療の発展　MP3 167

19 Artificial intelligence will lead to incredible improvements in medical science. For example, scientists have already developed smart computer programs that are better at reading X-rays than humans. As this technology continues to advance, AI programs will be able to fully diagnose and treat illnesses in humans. With intelligent nanorobots, we may be able to completely eliminate the majority of diseases.

宇宙開発

10 Content Block 宇宙関連研究の技術転用（食料）　MP3 168

20 Scientists claim many useful technological innovations have been made by trying to help astronauts in the harsh conditions of outer space. For example, NASA's efforts to provide astronauts with nutrient-rich foods in space have led to improvements in commercial food for newborn babies.

訳 10 17 たとえ人間が人工知能プログラムやロボットをコントロールできるとしても、極めて危険であることに変わりはないだろう。すでに多くの政府が、さまざまな軍事目的で人工知能を開発している。人間を殺すようにプログラムできるロボットは、どんなタイプのものであれあまりにも危険だ。テロリストや腐敗した政府が無辜の市民を殺害するのに使われる恐れもある。

Vocabulary

□ risky 危険な　□ corrupt 墜落した、腐敗した

訳 10 18 人工知能の発達は、地球上のすべての人々の生活をよりよいものにする。例えば、企業はすでに自動運転車を開発している。自動運転車は交通渋滞を減らし、時間を節約し、飲酒運転による事故件数を減らす。人工知能のプログラムがもっとよくなれば、危険な作業や退屈な作業をすべて自動化することができるだろう。

Vocabulary

□ drinking and driving 飲酒運転　□ automate 〜を自動化する　□ tedious 退屈な

訳 10 19 人工知能は、医療分野における著しい発展につながる。例えば、科学者たちはすでに、人間よりも精確にX線画像を読影できるスマートコンピュータープログラムを開発している。この技術が発展を続ければ、人工知能のプログラムは人間の病気を完全に診断し、治療することができるようになるだろう。インテリジェントナノロボットを使えば、私たちは大多数の病気を根絶できるかもしれない。

Vocabulary

□ eliminate 〜を排除する

訳 10 20 宇宙空間という過酷な環境にいる宇宙飛行士を助けようとして多くの有益な技術革新が生み出されたと、科学者たちは主張している。例えば、宇宙で宇宙飛行士に栄養価の高い食事を提供しようというNASAの取り組みは、新生児用の市販食品の改善につながった。

Vocabulary

□ harsh 過酷な　□ newborn baby 新生児

宇宙関連研究の技術転用（浄水）

21 Space technology research even leads to benefits for people in developing countries. For example, water purification systems developed to sustain life in outer space are now used to change wastewater into safe drinking water. This technology provides poor communities around the world with access to clean drinking water.

資金のより有効な使い道

22 We could spend the money used for space research on more important things like developing renewable energy or decreasing world poverty. These investments would have a direct benefit on human lives. For example, it is simply not logical to spend money building spaceships when there are millions of people in the world that are starving or do not have clean water.

より優先度の高い研究

23 Exploring our oceans is more important than exploring space. Several experts claim that exploring and studying the ocean might lead to many important discoveries. For example, it is believed that some of the creatures living in the ocean could be used to develop cures for many diseases. Discoveries like this are unlikely in space.

ロボットによる宇宙探査

24 A major problem with space-related technology is that it is developed for humans. But it would be cheaper and more effective to only send robots into outer space. It is difficult and costly to send humans into space because they need food, water, and oxygen. But a robot does not need any of these things. Also, robots never need to return to Earth.

訳 10 21　宇宙技術の研究は、発展途上国の人々にも恩恵をもたらしている。例えば、宇宙空間で生命を維持するために開発された浄水システムは、現在、廃水を安全な飲み水に変えるために活用されている。この技術のおかげで、世界中の貧しい地域の人々が清潔な飲み水を得られるようになっている。

Vocabulary

□ water purification system 浄水システム　□ sustain 〜を維持する、持続する

訳 10 22　私たちは宇宙研究に使われている資金を、再生可能エネルギーの開発や、世界の貧困の低減など、もっと重要なことに使うことができる。こうした投資は、人間の暮らしに直接的な恩恵をもたらす。例えば、世界では何百万人もの人々が飢えていたり、清潔な水が手に入れられなかったりする一方で、宇宙船の建造に費用を投じるというのはまったく理にかなっていない。

Vocabulary

□ starve 飢える

訳 10 23　海洋探査は宇宙探査よりも重要だ。海洋を探査し、研究することは、たくさんの重要な発見につながる可能性があると、複数の専門家が主張している。例えば、海に生息する生物の中には、多くの病気の治療薬を開発するのに使うことができるものもあると考えられている。このような発見は宇宙では見込みが薄い。

Vocabulary

□ creature 生物　□ unlikely ありそうにない

訳 10 24　宇宙関連技術の大きな問題は、それが人間用に開発されているということだ。しかし、宇宙にロボットだけを送り込むのであれば、費用を抑えられ、より効率的になるだろう。人間は食料と水、酸素を必要とするため、人間を宇宙に送り込むことは困難で費用がかかる。しかし、ロボットにはこれらのいずれも必要ない。それに、ロボットは地球に帰ってくる必要もない。

Vocabulary

□ costly 金のかかる　□ oxygen 酸素

11 | 医療・生命倫理

CHAPTER_2

医療

　医療の問題はこの10年ほどの試験で直接テーマになったことはないが、科学技術の進歩や高齢化社会、仕事への過度の傾斜といったテーマのPOINTとして**健康**（health）が複数回取り上げられている。当然、人口問題にも関わってくる。

　制度の面で見ると、日本には国民皆保険制度があり、患者が払う医療費は一部であるため、自己負担は比較的少ない（もちろん保険が適用されない高額医療も存在する）。一方、医師や医療機関への診療報酬は医療保険から点数制で支払われるため、過度の検査や投薬、長期入院が多くなるというデメリットもある。また**保険制度**（insurance system）の財源も大きな問題になっている。
（→1 現代日本社会「少子高齢社会」）

生命倫理

　クローン技術や再生医療、遺伝子組み換えといったバイオテクノロジーは生命科学の中でも現在最も注目されている分野の一つで、1級でも遺伝子組み換え作物やクローンに関する問題が直接テーマとして出題されている。バイオマスエネルギーのように環境問題に関連する場合もある。

　このトピックでポイントになるのは、細胞中で生物の特徴・性質を子孫に伝える役割を持つ**遺伝子**（gene）だ。その本体はDNAで、遺伝情報は塩基の配列順序で保持されている。

　生物が親から引き継いだ遺伝情報の全体は**ゲノム**（genome）と呼ばれ、その解読が治療に生かされるようになってきた。

　また、**クローン**（clone）とは親と同じ遺伝情報を持つ個体のことで、その研究は医療の発展を推進する一方で、人間に対する応用は倫理的観点から世界各国で禁止される方向にある。また、前臨床試験として行われる動物実験についても、動物福祉の観点から問題視する声がある。

　遺伝子を人為的に操作する遺伝子組み換え技術を使って作り出された**遺伝子組み換え作物**（genetically modified crops）は、除草剤や害虫に強く、安定した収穫を得られるという利点がある半面、生態系へ未知の影響を及ぼす危険性も指摘されている。
（→4 世界の問題「世界の飢餓」、→8 環境保護）

🔍 キーワード

●医療

□ 代替医療	**alternative remedy**
□ 処方箋	**prescription**（＜ **prescribe** ～を処方する）
□ 抗生物質	**antibiotic**
□ 薬剤、薬品	**pharmaceutical drug**
□ 新薬を開発する	**develop new drugs**
□ ジェネリック医薬品	**generic drug**

●再生医療

□ 再生医療	**regenerative medicine**
□ 幹細胞	**stem cell**
□ 組織	**tissue**
□ 遺伝形質	**genetic trait**
□ 拒絶反応	**rejection**（＜ **reject** ～に拒絶反応を示す）
□ 臓器売買	**organ trade**

●遺伝子組み換え作物

□ 収穫効率	**efficiency of crops**
□ 人体への影響	**influence on humans**
□ 無農薬の	**chemical-free**
□ 独占	**monopoly**
□ 製品の安全性	**product safety**
□ 農家の搾取	**exploitation of farmers**
□ バイオハザード	**biohazard**

●クローン

□ 倫理的問題	**ethical question**
□ 差別	**discrimination**（＜ **discriminate** ～を差別する）
□ 生態系の破壊	**ecological destruction**
□ 世界飢餓の解決	**solution to world hunger**

●動物実験

□ 動物の権利	**animal rights**
□ 実験の有効性への疑問	**doubts regarding experiments' effectiveness**

医療技術の発達

11-1 Content Block 寿命の伸長　MP3 173

The most obvious reason that medical technology is always beneficial to society is that it allows us to live longer. Every year, we find new cures and treatments for diseases, and the life expectancy of developed nations continues to increase. This means that we can spend more time with our family and friends.

11-2 Content Block 医療費の低下　MP3 174

As medical technology improves, it also becomes much cheaper, and more people can receive proper care. Right now many advanced medical treatments are still so expensive that only the world's richest people have access to them. However, thanks to the development of medical technology, we are approaching an era in which affordable healthcare is available to everyone.

11-3 Content Block 細菌の耐性　MP3 175

The more we create drugs for some illnesses, the worse they become. For example, antibiotics that fight bacterial infections can promote the development of drug-resistant bacteria, sometimes referred to as "superbugs." In other words, our drugs are making bacteria stronger and more dangerous. This could potentially lead to a disease that cannot be controlled, which could kill billions of people.

11-4 Content Block 伝統的な治療法　MP3 176

As we continue to rely on medical technology, more traditional healing methods are being ignored or forgotten. For example, many doctors give their patients various medications for illnesses that could be healed naturally with herbs, proper nutrition, and rest. Nowadays, most people do not acknowledge the power of natural healing methods, but many of them have been used effectively for thousands of years.

訳 11 1 医療技術が常に社会に有益である最も明白な理由は、そのおかげで私たちは長生きできるようになったということだ。毎年、病気の新しい治療薬と治療法が発見され、先進国の平均寿命は延び続けている。このことは、私たちがより長い時間を家族や友人と過ごせるということを意味している。

Vocabulary

☐ life expectancy 平均余命、寿命

訳 11 2 医療技術が発達するにつれて、費用も大幅に下がり、適切な手当てを受けられる人が増える。現在は、多くの先進医療はまだとても高額で、世界で最も裕福な人々しか治療を受けることができない。しかし、医療技術の発展のおかげで、誰もが手ごろな費用で医療を受けられる時代が近づいている。

Vocabulary

☐ era 時代

訳 11 3 治療薬をつくればつくるほど、悪化する病気もある。例えば、細菌の感染に対処する抗生物質は、時に「スーパーバグ」と呼ばれる抗生物質に耐性を持つ細菌を出現させることがある。言い換えると、私たちの医薬品が、細菌をさらに強く危険にしているのだ。このことは、コントロール不可能な病気を発生させかねず、何十億人もの人々が死亡するかもしれない。

Vocabulary

☐ antibiotic 抗生物質　☐ infection 感染　☐ drug-resistant 薬剤耐性の

訳 11 4 私たちが医療技術への依存を続けると、伝統的な治療法が見過ごされ、忘れられていく。例えば、多くの医師は、薬草や適切な栄養、休養をとれば自然に治る病気に対して、さまざまな医薬品を患者に与える。最近では、ほとんどの人が自然療法の力を認めていないが、その多くは数千年もの間、効果的に活用されてきたものなのだ。

Vocabulary

☐ medication 薬　☐ nutrition 栄養

クローン研究

11 Content Block 反自然 🎧 177

5 The main reason that cloning should be banned is that it is not natural. If people used cloning to produce and modify humans, then it would cause unnatural changes to the human species in general. There would likely be class divisions between cloned and non-cloned humans. Also, determining the traits of new generations upsets the natural balance of the world.

11 Content Block 遺伝的多様性の喪失 🎧 178

6 Decreases in genetic diversity are hazardous to animals. Plenty of scientific studies have shown that genetic diversity makes a species stronger. This is part of the evolutionary process. With cloning, however, plants and animals lose their genetic diversity, making them more vulnerable to problems such as diseases.

11 Content Block 医学への貢献 🎧 179

7 The main advantage of cloning research is its potential contribution to medical science. For example, it is theoretically possible that scientists could use cloning technology to replace organs such as kidneys and hearts. This type of technology would save countless lives, but it will be difficult to develop if cloning research is banned.

11 Content Block 絶滅危惧種の個体数増加 🎧 180

8 It is possible that cloning could be used to build populations of endangered and extinct animals. It is estimated that between 200 and 2,000 animal species become extinct every year. There is no denying that humans are largely responsible for this. With cloning, we can repair some of the damage that humans have caused.

訳 11 5 クローン技術が禁止されるべき主な理由は、自然に反するからだ。もし、クローン技術をヒトの繁殖や改変に使えば、ヒトという種全体に不自然な変化が起こることになる。クローンで生まれた人間とクローンでない人間の間に階級区分も生じるだろう。また、新しい世代の形質を決定することは、世界の自然なバランスを乱してしまう。

Vocabulary
□ modify 〜を(部分的に)変える　□ trait (遺伝)形質

訳 11 6 遺伝的多様性の低下は、動物にとって危険である。遺伝的多様性は種をより強固にしていると多くの科学研究が示している。これは進化のプロセスの一部だ。しかしながら、クローン技術によって動植物は遺伝的多様性を失い、このことで病気などの問題に対してより脆弱になる。

Vocabulary
□ genetic diversity 遺伝的多様性

訳 11 7 クローン研究の主なメリットは、医学に貢献する可能性があることだ。例えば、科学者がクローン技術を使って、腎臓や心臓といった臓器を取り換えることは、理論的には可能だ。このような技術ができれば無数の生命が救われるだろうが、クローン研究が禁止されれば開発は困難になる。

Vocabulary
□ kidney 腎臓

訳 11 8 絶滅危惧種や絶滅種の動物の個体数を増やすために、クローン技術を使用することが可能だ。毎年、200から2000種の動物が絶滅していると推定されている。人間がこの主たる原因となっていることは否定できない。クローン技術があれば、人間が引き起こしたダメージのいくつかを修復することができる。

Vocabulary
□ extinct 絶滅した　□ There is no denying that 〜 〜ということを否定することはできない

動物実験

Content Block 11-9 信頼性の乏しさ　MP3 181

The main reason that animal testing should be banned is that it is not reliable. Animals and humans are very different organisms. Because of this, some products that are harmful to humans are not harmful to animals, and vice versa. In fact, most potential pharmaceutical drugs that are shown by animal testing to be effective and safe do not pass clinical tests.

Content Block 11-10 代替手段　MP3 182

There are already more promising methods for testing goods. For example, testing methods that use human cells and tissues combined with special computer programs are more reliable. These methods can even be used to test the effects of various substances on specific organs and cells, which leads to more accurate results.

Content Block 11-11 人命の優先　MP3 183

The primary reason that animal testing should not be banned is that human lives are more valuable than animal lives. Before animal testing was introduced, humans used products without performing safety tests. This led to a considerable number of deaths and even more illnesses. Scientists do not wish to cause harm to animals, but it is a better option than allowing humans to be harmed.

Content Block 11-12 科学的な発見への寄与　MP3 184

Animal testing leads to valuable scientific discoveries. Animal testing has contributed to medical breakthroughs related to diseases like cancer, AIDS, and diabetes. Also, experimenting with animals has taught psychology researchers a great deal of information about basic learning processes and motivational factors such as hunger, thirst, and reproduction.

訳 11-9　動物実験が禁止されるべき主な理由は、信頼性に乏しいことである。動物と人間はかけ離れた生物だ。このため、人間に有害でも動物には無害な製品もあり、その逆もある。実際、動物実験では効果があり、安全であると示された開発中の医薬品のほとんどが、臨床試験を通過しない。

Vocabulary

□ animal testing 動物実験　□ pharmaceutical drugs 薬剤、薬品　□ clinical test 臨床試験

訳 11-10　製品を試験するのにはもっと確実な方法がすでに存在する。例えば、特別なコンピュータープログラムと組み合わせて人間の細胞と組織を使った実験方法は、より信頼性が高い。こうした方法は、特定の臓器や細胞への多様な物質の影響を実験するのに使うこともでき、さらに正確な実験結果をもたらす。

Vocabulary

□ tissue 組織

訳 11-11　動物実験を禁止するべきではない第一の理由は、人命は動物の命よりも価値があるということだ。動物実験が導入される前、人間は安全性を確認する実験を行わずに製品を使っていた。死亡に至るケースも相当数あり、病気を招くケースはさらに多かった。科学者たちは動物に害を与えることを望んではいないが、人間に害を与えるよりは好ましい選択肢だ。

Vocabulary

□ a considerable number of ～ 相当数の～

訳 11-12　動物実験は貴重な科学的な発見をもたらす。動物実験はこれまで、がんやエイズ、糖尿病といった疾病に関する医学的な発見に貢献してきた。また、動物を使った実験は、心理学の研究者に、基本的な学習プロセスと飢えや渇き、生殖のような動機づけ要因について非常に多くの情報をもたらしてきた。

Vocabulary

□ breakthrough (科学上の)大発見、画期的な進歩　□ diabetes 糖尿病　□ reproduction 繁殖、生殖

遺伝子組み換え作物

Content Block 情報の不十分さ

13. We do not have enough information about GMOs at this time. A large number of the scientific studies regarding GMOs have been funded by the large biotechnology companies that manufacture them. Reliable safety data can only be released by scientists without a conflict of interest, but such data is not yet available.

Content Block 過剰な除草剤

14. Producers of genetically modified crops use too many herbicides. One of the reported benefits of GMOs is that they are resistant to chemicals that kill weeds. This means that farmers can spray more of these chemicals onto genetically modified crops, which may be unhealthy for human consumption.

Content Block 世界人口をまかなう食糧生産

15. Without the use of genetically modified crops, we may be unable to feed all of the people on Earth. The human population is expected to reach around 10 billion by 2050. Experts predict we will need 70% more agricultural production to feed all of these people. Because of this growing number, we need to do everything we can to increase food production.

Content Block コストの低下

16. GMOs help keep food production costs down, which results in lower prices for consumers. Genetically modified crops are reliable, consistent, and highly resistant. This means that genetically modified crops are easier to harvest, so farms using genetically modified crops can save money on labor. In turn, this saves money for customers, too.

訳 11 13　私たちには遺伝子組み換え作物について、現時点で十分な情報がない。遺伝子組み換え作物に関する科学研究の多くは、遺伝子組み換え作物を製造している大手のバイオテクノロジー企業によって資金提供を受けてきた。信頼できる安全性についてのデータは、利害関係のない科学者にしか出せないものだが、そのようなデータはまだ入手できない。

Vocabulary

□ GMO 遺伝子組み換え生物（作物）（genetically modified organismの略）

訳 11 14　遺伝子組み換え作物の生産者は過剰な除草剤を使う。遺伝子組み換え作物について報告されている利点の一つは、雑草を枯らす化学物質に耐性があることだ。これはつまり、農業従事者はこうした化学物質をより多く遺伝子組み換え作物に散布できるということで、人間が摂取するには不健康である可能性がある。

Vocabulary

□ herbicides 除草剤　□ resistant to ～ ～に耐性のある

訳 11 15　遺伝子組み換え作物の使用がなければ、地球上のすべての人々を養うことはできないだろう。人口は2050年までに約100億人に達すると予想されている。専門家は、このすべての人々を養うには農業生産を70％増やす必要があると予測している。この人口増加のため、我々は食糧生産を増やすためにできるあらゆることをする必要がある。

Vocabulary

□ feed ～を養う

訳 11 16　遺伝子組み換え作物は、食糧生産コストを低く抑えるので、結果的に消費者が支払う価格は安くなる。遺伝子組み換え作物は、信頼性があり、安定しており、耐性が高い。つまり遺伝子組み換え作物は収穫が容易で、遺伝子組み換え作物を使う農家は労働コストを抑えることができる。このことは結局、消費者にとってお金の節約にもなる。

Vocabulary

□ consistent 着実な、一貫性のある　□ harvest ～を収穫する

12 経済・ビジネス

CHAPTER_2

労働

　仕事と生活の間で問題を抱える人が増加したことから、日本でも2007年に内閣府が「ワーク・ライフ・バランス憲章」を発表し、残業時間の削減や有給休暇・男性による育児休暇の取得率の向上などを目標として掲げた。また雇用の維持・創出のために労働者一人あたりの労働時間を短縮するワーク・シェアリングも広がりつつある。その一方で、フリーターや派遣労働者などの非正規雇用者を中心に、フルタイムで働いても生活の維持が困難な「ワーキングプア（働く貧困層）」が増加していることも問題になっている。

　過去の問題では、現代社会では仕事に重きが置かれすぎているかを問うテーマが出題されている。終身雇用制や能力制といったテーマについても考えておきたい。

税

　税とは、国や地方自治体が、国民・市民のためのサービスを提供するために強制的に徴収する金。国税／地方税、直接税（所得税・法人税など）／間接税（消費税・酒税など）といった分類がある。税には、富裕者から多く徴収すること（累進課税）で富を再分配する機能がある一方で、労働意欲を阻害する側面もあるとされる。

　直接テーマとして出題されてはいないが、社会の高齢化や多国籍企業の役割などのテーマの問題でPOINTとして取り上げられている。

マスメディアと広告

　マスメディアとは、不特定多数の人に情報を伝達する媒体。具体的には新聞やテレビ、ラジオ、雑誌などを指す。大衆に情報を伝え、世論を形成する役割も持つので、視聴者・読者に正確かつ公正な情報を提供することが求められるが、資本主義社会においてはマスメディアの多くが営利企業として運営されているため、利潤追求のため、広告主に有利になるように（あるいは不利にならないように）偏向する可能性がある。

　過去の問題ではマスメディアが社会に対して持つ影響の是非について出題されている。

🔍 キーワード

●労働

☐ ワーク・ライフ・バランス	work-life balance
☐ 賃金の低下	wage reduction
☐ サービス残業	unpaid overtime
☐ 基本給	base [basic] salary
☐ 最低賃金	minimum wage
☐ 残業手当	overtime allowance
☐ フルタイムの仕事	full-time job
☐ 労働条件	labor [work] conditions
☐ 有給休暇	paid leave
☐ 景気の悪化	economic deterioration
☐ 過労死	death from overwork
☐ フレックスタイム制	flexible working hours
☐ 自殺率の低下	decline in the suicide rate
☐ 規制緩和	deregulation
☐ 早期退職	early retirement
☐ 終身雇用制度	lifelong employment system
☐ 能力給制度	merit system

●税

☐ 累進課税	progressive taxes
☐ トリクルダウン効果	the trickle-down effect
☐ 遺産相続	inheritance
☐ 租税回避、節税	tax avoidance
☐ (違法な)脱税	tax evasion
☐ 均一税率の導入	the introduction of a flat tax rate
☐ 支出の増加	increased spending
☐ 公平性	fairness
☐ モチベーションの低下	fall of motivation
☐ 富の再分配	redistribution of wealth
☐ 自由競争	free competition
☐ 格差社会	social polarization

●マスメディアと広告

☐ 偏向報道	media bias
☐ 情報共有	information sharing
☐ 誤報	false report
☐ 速報性	quick reporting

高所得者と税

累進課税

1. Higher taxes are required for wealthier citizens because this is the best way to generate enough money for government expenses. It is common to hear people suggest flat-rate tax systems. However, expert economists have shown that these would result in heavier tax burdens for poor people and a lack of government funds.

比例しない所得と労働量

2. Many people argue that the rich should not pay higher taxes because they worked harder to earn their money, but this is not true. For example, someone making 1 million dollars per year makes more money than 20 teachers. It is impossible for that person to be working harder than all of those teachers.

資本主義の阻害

3. Raising taxes for rich people discourages capitalism. Generally speaking, people work harder when they want to make more money. However, there is less reason to work harder when there are higher tax rates for rich people. In other words, higher tax rates for the rich discourage capitalism.

租税回避の促進

4. Setting high tax rates for rich individuals encourages tax avoidance. If rich people are faced with higher tax rates, then they will search for ways to avoid paying taxes. This is one reason why rich citizens place their money and assets in overseas tax havens, which harms the local economies.

訳 12 1 裕福な市民にはより高い税金を求めるべきである理由は、これが政府の歳出をまかなうに足るお金を生み出す最善の方法だからだ。一律課税制度を提言する声もよく聞かれる。しかし、経済の専門家たちは、この制度では貧しい人々の税負担を増すことになり、政府の資金が不足することになると示している。

Vocabulary

□ flat-rate（料金・税などが）均一の

訳 12 2 多くの人々が、裕福な人々は高い税金を支払うべきではないと主張しており、その理由は、裕福な人々はお金を稼ぐためにより熱心に働いているからだというのだが、それは事実ではない。例えば、1年間に100万ドルを稼ぐ人は、20人の教員よりも多くのお金を稼いでいる。（だが）年収100万ドルの人が教員20人分よりもたくさん働くことは不可能だ。

Vocabulary

□ make money 稼ぐ

訳 12 3 裕福な人々への税金を上げることは、資本主義を阻害する。概して、人はお金をもっと稼ぎたくて、もっと熱心に働く。しかし、裕福な人への税率が高ければ、より勤勉に働く理由が減る。言い換えれば、富裕層への税率を高くすることは、資本主義を阻害する。

Vocabulary

□ discourage ～を阻害する

訳 12 4 裕福な個人に高い税率を設定するのは、租税回避の原因となる。裕福な人々は高い税率に直面すれば、税金の支払いを避ける方法を探る。これは、裕福な人々が海外の租税回避地に資金や財産を置く理由の一つで、地域経済に損害を与えている。

Vocabulary

□ tax avoidance 税金逃れ、租税回避　□ asset 資産、財産　□ tax haven 租税回避地

マスメディアの影響

12 Content Block 情報の偏向　　MP3 193

5　Mass media news programs tend to be biased and misleading. News programs should be unbiased, honest, and free from government and sponsor controls. Unfortunately, this is not the case. For example, government regulations have caused Japan's press freedom ranking to drop to embarrassingly low levels in recent years.

12 Content Block 広告の影響　　MP3 194

6　People cannot escape the influence of mass media advertising. This is a problem because a significant portion of advertising is designed to make people feel bad about themselves. For example, advertising often makes young girls overly self-conscious about their bodies. This has been linked to an increase in eating disorders such as anorexia, which is one of the most dangerous mental illnesses.

12 Content Block 教育的価値　　MP3 195

7　The greatest benefit of the media is its educational value. Thanks to news programs, we can learn about what is happening in other areas of the world. Even popular dramas and comedies teach us an incredible amount of things. Plus, the media includes a wide variety of educational programs that teach about topics such as science and history.

12 Content Block 娯楽の提供　　MP3 196

8　The media contributes to society by entertaining people. Entertainment has been an important part of every human civilization. Humans need stories in their lives. Most people would not want to quit watching television or films forever. This is because the media makes their lives more enjoyable. Surely this is a positive thing.

訳 12-5 マスメディアのニュース番組には偏りがあり、誤った認識を与える傾向がある。ニュース番組は公平、誠実で、政府やスポンサーのコントロールから自由であるべきだ。しかし残念ながら、現実はそうなっていない。例えば近年、政府の規制のために、日本の報道の自由度ランキングはあきれるほど低いレベルに落ちている。

Vocabulary

- □ unbiased 偏りのない、公平な　□ not the case 事実と異なる　□ regulation 規制
- □ embarrassingly 当惑するほどに

訳 12-6 人はマスメディアの広告の影響から逃れることができない。広告のうちのかなりのものは人々に自信を失わせるように作られているので、これは問題である。例えば、広告は若い女性に自分の身体について過剰に意識させることが多い。これが、拒食症のような摂食障害の増加につながっている。拒食症は最も危険な精神疾患の一つだ。

Vocabulary

- □ eating disorder 摂食障害　□ anorexia 拒食症

訳 12-7 メディアの最大の長所は教育的な価値があることだ。ニュース番組のおかげで、私たちは世界の他の地域で何が起こっているのかを知ることができる。人気のドラマやコメディでさえも、私たちに驚くほど多くの物事を教えてくれる。さらに、メディアには、科学や歴史などのテーマについて教えてくれる幅広い教育番組がある。

Vocabulary

- □ incredible 信じられないほどの、途方もない

訳 12-8 メディアは人々を楽しませることによって社会に貢献している。娯楽は人類のあらゆる文明において重要な要素である。人間の暮らしには物語が必要だ。ほとんどの人は、テレビや映画を今後まったく見ないようにしたいとは思わないだろう。それは、メディアが人の生活をもっと楽しめるものにしているからだ。確かにこれは好ましいことだ。

Vocabulary

- □ entertain 〜を楽しませる

有害物質の広告

Content Block 12 若者への広告の影響　MP3 197

9　Research suggests that teenagers are easily affected by alcohol and tobacco advertising. Younger people see various advertisements every day, and in these ads it seems like buying these products is fashionable and normal for adults. Consequently, young people want to try drinking and smoking at an early age, which is bad for their health and education.

Content Block 12 飲酒と喫煙の成人への影響　MP3 198

10　Drinking and smoking too much is bad for the health and safety of adults, too. For example, in Japan, driving-related deaths involving alcohol are almost eight times more common than deaths without alcohol, and tobacco can cause cancer. Addiction to alcohol is also linked to child abuse. Surely, less alcohol and tobacco advertising will contribute to healthier habits among all age groups.

Content Block 12 広告と飲酒・喫煙の関係　MP3 199

11　Several studies show that people do not drink or smoke less when they do not see commercials. In fact, France banned all alcohol advertisements from television in 1991. However, France reported that people drank more alcohol after the ban. Clearly, advertisements do not cause people to take harmful substances.

Content Block 12 広告の自由　MP3 200

12　It is unethical to heavily restrict the advertisement of tobacco and alcohol. Since these are harmful substances, it makes sense to force companies to clarify the health risks involved with these products. But as long as they are being honest about the effects of their products, then they should be permitted to advertise freely.

訳 12-9 調査によると、若者はアルコールやタバコの広告の影響を受けやすいことが示されている。若者は毎日さまざまな広告を目にし、こうした広告では、これらの製品を買うことはおしゃれで、成人にとっては普通のことのように見える。その結果、若い人々は低年齢で飲酒や喫煙をしてみたがるが、これは若者の健康と教育に悪い。

Vocabulary

□ consequently その結果

訳 12-10 過度の飲酒と喫煙は、成人の健康と安全にもよくない。例えば、日本では飲酒に関連した交通事故死は飲酒を伴わない事故死の約8倍にのぼり、タバコはがんの原因になる。アルコール中毒は児童虐待とも関連がある。アルコールとタバコの広告を減らせば、あらゆる年齢層により健康的な習慣をもたらすのは間違いない。

Vocabulary

□ addiction to alcohol アルコール中毒　□ child abuse 児童虐待

訳 12-11 複数の研究で、人はコマーシャルを見ない場合にも飲酒や喫煙を減らすことはないと示されている。実際、フランスは1991年にアルコールのテレビ広告を全面禁止にした。しかし、この禁止後、国民の飲酒量は増えたとフランスでは報告されている。明らかに、広告が人に有害物質を摂取させているわけではない。

Vocabulary

□ harmful substance 有害物質

訳 12-12 アルコールやタバコの広告を厳しく規制することは道義に反する。これらは有害物質なので、企業に対してこれらの製品が持つ健康上のリスクを明示させるのは理にかなっている。しかし、企業が製品の影響について正直に伝える限りにおいて、企業はそれを自由に広告することが許されるべきだ。

Vocabulary

□ unethical 非倫理的な、道義にもとる

現代における仕事のあり方

Content Block 多様な選択肢 MP3 201

Modern society has many options for those who do not want full-time jobs. For example, people who feel overworked can always switch to a different company. They can choose a job with fewer hours in a less stressful environment, sometimes without a major decrease in salary. Society might pressure people to work many hours, but ultimately it is a free choice.

Content Block 資本主義的な労働観 MP3 202

Business culture in a capitalist society always benefits the company, not the employees. This can be harmful because companies control the schedule and lifestyle of their workers and usually value profits over employees' happiness. Thus, as modern society continues to become more capitalistic, it is also becoming more common for employees to work long hours and fulfill highly demanding job requirements.

労働時間の短縮

Content Block 効率の向上 MP3 203

Several studies have shown that happy, well-rested workers are more productive, engaged and successful at their jobs. Also, happy workers take fewer sick days than unhappy workers, and employees that get adequate sleep are less likely to make mistakes. For this reason, decreasing weekly working hours will make offices more efficient.

Content Block フリーランサーの活用 MP3 204

When full-time employees cannot complete jobs on their own, companies can employ skilled freelancers to assist them. Thanks to advances in technology, millions of skilled workers are available for short-term projects online. This new system of work has been shown to increase company profits in many situations.

訳 12 13 現代社会には、正規の仕事を求めない人々に多くの選択肢がある。例えば、過労だと感じている人は、いつでも別の会社に転職することができる。ストレスのより少ない環境で労働時間がより短い仕事を選ぶことができ、給料がそれほど下がらない場合もある。社会は長時間労働を強いているかもしれないが、最終的に選択は個人の自由だ。

Vocabulary

□ feel overworked 働きすぎだと感じる

訳 12 14 資本主義社会におけるビジネス文化は、常に、従業員にではなく企業に恩恵をもたらす。このことは有害である可能性がある。企業が従業員のスケジュールやライフスタイルを支配し、従業員の幸福よりも利益に価値を置くことが多いからだ。そのため、現代社会の資本主義化が続けば、従業員が長時間働いて、非常に厳しい仕事の要件を満たすという状況が増えるだろう。

Vocabulary

□ capitalist society 資本主義社会　□ value A over B AをBより重んじる　□ capitalistic 資本主義的な
□ fulfill 〜を果たす

訳 12 15 満足していて休息がよくとれている労働者は、より生産性が高く、積極的で、仕事に成功していると、複数の研究が示している。また、満足している労働者は、不満を抱えた労働者よりも病気での欠勤が少なく、睡眠時間が十分な従業員のほうがミスをする可能性が低い。こうした理由から、週の労働時間を減らすことは、職場の効率を高める。

Vocabulary

□ well-rested よく休息をとった

訳 12 16 正社員が自力で仕事を完了することができない場合、企業はフリーランスの熟練労働者を活用して正社員をサポートしてもらえばいい。技術の進歩により、インターネットを通じて、何百万もの熟練労働者に短期間のプロジェクトを依頼することができる。この新しい仕事のシステムは、さまざまな状況で企業の利益を増すことが示されている。

Vocabulary

□ freelancer フリーランサー

12 Content Block 経済へのダメージ

17 The main reason that the number of weekly working hours should not be decreased is that it would hurt the economy. In a healthy economy, workers produce more value than they consume. If people worked less, then they would create less value for society. In other words, decreasing working hours would not be beneficial for the economy.

12 Content Block 会社の損失

18 Even if the working hours are reduced, the amount of work that needs to be completed will not decrease. In order to get all of this work completed, companies would be forced to hire more employees, and their profit margins would decrease. This would most likely lead to lower salaries and fewer benefits for companies' employees.

12 Content Block 経済的効果

19 Research suggests that decreasing working hours could improve the economy. For example, by switching to shorter workweeks, more single parents would be able to work "full-time" jobs. This is especially important in countries like Japan, where female workers are essential to the future of the economy.

12 Content Block 残業代の支払い

20 Although it is not necessary to decrease limits on working hours, the government should force companies to pay salaried workers for overtime. A large percentage of employees that work overtime have special skills, so they cannot be replaced easily. These workers deserve to receive extra incentives for completing their work.

訳 12-17 週の労働時間を減らすべきではない主な理由は、経済に悪影響を及ぼすからだ。健全な経済では、労働者は消費するよりも多く生産する。人々の働く時間が減れば、社会にもたらす価値が少なくなる。言い換えれば、労働時間を減らすことは、経済に有益ではないだろう。

Vocabulary
- healthy economy 健全な経済

訳 12-18 仮に労働時間が減ったとしても行うべき仕事の量が減るわけではない。行うべき仕事すべてを終わらせるために、企業はより多くの従業員を雇わなければならなくなり、利幅は減るだろう。このことは結果的に従業員の給料を下げ、手当を減らすと考えられる。

Vocabulary
- profit margin 利ざや

訳 12-19 研究によると、労働時間を減少させると経済が改善される可能性があると示されている。例えば、1週間の労働時間を減らすことによって、「フルタイムの」仕事ができる一人親が増える。このことは、経済の未来にとって女性労働者が絶対に必要な日本のような国では特に重要だ。

Vocabulary
- workweek 1週間の労働時間　□ single parent 一人親

訳 12-20 労働時間の制限を減らす必要はないが、政府は企業に対し、給与所得者に残業代を支払うように強制するべきだ。残業する従業員の大半は特別な技能を持っているので、別の人に代わってもらうことは容易ではない。こうした労働者は、業務の遂行に対して、追加報酬を受ける権利がある。

Vocabulary
- salaried worker 給与所得者、サラリーマン　□ incentive 奨励金

起業

12 Content Block 失敗を受け入れない風土　MP3 209

21　Japanese people do not typically start their own companies because they worry about failing. Generally speaking, Japanese society does not accept failure. Unless Japan starts to accept failure more as a natural part of building a business, then it is unlikely that the number of entrepreneurs will increase significantly.

12 Content Block 増えつつある起業　MP3 210

22　The amount of funding and support for new businesses is increasing in Japan. Funding for startups doubled between 2014 and 2015. Although new businesses do not receive nearly as much money in Japan as in the U.S., for example, this is a sign that support for entrepreneurs is already improving at a steady rate. Consequently, more entrepreneurs will seek to start their own businesses.

12 Content Block 地方自治体による支援　MP3 211

23　Local governments in Japan are working hard to support new businesses. For example, the Tokyo city government has invested hundreds of millions of yen in a center to support entrepreneurs that are developing new business plans. Also, the national government is working on programs to provide funds for businesses started by elderly citizens.

12 Content Block 不十分な国の支援　MP3 212

24　There is much less funding for new businesses in Japan than in other developed countries. The United States is the home of dozens of multibillion-dollar ventures like Uber and Airbnb. China's startup companies have had similar success. But Japan has had hardly any hugely successful startup companies in recent years. This alone is evidence that entrepreneurship is not supported enough in Japan.

訳 12 21 日本人は概して、失敗することを恐れて起業しない。一般的に言って、日本社会は失敗を受け入れない。日本人が、事業を立ち上げれば当然、失敗することもあると認めるようにならなければ、起業家の数が著しく増える可能性はないだろう。

Vocabulary

□ typically 典型的に、普通　□ entrepreneur 起業家

訳 12 22 日本では、新規事業に対する資金提供と支援の量が増えている。2014年から2015年の間に、起業に対する資金提供は2倍になった。例えば、新規事業はアメリカほどの資金提供は受けていないものの、資金提供が2倍になったことは起業家に対する支援がすでに着実に改善していることの現れだ。その結果、もっと多くの起業家が自分のビジネスを立ち上げようとするようになるだろう。

Vocabulary

□ startup 新規事業、新興企業　□ at a steady rate 一定して、着実に

訳 12 23 日本の地方自治体は新規事業の支援に懸命に取り組んでいる。例えば東京都は、新規事業計画を立てている起業家を支援するセンターに何億円も投じている。また、中央政府も、高齢者が始める事業に資金提供をするプログラムに取り組んでいる。

Vocabulary

□ hundreds of millions of ～ 何億もの～

訳 12 24 日本では新規事業への資金提供が、ほかの先進国よりも大幅に少ない。アメリカでは、ウーバーやエアビーアンドビーなど、数十億ドル規模のベンチャー企業が何十社も生まれている。中国の新興企業も同様の成功を収めている。しかし日本では、近年、大成功を収めた新興企業はほとんどない。このこと一つをとっても、日本では起業支援が十分でないのは明らかだ。

Vocabulary

□ home 本拠地　□ entrepreneurship 起業家精神

column

bodyを考え出すのに困ったら

　Chapter 2では、分野別に200を超えるコンテンツブロックを紹介しました。これだけたくさんのトピックが頭に入っていれば、たいていの問題に対処することができるでしょう。しかしすべてを覚えるのは大変ですし、対処できない問題が出題されることもあり得ます。そこでbodyを考え出すのに困ったときに思い出してほしい、いくつかのポイントを挙げておきましょう。

● グローバリゼーションが進んでいる
とりわけインターネットによって、世界中の情報が手に入り、教育を受けることができ、人材を集めることができるといった論点は、事態が改善すると論じる際にしばしば有力な論拠になります。一方で、それが犯罪に利用され、対人コミュニケーションの劣化を招くといったネガティブな側面を取り上げることも可能です。

● イノベーション（技術革新）が起きる
この先、イノベーションが起きれば、生活が改善され、ものの価格が下がる（可能性がある）というのは、問題が解決すると主張するときの論点になります。

● 環境破壊・人口問題が深刻化している
これらの問題はその他のテーマともしばしば連動しているので、関連がないか考えてみるとトピックが思い浮かぶ場合があります。

● 経済的なメリット／デメリットがある
何かの施策を行うべきだ／行うべきではないと論じる際に、経済的な側面を取り上げるのは有力な切り口です。

● 関心が高まっている
一般によく知られていないようなテーマが取り上げられることはありません。したがって、すでに社会的な関心は高まっており、それは問題解決の兆しであると論じることができるでしょう。

● 伝統が失われる
主に科学技術の進歩の是非を問う問題で、否定の立場で答えるときに使える論点です。伝統的な技法で十分用は足りているといった議論をすることもできます。

実践問題30

CHAPTER 3

このChapterでは、
過去問の分析を基に作成した30問のオリジナル問題と
それに対する肯定・否定60の答案例を挙げた。
まずは自分の力で答案を作成してみよう。
そして答案例を確認し、
さらに自分のオリジナル模範解答例も作ってみよう。
最高の試験対策になるはずだ。

1 社会問題

CHAPTER_3

- Write an essay on the given TOPIC.
- Give THREE reasons to support your answer.
- Structure: Introduction, main body, and conclusion
- Suggested length: 200–240 words

TOPIC

1. Will societies with low birthrates face a crisis in the future?

2. Agree or disagree: Extreme social inequality will never be eliminated

3. Should advertising for harmful substances such as alcohol and tobacco be more heavily restricted?

4. Is maintaining public safety more important than respecting citizens' privacy?

5 Should there be restrictions to freedom of speech in some cases?
　　　　　　　　　　　　　　　　　＞解答・解説は178-181ページ

6 Should people be punished for downloading music and movies illegally?
　　　　　　　　　　　　　　　　　＞解答・解説は182-185ページ

7 Agree or disagree: A lack of women's rights is a serious problem in Japan
　　　　　　　　　　　　　　　　　＞解答・解説は186-189ページ

8 Should rich people be required to pay higher taxes?
　　　　　　　　　　　　　　　　　＞解答・解説は190-193ページ

9 Should minors receive life imprisonment for serious crimes?
　　　　　　　　　　　　　　　　　＞解答・解説は194-197ページ

10 Agree or disagree: Hosting international sporting events is good for local communities
　　　　　　　　　　　　　　　　　＞解答・解説は198-201ページ

TOPIC

1. Will societies with low birthrates face a crisis in the future?

モデルエッセイ 👍 Affirmative 🎧 213

Societies with low birthrates will face a number of issues in the future. Among these are healthcare problems, economic burdens forced onto the youth, and less scientific and technological innovation.

A consequence of an aging population is that more people need medical care. However, countries like Japan with aging populations are not equipped to deal with an increased demand for costly healthcare. This is a huge problem because there are not enough medical staff and not enough funds to hire them.

Furthermore, when the population of young workers is less than that of the elderly, this means the smallest group of people carries the heaviest economic responsibility. The younger working population must do all the work to support the older generation, who receive pensions and expensive medical care. The government cannot support the elderly without forcing young people to work unreasonable hours.

Last, countries with a limited number of young workers are likely to have less scientific and technological innovation. Young people tend to experiment more with new forms of technology, and this had led to the creation of several impressive online companies. Countries without many innovative young minds may fall behind economically.

Considering these issues, governments will need to find new ways to provide support for people who wish to start families in order to lessen the future economic and social problems resulting from a low birthrate.

(228 words)

訳 1 出生率が低い社会は、将来危機に直面するか
👍 Affirmative

　出生率の低い社会は、将来、数多くの課題に直面するだろう。その中には、保健医療の問題、若者への経済的負担、科学技術のイノベーションの減少が挙げられる。

　人口の高齢化の結果、医療を必要とする人が増える。しかし日本のような国民の高齢化が進む国は高額医療の需要の増加に対処する備えができていない。医療従事者の数が足りず、彼らを雇用する資金も足りないので、これは非常に大きな問題だ。

　さらに若い労働者の人口が高齢者よりも少なくなると、最も数が少ない集団に属する人々が最も重い経済的責任を負うことになる。年金を受給し、高額な医療を受ける上の世代を支えるためのあらゆる仕事を、若い労働者人口が引き受けなければならない。政府は、若者に法外な長時間労働を強いることなしに高齢者を支えることができない。

　最後に、若い労働者の数が限られた国では、科学や技術の分野でのイノベーションが減るだろう。若者は新しいタイプの技術にチャレンジする傾向があり、このことがいくつもの素晴らしいオンライン企業を作り出してきた。革新的な若いマインドを持たない国は経済的に後れをとるかもしれない。

　こうした点を踏まえると、政府は、低い出生率から生じる将来の経済的、社会的問題を緩和するために、家庭を築きたいと願う人々を支援する新しい方法を見出す必要が出てくるだろう。

Vocabulary
□ be equipped to *do* 〜する備えができている　□ pension 年金　□ fall behind 後れをとる

解説
　少子高齢化の問題はまさに日本が今、直面している問題であり、私たちが常に意識すべき、あるいは意識せざるを得ない問題である。

　まずは社会が危機に直面するとする立場から。年金制度が破たんするといった結果だけでなく、その背景やプロセスを意識するようにしよう。モデルエッセイでは、増加する高齢者を支える体制が整っていないこと、高齢者を支える若者の負担が法外なまでに大きくなること、最後に若者が減ることで科学や技術分野でのイノベーションが起こりづらくなることをトピックとして挙げた。

Structure
- Introduction
- 1-1 高齢者と医療費
- 1-2 若者の負担
- オリジナル イノベーションの減少
- Conclusion

TOPIC

1 Will societies with low birthrates face a crisis in the future?

モデルエッセイ ♠ Negative

Some argue that societies with low birthrates will face a crisis in the future. However, there are many benefits of a lower population, such as less spending on raising children, better food security, and less burden on the environment.

Taking care of children is expensive in developed countries because parents need to pay for education, healthcare, and bigger houses. Families with fewer children spend less money. As a result, they are more capable of purchasing goods and services, which improves their quality of life.

Second, countries with lower populations may have an advantage in the future because they will need less food. Experts predict that there will be major worldwide food shortages only a few decades from now. This is especially frightening for countries like Japan that do not produce enough food to feed their citizens. Decreased population will alleviate this problem.

Finally, studies show that overpopulation is one of the main causes of environmental problems. Humans' activities have a variety of harmful impacts on the planet, including pollution, global warming, and deforestation. A world with fewer people will put less burden on the environment.

In conclusion, a low birthrate does not mean that countries will face a crisis in the future since there are many advantages to maintaining a lower population. (212 words)

ワンポイントアドバイス

第1パラグラフ第2文のbetter food securityは、better self-sufficiency（自給率の向上）、あるいはdecreased risk of food shortages（食糧不足の危険の減少）などとしてもよい。

訳 **1** 出生率が低い社会は、将来危機に直面するか
🌧 Negative

　出生率が低い社会は将来、危機に直面すると言う人もいる。しかし、子育てにかかる費用の減少、食糧安全保障の向上、環境への負荷の減少など、人口が減少することによる利点はたくさんある。

　子どもの面倒をみることは、先進国では高くつく。親は教育、医療、より広い住居にお金をかける必要があるからだ。子どもが少ない家庭では出費が少ない。その結果、より多くの製品やサービスを購入できるようになり、生活の質が向上する。

　第二に、人口の少ない国は必要となる食糧も少ないので将来有利になるかもしれない。専門家はほんの数十年先には深刻な食糧不足が世界的に起こると予測している。これは自給率の低い日本のような国にとっては特に脅威である。人口の減少はこの問題を軽減する。

　最後に、人口過剰が環境問題の主な原因の一つであることを研究は示している。人間の活動は、汚染、地球温暖化、森林破壊などのさまざまな悪影響を地球に及ぼしている。世界の人口が少なくなれば、環境への負荷は減る。

　結論として、より少ない人口を維持していく利点は数多くあるため、出生率の低さによって、国が将来危機に直面するということにはならない。

Vocabulary

- be capable of *doing* 〜することができる　□ frightening 恐ろしい　□ alleviate 〜を緩和する
- overpopulation 人口過剰

解説　少子高齢化は大きな問題として論じられることが多いが、人口の減少は必ずしも悪いことではないとする立場も成り立つだろう。特に、日本では人口が減少に転じた一方で世界では人口増加が続いている点を念頭に置いておくといい。

　モデルエッセイでは、育児のための費用が減るので個々人の生活に余裕が生じる、また人口の減少は食糧不足の問題に対してポジティブな意味を持つ、さらに環境への負荷も減るといった点をトピックとして挙げた。

● Structure

Introduction
1/3　子どもの養育費
1/4　食糧問題の軽減
オリジナル　環境負荷の減少
Conclusion

TOPIC

2 Agree or disagree: Extreme social inequality will never be eliminated

モデルエッセイ 👍 Affirmative

I agree that extreme social inequality will never be eliminated. The world's population is growing, and its resources are diminishing. Also, solving poverty will not change society's large gaps in income, which are actually rising.

First, the human population will continue to expand in the future, causing the depletion of resources. The world population is expected to be around 10 billion by 2050. Experts predict that there will also be major food shortages around this time. These problems are likely to get worse, worsening equality.

Second, fixing poverty does not fix inequality. Thanks to technological developments, it is theoretically possible that poverty can be eliminated eventually. However, this does not mean that inequality will disappear. The world will always have extremely rich people with much more money than the average person. In fact, wealth inequality is at record highs in countries like the U.S.

Third, people are largely incapable of caring about strangers living in poor conditions. Humans evolved as a small tribal species, and even today people mostly only worry about their small "tribe" of family and friends. The large majority of people would choose to use their resources to increase a family member's comfort before using them to help a stranger who is suffering.

When considering the points mentioned above, it is unrealistic to expect that extreme social inequality will ever be eliminated.

(225 words)

訳 **2** 賛成か反対か：社会の著しい不平等は決してなくならない
👍 Affirmative

　極度の社会的不平等は決してなくなることはないという意見に賛成だ。世界の人口は増加しており、資源は減少している。また、貧困を解決しても社会における大きな収入格差は変わらないだろう。実際のところ、収入格差は広がっている。

　第一に、将来人口は増加を続け、資源の枯渇を引き起こす。世界の人口は2050年までに約100億人になると予想されている。このころには大規模な食糧不足も起こると専門家たちは予測している。こうした問題はさらに悪化する見込みで、その結果、不平等は拡大する。

　第二に、貧困の是正は不平等の是正にはならない。技術の発達のおかげで、理論的には、いずれは貧困を根絶することが可能とされる。しかし、これは不平等がなくなることを意味するわけではない。世界には、平均的な人よりもはるかに多くのお金を持つ極端に裕福な人々が今後も常にいるだろう。実際、アメリカなどでは富の不平等は記録的なものになっている。

　第三に、人は概して、貧しい状況にある知らない人を思いやることができない。人類は小さな部族で生活する種として進化してきた。そして今日なお、ほとんどの人は家族や友人といった小さな「部族」のことばかりを気にかけている。大部分の人は、自らの資金を、苦しんでいる知らない人を助けるために使う前に、家族がより快適に暮らすために使うことを選ぶだろう。

　上述の点を考慮すると、極度の社会的不平等がいずれなくなると考えることは非現実的である。

Vocabulary
□ diminish 減少する　□ depletion（資源などの）枯渇　□ worsen 〜を悪化させる　□ tribal 部族の

解説　「社会的不平等」というと漠然とした問題のように聞こえるが、「経済格差（economic disparity）の問題」と言い換えると話が少し具体的になるだろう。現在、日本でも貧困層が増加し、経済格差が広がっている。

　モデルエッセイでは、世界の人口増加と資源の枯渇から食糧不足が起こり格差は広がる、また貧困が是正されたとしても富裕層がいなくなるわけではなく、不平等はなくならない、人はそもそも身近な人しか思いやることができない、というトピックを挙げた。

　なお、この問題はp.190-193の税の問題と関連づけて考えることも可能だ。

● Structure

Introduction
4-1 人口増加と不平等の拡大
4-2 貧困の是正と不平等
オリジナル 見知らぬ人に対する想像力の欠如
Conclusion

TOPIC

2 Agree or disagree: Extreme social inequality will never be eliminated

モデルエッセイ ♣ Negative

I am of the opinion that extreme social inequality will be eliminated in the future. This is mainly due to the growing fair trade movement, improved technology, and free education.

First, as the fair trade movement continues to gain popularity, working conditions and trade agreements for people in developing countries will get better. More and more countries are starting to use labeling for fair trade products, and a higher number of consumers are demanding products with these labels, as well.

Second, developments in technology will lead to less work for all people. For example, experts estimate that in the near future, robots will be able to perform nearly half of all jobs. This low-cost productivity will boost the economy, and the extra money can be spent to improve the lives of the poor. As a result, inequality will decrease.

Third, education will become accessible to everyone. The main reason that poor people stay in poverty is that they do not know how to improve their lives. They have never received professional training related to saving and investing money, acquiring valuable skills, and so on. Eventually, all of this information will be available for free on the Internet.

In conclusion, I believe that it is realistic to claim that extreme social inequality will be eliminated someday. (215 words)

訳 2 賛成か反対か：社会の著しい不平等は決してなくならない
🌧 Negative

　私は極度の社会的不平等は将来、根絶されるだろうという考えだ。これは主にフェアトレード運動の成長、技術の発展、無料の教育によるものである。

　第一に、フェアトレード運動が支持を拡大するにしたがい、途上国の人々の労働条件や取引契約は改善されるだろう。フェアトレード商品のラベル表示を始める国は増えており、このラベルのついた商品を求める消費者も増加している。

　第二に、技術の発展は、すべての人にとって労働を減らすことにつながる。例えば、専門家たちは近い将来、ロボットがすべての仕事のうちの半分近くを行えるようになるだろうと推定している。このコストの低い生産力は、経済を上向かせ、余剰の資金は貧しい人々の生活を改善するのに使うことができる。その結果、不平等は縮小するだろう。

　第三に、誰もが教育を受けられるようになるだろう。貧しい人々が貧困状態から抜け出せない主な理由は、どうすれば生活を改善できるのかを知らないことだ。貧しい人たちは貯蓄や投資、役に立つスキルの獲得などに関する専門的な訓練を受けたことがない。いずれは、こうした情報のすべてがインターネットで無料で得られるようになるだろう。

　結論として、極度の社会的不平等はいつかなくなるだろうと主張するのは現実性があると思う。

Vocabulary
□ labeling ラベル表示　□ accessible 手に入る　□ related to 〜 〜に関して

解説　モデルエッセイでは、第2パラグラフでフェアトレード運動を取り上げたが、それだけで不平等がなくなるとするのは非現実的だ。不平等がなくなるという立場を取る場合は、何らかのイノベーションが起こる可能性を考える必要があるだろう。

　ここでは、安いコストで働くロボットの開発によって経済が上向き、余剰の資金を人々の生活改善に役立てることができる、技術の発展ですべての人が教育を受けられるようになり、貧しい人が貯蓄や投資などのスキルを身につけられるようになるというトピックを取り上げた。

● Structure

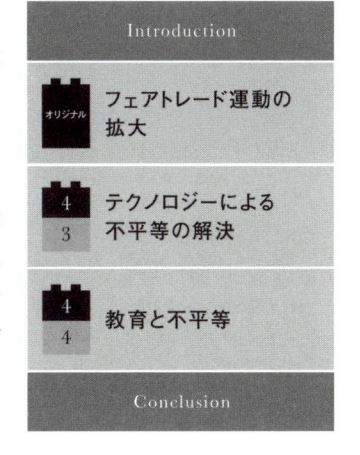

| Introduction |
| オリジナル　フェアトレード運動の拡大 |
| 3　テクノロジーによる不平等の解決 |
| 4　教育と不平等 |
| Conclusion |

TOPIC

3 Should advertising for harmful substances such as alcohol and tobacco be more heavily restricted?

モデルエッセイ 👍 Affirmative 　　　　　　　　　　MP3 217

　　　　Advertising for harmful substances like alcohol and tobacco should be restricted for many reasons. Restricting alcohol and tobacco advertisements benefits public health and safety, while motivating companies to invest in healthier alternatives.

　　　　Research suggests that teenagers are easily affected by alcohol and tobacco advertising. Younger people see various advertisements every day, and in these ads it seems like buying these products is fashionable and normal for adults. Consequently, young people want to try drinking and smoking at an early age, which is bad for their health and education.

　　　　Furthermore, drinking and smoking too much is bad for the health and safety of adults, too. For example, in Japan, driving-related deaths involving alcohol are almost eight times more common than deaths without alcohol, and tobacco can cause cancer. Addiction to alcohol is also linked to child abuse. Surely, less alcohol and tobacco advertising will contribute to healthier habits among all age groups.

　　　　Last, alcohol and tobacco companies make less money when advertising has limits, so they invest in different products to recover lost profits. As a result, healthier drinks and activities are featured in advertisements, leading to decreases in drinking and smoking. This means that these companies can stay profitable while also lessening their negative effects on society.

　　　　In conclusion, there should be stronger restrictions for advertising alcohol and tobacco. These products are harmful to everyone, and advertising only increases their popularity.　　(231 words)

ワンポイントアドバイス

第2パラグラフ1文目はResearch suggests that advertisements can make teenagers want to use alcohol and tobacco.などと言い換えてもよい。

訳 **3** アルコールやタバコのような有害物質の広告はもっと厳しく規制されるべきか
👍 Affirmative

　アルコールやタバコのような有害な物質の広告は、多くの理由から規制されるべきである。アルコールとタバコの広告を規制することは、国民の健康と安全に寄与し、他方、より健康的な別の製品に資金を投入するよう企業に促すだろう。

　調査によると、若者はアルコールやタバコの広告の影響を受けやすいことが示されている。若者は毎日さまざまな広告を目にし、こうした広告では、これらの製品を買うことはおしゃれで、成人にとっては普通のことのように見える。その結果、若い人々は低年齢で飲酒や喫煙をしてみたがるが、これは若者の健康と教育に悪い。

　さらに、過度の飲酒と喫煙は、成人の健康と安全にもよくない。例えば、日本では飲酒に関連した交通事故死は飲酒を伴わない事故死の約8倍にのぼり、タバコはがんの原因になる。アルコール中毒は児童虐待とも関連がある。アルコールとタバコの広告を減らせば、あらゆる年齢層により健康的な習慣をもたらすのは間違いない。

　最後に、アルコールやタバコの企業は、広告が規制されると収益が減るので、逸失利益を取り戻すため、別の製品に資金を投入するようになる。その結果、より健康的な飲料や活動が広告で取り上げられるようになり、飲酒と喫煙を減らすことになる。これはつまり、こうした企業は社会へ及ぼす悪影響を減らしながら利益を維持できるということだ。

　結論として、アルコールとタバコの広告はもっと厳しく規制されるべきである。こうした製品は誰にとっても有害であり、宣伝すれば飲酒と喫煙を増加させるだけである。

Vocabulary

☐ addiction to alcohol アルコール中毒　☐ child abuse 児童虐待　☐ lost profit 逸失利益
☐ profitable 利益になる

解説　アルコールやタバコの広告の是非を問う問題。規制を強化すべきだという立場の答案では、アルコールやタバコの害を具体的に説明するのが一番わかりやすい方法だ。モデルエッセイでは、10代の若者への広告の影響、成人に対するアルコールとタバコの影響に分けて説明し、第4パラグラフでは広告の規制が、メーカーにほかの商品の製造販売を促す効果を上げてトピックとしている。両者には依存性があるといったトピックを挙げることも可能だろう。

Structure

| Introduction |
| 12 / 9　若者への広告の影響 |
| 12 / 10　飲酒と喫煙の成人への影響 |
| オリジナル　他の製品の販売促進 |
| Conclusion |

TOPIC

3. Should advertising for harmful substances such as alcohol and tobacco be more heavily restricted?

モデルエッセイ ◆ Negative

MP3 218

　Advertising for alcohol and tobacco products should not be restricted. Fewer advertisements do not lead to less drinking or smoking. Also, many rules already exist, and many types of companies would lose money.

　First, several studies show that people do not drink or smoke less when they do not see commercials. In fact, France banned all alcohol advertisements from television in 1991. However, France reported that people drank more alcohol after the ban. Clearly, advertisements do not cause people to take harmful substances.

　Additionally, it is unethical to heavily restrict the advertisement of tobacco and alcohol. Since these are harmful substances, it makes sense to force companies to clarify the health risks involved with these products. But as long as they are being honest about the effects of their products, then they should be permitted to advertise freely.

　Finally, limiting the advertising of harmful products has economic disadvantages. Alcohol and tobacco companies invest billions of dollars per year in advertising, which contributes to the economy. Moreover, instead of limiting advertising, the government should just raise taxes on these harmful products, which both increases government funding and lowers the popularity of these products.

　People should definitely drink and smoke less, since these activities are unhealthy. However, heavily regulating alcohol and tobacco advertisements is not the best way to stop people from buying them.

(222 words)

訳 **3** アルコールやタバコのような有害物質の広告はもっと厳しく規制されるべきか
　　　💭 Negative

　アルコールやタバコ関連製品の広告は規制されるべきではない。広告が減っても、飲酒や喫煙が減ることにはならない。また、すでに多くの規則があり、（もし規制が強化されれば）さまざまな業種の企業が収益を減らすだろう。

　まず、複数の研究で、人はコマーシャルを見ない場合にも飲酒や喫煙を減らすことはないと示されている。実際、フランスは1991年にアルコールのテレビ広告を全面禁止にした。しかし、この禁止後、国民の飲酒量は増えたとフランスでは報告されている。明らかに、広告が人に有害物質を摂取させているわけではない。

　加えて、アルコールやタバコの広告を厳しく規制することは道義に反する。これらは有害物質なので、企業に対してこれらの製品が持つ健康上のリスクを明示させるのは理にかなっている。しかし、企業が製品の影響について正直に伝える限りにおいて、企業はそれを自由に広告することが許されるべきだ。

　最後に、有害な製品の広告を制限することは経済的にデメリットがある。アルコールやタバコの会社は、毎年何十億ドルも広告に資金を投入しており、それは経済によい影響を与えている。さらに、政府は広告を制限するのではなく、これらの有害な製品にかける税を重くすればいいのだ。そうすれば、政府の収入は増え、かつこれらの製品の人気は落ちる。

　飲酒と喫煙は不健康なので、飲酒と喫煙を減らすべきなのは言うまでもない。しかし、アルコールとタバコの広告を厳しく規制することは、人にアルコールやタバコを買わせないようにする最善の策ではない。

Vocabulary

□ unethical 非倫理的な、道義にもとる　□ raise taxes on ～ ～の税を上げる

解説　今度はアルコールやタバコの広告は今よりも厳しく規制されるべきではないとする立場の答案。設問に harmful substances such as alcohol and tobacco（アルコールやタバコのような有害物質）とあるので、そもそもアルコールやタバコにはメリットもあるといったトピックを挙げるのは的外れとなる。

　モデルエッセイでは、規制しても飲酒や喫煙が減るわけではない、有害である点を明示している限り広告することは許されるはずだ、広告を制限すれば経済的なデメリットがあるというトピックを挙げている。

● Structure

| Introduction |
| 12 / 11　広告と飲酒・喫煙の関係 |
| 12 / 12　広告の自由 |
| オリジナル　経済への影響 |
| Conclusion |

TOPIC

4 Is maintaining public safety more important than respecting citizens' privacy?

モデルエッセイ 👍 Affirmative　　　MP3 219

　　I think that maintaining public safety is more important than respecting the privacy of citizens. The lives of people will always be more significant than privacy. Also, monitoring the digital world is necessary in order to fight criminals and terrorists.

　　Although protecting personal privacy is vital, it is not as valuable as maintaining public safety. If human lives can be saved by violating the privacy of one or more people, then it is acceptable to do so. Governments and police only access private personal information in order to protect people.

　　In addition, limiting the amount of private information that governments and police can access aids criminals and terrorists. For example, when prepaid cellphones were introduced, they quickly became popular among drug dealers, because they are difficult to track. If everyone has more privacy, then criminals and terrorists will have more privacy, too.

　　Finally, the government should be able to put more restrictions on people's ability to access the Internet anonymously. Even without technical expertise, it is quite simple to hide one's identity online, which is what many people do when engaging in criminal activities. Although it will decrease privacy, there should be more barriers to concealing identity on digital platforms.

　　In conclusion, I believe that sometimes privacy must be sacrificed to protect public safety. Saving lives and catching criminals are a higher priority than respecting privacy. (226 words)

ワンポイントアドバイス

第3パラグラフの最後の文は〈the 比較級＋the 比較級〉の構文を使い、The more privacy everyone has, the more privacy criminals and terrorists have, too. としてもよい。

訳 **4** 公衆の安全の維持は市民のプライバシーの尊重よりも重要か
👍 Affirmative

　私は公衆の安全の維持のほうが市民のプライバシーの尊重よりも重要だと思う。人命は常にプライバシーよりも重要だろう。それに、犯罪者やテロリストと闘うためにはデジタルの世界を監視することが必要だ。

　個人のプライバシーを保護することは不可欠だが、公衆の安全を維持することに比べれば重要度は低い。もし、個人のプライバシーを侵すことで人命が守られるならば、そうすることは許容できる。政府と警察が個人情報にアクセスするのは、あくまで人々を保護するためなのだ。

　さらに、政府と警察がアクセスできる個人情報の量を限定すれば、犯罪者やテロリストを利することになる。例えば、プリペイド携帯電話が導入されたとき、プリペイド携帯電話は追跡が難しいため、すぐに麻薬ディーラーの間で広まった。すべての人々にもっとプライバシーが認められれば、犯罪者やテロリストにもより多くのプライバシーが認められることになる。

　最後に、政府は人々が匿名でインターネットにアクセスする権限をもっと制限できるべきだ。技術的な専門知識がなくてもオンライン上で正体を隠すことはとても簡単で、多くの人が犯罪行為に関わるときにそうしている。プライバシーは減るが、デジタルプラットフォーム上で正体を隠すことにはもっと障壁が必要だ。

　結論として、公衆の安全を守るためにプライバシーを犠牲にしなければならないこともあると思う。人命を守ることと犯罪者を捕らえることは、プライバシーを尊重することよりも優先度が高い。

Vocabulary

□ vital 必須の、不可欠の　□ aid ～を助ける　□ anonymously 匿名で　□ expertise 専門知識
□ conceal ～を隠す

解説　公衆の安全とプライバシーの尊重の優先度を問う設問。普段きちんと読むことは少ないかもしれないが、企業などのプライバシーポリシーには、個人情報保護法に基づき、公衆の安全を守るために断りなく個人情報を開示することがあると記されていることが多い。肯定の立場はこれに準ずる立場と言える。モデルエッセイでは、人命はプライバシーの保護にまさる点、政府や警察のアクセス権の制限は犯罪者やテロリストを利することになる点、一般人が匿名でインターネットにアクセスするのを制限するべきだとする点をトピックとして挙げた。

● Structure

| Introduction |
| 2-1 人命の重要性 |
| 2-2 犯罪者とプライバシー |
| オリジナル インターネットへの匿名アクセス権限 |
| Conclusion |

TOPIC

4 Is maintaining public safety more important than respecting citizens' privacy?

モデルエッセイ ♠ Negative

I believe that respecting the privacy of citizens is more important than maintaining public safety. Privacy is a fundamental human right that must not be violated. Additionally, less privacy and more government power can actually decrease public safety.

The primary reason privacy must be respected is that humans need privacy to live happy, healthy lives. Privacy is a fundamental human right recognized in the Universal Declaration of Human Rights. When privacy rights are violated, people feel vulnerable, insecure, and afraid. Protecting the mental health of people is just as crucial as maintaining public safety.

Second, human rights should never be sacrificed because of fear. Throughout history, governments have used fear to control their citizens. The argument of these oppressive governments is that personal freedom must be sacrificed for public safety. In modern society, the personal freedom being sacrificed is personal privacy.

Third, removing privacy protections does not necessarily lead to increased public safety. For example, recently many government agencies have demanded that large tech companies create methods for breaking into devices such as smartphones. Decreasing the security features of devices like this would make it easier to conduct investigations, but it would also make it easier for criminals to steal information from private citizens.

For the reasons mentioned above, I believe that maintaining public safety is not a justifiable excuse for violating the privacy of people. (226 words)

ワンポイントアドバイス

冒頭の1文はThe privacy of citizens should not be sacrificed in order to maintain public safety.のように直截的な言い方にしてもよい。

訳 **4** 公衆の安全の維持は市民のプライバシーの尊重よりも重要か
　　🌧 Negative

　私は市民のプライバシーを尊重することのほうが公衆の安全を維持することよりも重要だと思う。プライバシーは、侵害されてはならない基本的な人権だ。さらに、プライバシーが減って政府の権限が増すことは、実際には公衆の安全を低下させる。

　プライバシーが尊重されなければならない第一の理由は、人間が幸福で健康的な生活を送るためにはプライバシーが必要だからだ。プライバシーは、世界人権宣言で認められた基本的人権である。プライバシーが侵害されると、人は弱さと危険と恐れを感じる。人々の精神衛生を守ることは、公衆の安全を維持するのとまったく同等に重要だ。

　第二に、人権は決して恐怖感によって犠牲にされるべきではない。歴史を通じ、政府は市民をコントロールするのに恐怖感を利用してきた。抑圧的な政府の主張は、個人の自由は公衆の安全のためには犠牲にされなければならないというものだ。現代社会において、犠牲にされる個人の自由は、個人のプライバシーである。

　第三に、プライバシーの保護を取り払っても、必ずしも公衆の安全を高めることにはならない。例えば、最近、多くの政府機関がスマートフォンなどの機器のロックを解除する方法を開発するよう大手テクノロジー企業に要求している。このように機器のセキュリティー機能を低下させることは、捜査をしやすくするだろうが、犯罪者が市民の情報を盗むことも容易にするだろう。

　上記の理由から、公衆の安全の維持は、人々のプライバシーを侵害する弁明として正当化されうるものではないと思う。

Vocabulary
□ conduct investigation 捜査する　□ justifiable 正当化できる

解説　今度は、公衆の安全をプライバシー保護よりも上位に置くことに反対する立場で考えよう。

　プライバシーの権利の重要性を主張するところまでは容易に思いつくだろうが、公衆の安全の重要性がそれを下回るという議論を組み立てるのはかなり難しい。モデルエッセイでは、公衆の安全という大義名分が政治権力の抑圧装置として利用されてきたこと、またプライバシーの保護を緩めることが必ずしも公衆の安全を高めることにはならないと対論の論拠を切り崩す議論をトピックとした。

● Structure

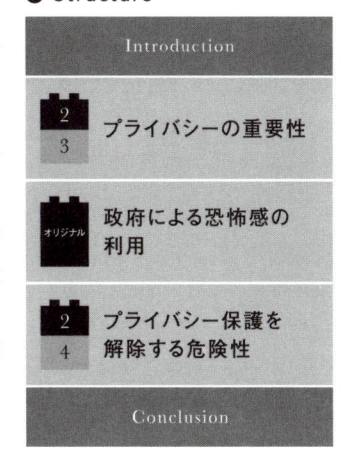

	Introduction
2 3	プライバシーの重要性
オリジナル	政府による恐怖感の利用
2 4	プライバシー保護を解除する危険性
	Conclusion

TOPIC

5 Should there be restrictions to freedom of speech in some cases?

モデルエッセイ 👍 Affirmative

Most would agree that freedom of speech is a valuable human right. However, there should be restrictions to freedom of speech in some cases. For example, speech should be restricted if it causes violence, spreads social inequality, or misleads consumers.

First, there should be laws against speech that directly harms other people. These laws already exist in many countries. In these places, it is illegal to falsely accuse someone of a crime or to harm their public reputation by lying. Officials have established laws like these because words can sometimes be just as harmful as violence.

Second, there should be restrictions to hate speech and racial intolerance. Some of the greatest human crimes in history were committed because of racial intolerance. Allowing people to spread false, racist ideas in public places spreads hate. This has led to tragedies such as slavery, the Holocaust, and the genocide in Rwanda.

Third, lies to the public such as false advertising should be banned. For example, companies should not be allowed to lie about the benefits of their products or services. This type of speech can trick customers into purchasing things that they do not actually want, which is a type of stealing.

The examples mentioned above exhibit why restrictions to freedom of speech are sometimes necessary.

(213 words)

訳 5 場合によっては言論の自由は制限すべきか
👍 Affirmative

　言論の自由が重要な人権であるということには、ほとんどの人が同意するだろう。しかし、言論の自由を規制すべき場合がある。例えば、暴力を引き起こす場合や、社会的不平等を拡大する場合、または、消費者に誤解を与える場合、言論は規制されるべきである。

　第一に、他者に直接的な被害を与える言論を取り締まる法律を設けるべきである。このような法律はすでに多くの国に存在している。こうした国々では、虚偽の告発をすることや、虚偽によって人の世評を傷つけることは違法とされている。当局がこのような法律を制定しているのは、言葉が暴力とまったく同じくらいの被害をもたらす場合がありうるからだ。

　第二に、ヘイトスピーチや人種的不寛容には規制を設けるべきだ。人類史上最大の罪のいくつかは、人種的不寛容に起因するものだ。誤った人種差別的考えを公共の場で広めることを許せば、憎しみが広がる。このことは奴隷制やナチスによるユダヤ人大虐殺、ルワンダの大量虐殺などのような悲劇につながってきた。

　第三に、虚偽広告のような一般市民への嘘は禁止されるべきだ。例えば、企業に、自社の製品やサービスの長所について嘘をつくことを許すべきではない。このような言論は、顧客をだまして本当は必要のないものを買わせる可能性があるが、これは一種の盗みである。

　上述の例は、言論の自由に対する規制が時として必要である理由を示している。

Vocabulary

□ falsely 不当に、偽って　□ accuse 〜を告発する、非難する　□ intolerance 不寛容　□ racist 人種差別(主義)の　□ slavery 奴隷制　□ holocaust 大量虐殺(特にthe Holocaustでナチスによるユダヤ人大虐殺を指す)　□ genocide 大虐殺、集団殺戮

解説　今度は言論の自由に関する設問。言論の自由は、民主主義国家では（少なくとも建前上は）保障されている権利である。しかし民主主義国家においても濫用すれば名誉棄損罪になるなど、抵触するケースはある。現在問題になっているリベンジポルノやヘイトスピーチの問題も密接に絡んでくるだろう。

　モデルエッセイでは、相手に直接の被害を与える場合、人種的不寛容、虚偽広告などの場合、言論の自由は制限されるべきであるとした。

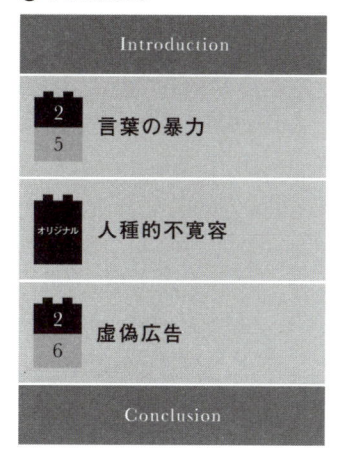

Structure

Introduction	
2/5	言葉の暴力
オリジナル	人種的不寛容
2/6	虚偽広告
Conclusion	

TOPIC

5 Should there be restrictions to freedom of speech in some cases?

モデルエッセイ ♠ Negative

I do not believe that there should be restrictions to freedom of speech. People cannot agree on what type of speech should be restricted, and governments cannot be trusted to use the power to restrict free speech responsibly. Also, people should be free to share any ideas or opinions.

The main reason that freedom of speech should not be restricted is that people cannot agree on what type of speech is unacceptable. The large number of debates surrounding this topic is evidence of this. Even if people have strange or offensive ideas, they should be able to express them freely.

Second, governments cannot be trusted with the power to limit speech. Historically, governments have repeatedly abused their power to limit speech. A modern-day example of this is North Korea, where criticism of the country's leaders can result in your entire family being arrested. No governments should have the capability of limiting freedom of speech like this.

Last, the world needs controversial—and sometimes offensive—art, ideas, and politics. For example, hundreds of famous books that are now used in literature classes were once banned by governments. The reason that governments usually restrict these books is because they want to control the ideas and principles of society in general, which is unacceptable. Freedom of speech supports freedom of thought.

For the reasons mentioned above, freedom of speech should not be restricted under any circumstances. (233 words)

訳 5 場合によっては言論の自由は制限すべきか
☂ Negative

　言論の自由に規制が設けられるべきだとは思わない。どのような言論が規制されるべきかについて合意を形成することはできないし、政府が自由な言論を規制する権限を、責任を持って行使すると信用することはできない。それに、いかなる考えや意見でも自由に表明できるべきだ。

　言論の自由が規制されるべきではない主な理由は、どのような言論が受け入れられないのかについて、人々が合意を形成することはできないということだ。このテーマをめぐって議論が百出していることがその証拠だ。たとえ誰かが、奇妙で不快な考えを持っていたとしても、自由にそれを表現できるようにすべきである。

　第二に、言論を制限する権限について政府を信用することはできない。歴史的に、政府は言論を制限する権力を繰り返し濫用してきた。これについての現代の例は北朝鮮で、この国では国の指導者を批判すると家族全員が逮捕される結果になることがある。このような言論の自由を制限する力を、いかなる政府も持つべきではない。

　最後に、世界には異論の多い──そして時には不快な──芸術や考え、政治信条が必要だ。例えば、今日の文学の授業で使われている何百という著名な書籍は、かつては政府が発禁としていたものだ。政府がこうした本を規制する理由はたいてい、社会全体の考えや信条をコントロールしたいからであり、これは受け入れがたいことだ。言論の自由は思想の自由を支える。

　上述の理由から、言論の自由はいかなる状況においても規制されるべきではない。

Vocabulary
□ responsibly 責任を持って　□ offensive 不快な　□ controversial 異論の多い、物議をかもす

解説
　言論の自由は制限すべきではないとする立場では、制限するデメリットを中心に論じることになるだろう。現在、民主主義国家において言論の自由が保障されているとはいえ、これはおのずと与えられた権利ではなく、人類が長い時間をかけて勝ち取ってきた権利である点を念頭に置くといいだろう。

　モデルエッセイでは、制限の線引きができないこと、政治権力は制限する権限を濫用する危険性があること、そして言論の自由こそが思想の自由を支え、歴史を切り拓いてきたことをトピックとして取り上げた。

◆ Structure

| Introduction |
| 2/7 言論の自由の規制の難しさ |
| オリジナル 政府による言論制限 |
| 2/8 言論の自由と思想の自由 |
| Conclusion |

TOPIC

6 Should people be punished for downloading music and movies illegally?

モデルエッセイ 👍 Affirmative　　　🎵 223

People who download music and movies illegally should be punished. Illegal downloading is theft, and it harms artists, companies, and ordinary people.

First, people need to realize that downloading copyrighted music and movies without purchasing them is a crime. Stealing digital products online is the same as stealing physical products from a store. Society will fall apart if people are allowed to break the law. So it makes sense to punish people for stealing this type of content.

Additionally, illegal downloading is a threat to the music and film industries. For example, in the last twenty years the number of singles purchased in the U.K. has decreased significantly. This is partly due to illegal downloading. This crime causes damage to artists and companies working hard to produce entertainment products.

Finally, illegal downloading does not only affect rich artists and entertainment companies. The people it hurts the most are average workers. Illegal downloading has been linked to layoffs in the entertainment industry, as companies are no longer able to afford their employees. This means that people who download music and movies illegally are responsible for higher unemployment rates.

Clearly, illegal downloading of music and movies should be punished. Aside from being against the law, it hurts artists, entertainment companies, and hard-working people.　　　　　　　　　(211 words)

ワンポイントアドバイス

第2パラグラフの第3文はTo maintain social stability, laws need to be respected. あるいはWe cannot have social stability if people are allowed to break the law. などとしてもよい。

訳 6 音楽や映画を違法にダウンロードする人を罰するべきか
　👍 Affirmative

　音楽や映画を違法にダウンロードする人は罰せられるべきだ。違法ダウンロードは窃盗であり、アーティストや企業、一般の人々に損害を与える。

　まず、著作権のある音楽や映画を購入することなくダウンロードすることは犯罪であるということを、人々は認識する必要がある。電子版の製品をオンラインで盗むことは、物的な製品を店舗で盗むのと同じだ。人々が法律を破ることを許されれば、社会は崩壊するだろう。ゆえに、この種のコンテンツを盗む人を罰することには意味がある。

　さらに、違法ダウンロードは音楽業界と映画業界への脅威だ。例えば、イギリスでは過去20年間で、購入されるシングルCDの枚数が著しく減っている。これは違法ダウンロードに一因がある。この犯罪は、エンターテイメント製品を作るために懸命に努力しているアーティストや企業にダメージを与えている。

　最後に、違法ダウンロードは裕福なアーティストやエンターテイメント会社に悪影響を及ぼしているだけではない。違法ダウンロードが最も損害を与えているのは、普通の労働者だ。違法ダウンロードは、エンターテイメント業界での解雇につながっている。企業にはもう従業員を雇う余裕がなくなっているからだ。これはつまり、違法に音楽や映画をダウンロードする人々は、失業率の増加の原因にもなっているということだ。

　明らかに、音楽や映画の違法ダウンロードは罰せられるべきだ。法に反しているだけでなく、アーティストとエンターテイメント企業、勤勉に働く人々に損害を与えている。

Vocabulary

□ fall apart バラバラになる、崩壊する　□ layoff 解雇　□ unemployment rate 失業率

解説　音楽や映画の違法ダウンロードを罰するべきかという設問。物的な商品と違い、ネット上のデジタル商品には無料のものも多く、違法ダウンロードに対しても人々の違法性の意識が低い点が問題を大きくしている。

　罰するべきとする立場では、罰しないとどのような被害が生じるか具体的に挙げていくといいだろう。モデルエッセイでは、法が順守されなければ社会が崩壊する、違法ダウンロードによってアーティストやメーカーが大きなダメージを受ける、被害はメーカーに勤める一般社員など業界全体に波及するというトピックを挙げた。

● Structure

| Introduction |
| 3-13 無許可ダウンロードの犯罪性 |
| 3-14 音楽業界と映画業界のダメージ |
| オリジナル 一般労働者へのダメージ |
| Conclusion |

TOPIC

6 Should people be punished for downloading music and movies illegally?

モデルエッセイ ◆ Negative

People should not be punished for downloading music and movies illegally. There is no effective method for punishing all of these people, and illegal downloading may not affect the entertainment industry negatively.

First, it is not possible to punish everyone that downloads music and movies illegally. Millions of people in hundreds of countries download music and movies without permission. The costs of capturing and fining all of them would be astronomical. Also, it is unfair to only fine or imprison a small percentage of these people.

Furthermore, the entertainment industry is already sufficiently profitable. Famous artists and actors make millions of dollars per year. And large entertainment companies make billions of dollars. Their continued success shows that illegal downloading does not affect them too much. The government should worry more about punishing people for worse crimes like murder, rape, and kidnapping.

Finally, there is not enough evidence to prove that pirating is harmful. A recent study in Europe has shown that pirating actually has very little influence on legal music downloads. According to this study, the majority of people who listen to illegal downloads would not have purchased the music even if they could not obtain it illegally. Plus, illegal downloads increase the popularity of music, which leads to higher revenue.

Upon taking the above points into consideration, it is clear that punishing people for downloading music and movies illegally is unrealistic and unnecessary.

(234 words)

訳 **6** 音楽や映画を違法にダウンロードする人を罰するべきか
　　　 🌧 Negative

　音楽や映画を違法にダウンロードすることで、人は罰を受けるべきではない。こうした人々全員を罰するのに実効力のある方法はなく、また、違法ダウンロードはエンターテイメント業界に悪影響を与えていない可能性がある。

　まず、音楽や映画を違法にダウンロードするすべての人を罰することは不可能だ。何百という国の何百万人もの人々が、許可なく音楽や映画をダウンロードしている。そのような人々全員を捕まえて罰金を支払わせるコストは、天文学的な数字になるだろう。また、このうちのごくわずかな割合の人々にだけ罰金を科したり投獄したりするのは不公平だ。

　さらに、エンターテイメント業界はすでに十分に利益を上げている。有名なアーティストや俳優は、年間何百万ドルも稼いでいる。それに、大手エンターテイメント企業は何十億ドルも儲けている。彼らが引き続き成功していることは、違法ダウンロードが彼らにそれほど大きな悪影響を与えていないことを示している。政府は、殺人やレイプ、誘拐といった、より悪質な犯罪に関する処罰のほうにもっと気を向けるほうがいい。

　最後に、違法コピーが有害だということを証明する十分な証拠がない。ヨーロッパで実施された最近の研究で、違法コピーは実は、合法的な音楽ダウンロードにほとんど影響を与えていないことが示されている。この研究によると、違法ダウンロードされた音楽を聞いている人々の大多数は、仮にそれらを違法に入手できなかったとしてもその音楽を買ってはいなかったという。加えて、違法ダウンロードは音楽の人気を高めており、収益を上げることにつながっている。

　上記の論点を考慮に入れると、音楽や映画を違法にダウンロードする人を罰することは、非現実的であり、不必要であることは明らかだ。

Vocabulary

□ capture ～を捕まえる　□ fine ～に罰金を科す　□ astronomical 天文学的な、けた外れに多い
□ imprison ～を投獄する　□ pirate 海賊行為をする、著作権を侵害する

解説　今度は違法ダウンロードを罰するべきではないとする立場。違法なものを罰しないという立場が成り立つのか不思議かもしれないが、現実世界でもデジタル商品の課金モデルをあきらめる企業は多く、ネットビジネスのモデルチェンジが起こっていることは念頭に置いておいてよい。

　モデルエッセイでは、そもそも違法ダウンロードの件数が多すぎて罰するのが現実的でないこと、コンテンツの違法ダウンロードは必ずしもメーカーやアーティストにとってデメリットではないことをトピックとして取り上げた。

◆ Structure

Introduction
3 / 15　処罰の非現実性
オリジナル　潤っているエンターテイメント業界
3 / 16　違法ダウンロードの有害性に関する疑問
Conclusion

TOPIC

7 Agree or disagree: A lack of women's rights is a serious problem in Japan

モデルエッセイ 👍 Affirmative 🎧 225

It is vital for Japan to improve women's rights. There are currently too few women leaders in both business and politics, and it is difficult for mothers in Japan to contribute as working members of society.

First, the number of women in executive positions at companies is embarrassingly low in Japan compared to other developed nations. According to a recent study, only about 10% of management positions at Japanese companies were held by women, and only 1% of senior, executive-level positions.

Second, Japan has one of the worst levels of political gender equality among developed countries. According to one survey, the percentage of female lower house members in Japan was less than that of over 100 other countries, including both China and North Korea. Discriminatory policies are not likely to change unless women have more representation in politics.

An additional problem in Japan is that it is extremely difficult to be a working mother. About 70% of women in Japan leave the workforce after having their first baby, compared to less than half that number in the United States. There are a number of causes for this, including a shortage of affordable childcare centers and outdated views about the roles of mothers in society.

Overall, it is clear that Japan needs to work more to increase women's rights and opportunities. Doing so will promote equality and improve Japan's economy and international reputation.

(232 words)

ワンポイントアドバイス

第3パラグラフの第1文は、短くWomen are also underrepresented in politics.（女性はまた、政界においても数が少ない）とすることもできる。underrepresentedは「十分に代表されていない」という意味。

訳 **7** 賛成か反対か：女性の権利の欠如は日本において深刻な問題である
👍 Affirmative

　日本における女性の権利の向上は極めて重要である。現在、日本ではビジネスにおいても政治においても、女性のリーダーがあまりにも少なく、また母親は働き手として社会に貢献しにくい状況である。

　第一に、日本の企業では、女性の重役の数が、他の先進国に比べてあきれるほど少ない。最近の調査によると、日本企業の女性管理職の割合はわずか10%ほどで、シニアレベル、エグゼクティブレベルに至ってはわずか1%ほどに過ぎない。

　第二に、日本は、政治におけるジェンダーの公平性が先進国の中で最低レベルの国の一つだ。ある調査によれば、日本の衆議院議員の女性の割合は中国や北朝鮮を含む100以上の諸外国よりも低かった。差別的な政策は、政界にもっと女性が進出しない限り、変わりそうにない。

　日本でさらに問題なのは、仕事と母親業を同時に行うのが極めて難しいことだ。日本では、女性の約70%が第1子の出産後に離職するが、アメリカではその半分にも満たない。これには、手ごろな費用で利用できる保育所の不足や、社会における母親の役割についての時代遅れの考え方を含め、数多くの原因がある。

　概して、日本は女性の権利と機会を向上させるためにもっと努力する必要があることは明らかだ。そうすることは、平等を推進し、日本の経済を上向かせ、国際的な評価を高めるだろう。

Vocabulary

☐ embarrassingly 当惑するほどに　☐ lower house 衆議院　☐ discriminatory 差別的な
☐ affordable 入手可能な　☐ childcare center 保育所　☐ workforce 労働力、従業員

解説　日本における女性の権利に関する設問。男性の育児休暇や少子化の問題とも関連するテーマだ。女性の権利が欠如しているとする立場で論じる場合は、具体的にどのような場面で女性の権利が認められていないか、またなぜそのような状況になっているのかといった側面から考えるといいだろう。

　モデルエッセイでは、企業の管理職に占める女性の割合、政治（衆議院）における女性の割合、そして女性の社会進出を阻害している要因の3点をトピックとして取り上げた。

● Structure

| Introduction |
| 2 ⑨ 日本企業の女性管理職 |
| 2 ⑩ 政界の女性 |
| オリジナル 産後の離職 |
| Conclusion |

TOPIC

7. Agree or disagree: A lack of women's rights is a serious problem in Japan

モデルエッセイ ● Negative

I do not believe that a lack of women's rights is a serious problem in Japan. Women's rights are already improving, and problems related to women advancing in companies are mostly due to Japan's work culture.

First, although women in Japan do not yet have as many opportunities as men, they are not victims of any human rights violations. In countries that are extremely prejudiced against women, females are treated as second-class citizens that cannot attend schools or acquire valuable skills. But in Japan women receive the same world-class education as men.

Second, Japan does need to work to improve the opportunities for women in society, but this change is already taking place. Specifically, women need more chances to obtain respectable, high-paying jobs and leadership positions, especially after having children. The majority of both men and women in Japan appear to agree on this issue. Accordingly, policymakers are already working to create a fairer system for women.

Finally, most of the "women's rights issues" in Japan are not really about women at all. It is common to hear that Japan needs to get more women to contribute to the workforce. The main reason that women leave companies, though, is not because of discrimination. Rather, the general work culture in Japan is too demanding for anyone to raise children while working full-time.

In conclusion, Japan does not need to work more to improve women's rights.

(234 words)

訳 **7** 賛成か反対か：女性の権利の欠如は日本において深刻な問題である
🌧 Negative

　私は女性の権利の欠如は日本において深刻な問題だとは思わない。女性の権利はすでに向上しつつあり、企業における女性の昇進に関わる問題は、ほとんどが日本の労働文化に起因している。

　第一に、日本の女性はまだ男性並みには機会を持っていないが、人権侵害の犠牲者になっているわけではない。女性に対する偏見の激しい国々では、女性は学校にも通えず、有用なスキルを身につけることもできない二流の市民として扱われている。しかし日本では、女性は男性と同じ世界レベルの教育を受けている。

　第二に、日本が社会における女性の機会改善のために努力しなければならないのは確かだが、こうした変化はすでに起こっている。具体的に言うと、女性は、とりわけ出産後、きちんとした高給の仕事と指導的な地位を得るためのより多くの機会が与えられるべきだ。日本の大半の男性と女性の両方がこの問題について意見が一致していると思われる。そしてそれを受けて、政策立案者たちはすでに、女性により公平なシステムを作ることに取り組んでいる。

　最後に、日本における「女性の権利の問題」の大部分は、本当は女性に関するものではまったくない。日本は、もっと多くの女性に労働力として貢献してもらう必要があるという意見をよく耳にする。だが、女性が会社を辞める主な理由は、差別のせいではない。そうではなく、日本の一般的な労働文化では、フルタイムで働きながら子育てをする人すべてにとって負担が大きすぎるということなのだ。

　結論として、日本は女性の権利を向上するために取り組みを増やす必要はない。

Vocabulary

□ prejudiced 偏見のある　□ policymaker 政策立案者

解説　今度は女性の権利の欠如は深刻な問題ではないとする立場。男女が平等に扱われるべきなのは前提であり、すでに行われている施策を取り上げることで、「深刻とは言えない」と論じるのが基本的なスタンスになるだろう。

　モデルエッセイでは、日本の女性は男性と同じ水準の教育を受けており、また男性と同じ職業の機会が女性に与えられるよう、政策的な取り組みも始まっていると論じている。そして最終トピックでは、現在の労働文化がフルタイムで働きながら子育てをする（男性を含む）すべての人にとって過酷であるとした。

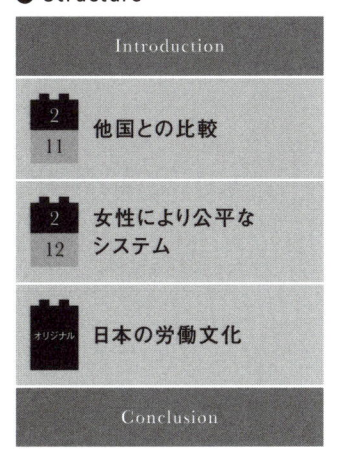

💬 Structure

| Introduction |
| 2-11　他国との比較 |
| 2-12　女性により公平なシステム |
| オリジナル　日本の労働文化 |
| Conclusion |

TOPIC

8 Should rich people be required to pay higher taxes?

モデルエッセイ 👍 Affirmative

I believe that rich people should be required to pay higher taxes. This is necessary for government funding, and it is a fairer system overall.

First, higher taxes are required for wealthier citizens because this is the best way to generate enough money for government expenses. It is common to hear people suggest flat-rate tax systems. However, expert economists have shown that these would result in heavier tax burdens for poor people and a lack of government funds.

Second, many people argue that the rich should not pay higher taxes because they worked harder to earn their money, but this is not true. For example, someone making 1 million dollars per year makes more money than 20 teachers. It is impossible for that person to be working harder than all of those teachers.

Finally, more needs to be done to ensure that rich people pay their fair share of taxes. Since they have access to more resources and information, rich people can lower their taxes using various tax deductions and loopholes. As a result, lower-income earners pay a higher percentage in combined income, property and sales taxes. There should be laws to prevent this.

In conclusion, I believe that rich people should pay higher taxes. This is the most effective way to fund the government, and it is the fairest system for income taxes.

(224 words)

訳 8 富裕層は税負担を重くするべきか
👍 Affirmative

裕福な人々には、より高い税金の支払いを求めるべきだと思う。これは政府の財源に必要であり、全体としてより公平な制度だ。

第一に、裕福な市民にはより高い税金を求めるべきである理由は、これが政府の歳出をまかなうに足るお金を生み出す最善の方法だからだ。一律課税制度を提言する声もよく聞かれる。しかし、経済の専門家たちは、この制度では貧しい人々の税負担を増すことになり、政府の資金が不足することになると示している。

第二に、多くの人々が、裕福な人々は高い税金を支払うべきではないと主張しており、その理由は、裕福な人々はお金を稼ぐためにより熱心に働いているからだというのだが、それは事実ではない。例えば、1年間に100万ドルを稼ぐ人は、20人の教員よりも多くのお金を稼いでいる。(だが)年収100万ドルの人が教員20人分よりもたくさん働くことは不可能だ。

最後に、裕福な人々が適正な税を確実に負担するように、より多くのことがなされるべきだ。裕福な人々は、より多くの手段や情報を利用できるため、さまざまな税控除や抜け道を使って税金を下げることができる。その結果、稼ぎの少ない人のほうが、所得税、固定資産税、売上税を合わせると、より高い割合の税金を支払っている。こうしたことを防止する法律が必要だ。

結論として、裕福な人々はより高い税金を支払うべきだと思う。これは政府の収入を確保する最も効果的な方法であり、また最も公平な所得税のシステムである。

Vocabulary
☐ flat-rate (料金・税などが)均一の ☐ tax burden 税負担 ☐ deduction 控除 ☐ loophole 抜け穴、抜け道

解説
税にはさまざまな種類や側面があるが、この設問で問われているのは累進課税(高所得者に高い税を課す)の是非である。「たくさん稼いでいるのだからその分多く払うのは当たり前だ」といった素朴な議論で終わらせないため、いくつかのポイントを押さえておきたい。一般的に累進課税には「富の再配分」「経済格差の是正(社会の安定化)」「消費の拡大」といったメリットがあるとされる。モデルエッセイでは、所得は労働量に比例しているという論を否定し、法の整備によって適切な納税を促すべきだとした。

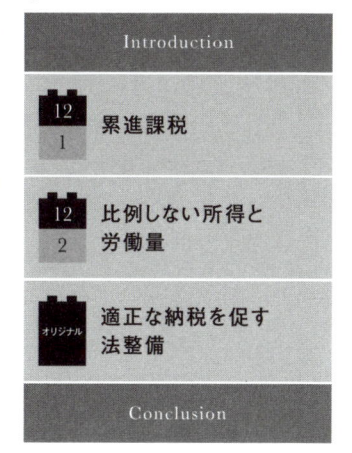

Structure
- Introduction
- 12-1 累進課税
- 12-2 比例しない所得と労働量
- オリジナル 適正な納税を促す法整備
- Conclusion

TOPIC

8 Should rich people be required to pay higher taxes?

モデルエッセイ ◆ Negative

I disagree with the opinion that rich people should be required to pay higher taxes. Supporting a system like this is the same as supporting discrimination. Also, this type of system would decrease incentives to work hard and increase incentives to avoid paying taxes.

The primary reason that rich people should not be required to pay higher taxes is that it is discriminatory. People seem to understand that poor treatment of people based on their religion, ethnicity, or physical appearance is wrong. But charging higher taxes for rich people is also a form of discrimination.

Additionally, raising taxes for rich people discourages capitalism. Generally speaking, people work harder when they want to make more money. However, there is less reason to work harder when there are higher tax rates for rich people. In other words, higher tax rates for the rich discourage capitalism.

Last, setting high tax rates for rich individuals encourages tax avoidance. If rich people are faced with higher tax rates, then they will search for ways to avoid paying taxes. This is one reason why rich citizens place their money and assets in overseas tax havens, which harms the local economies.

In conclusion, I believe that requiring rich people to pay higher taxes is a bad idea. Aside from being discriminatory, this type of system discourages tax compliance.

(221 words)

訳 8 富裕層は税負担を重くするべきか
🌧 Negative

裕福な人々により高い税金の支払いを求めるべきだという意見には反対だ。このような制度を支持することは、差別を支持するのと同じだ。それに、この種の制度は熱心に働こうという動機を減らし、税金の支払いを回避する誘因となるだろう。

裕福な人々により高い税金の支払いを求めるべきではない主たる理由は、それは差別的だからだ。宗教、民族、身体的な外見に基づいて人々を劣悪に扱うことが間違っているということに異論はないと思われる。しかし、裕福な人々により高い税金を課すこともまた、差別の一種だ。

さらに、裕福な人々への税金を上げることは、資本主義を阻害する。概して、人はお金をもっと稼ぎたくて、もっと熱心に働く。しかし、裕福な人への税率が高ければ、より勤勉に働く理由が減る。言い換えれば、富裕層への税率を高くすることは、資本主義を阻害する。

最後に、裕福な個人に高い税率を設定するのは、租税回避の原因となる。裕福な人々は高い税率に直面すれば、税金の支払いを避ける方法を探る。これは、裕福な人々が海外の租税回避地に資金や財産を置く理由の一つで、地域経済に損害を与えている。

結論として、裕福な人々により高い税金の支払いを求めるのはよくない考えだと思う。差別であるだけでなく、このようなシステムは納税の順守を阻害する。

Vocabulary

□ discrimination 差別　□ incentive 動機づけ　□ ethnicity 民族性　□ discourage 〜を阻害する
□ tax avoidance 租税回避　□ asset 資産、財産　□ tax haven 租税回避地　□ compliance 順守

解説

今度は累進課税に反対する立場で考える。累進課税の問題点としてよく言われるのは、経済効率性の阻害である。働いて収入が上がれば上がるほど税の割合が上がっていくと、働く意欲がそがれるという問題だ。また税率の高い場所からは富裕層は出て行ってしまう。

モデルエッセイでは、第2パラグラフで裕福な人に高い税率を課すのは一種の差別であるというトピックを挙げ、上記の2点と合わせて三つのBodyとした。

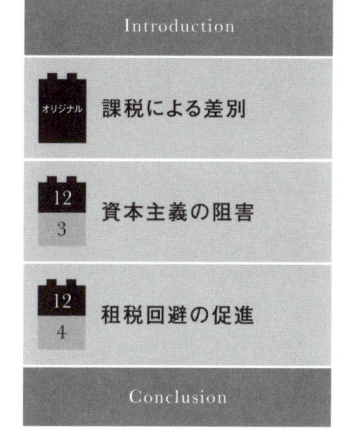

● Structure

Introduction	
オリジナル	課税による差別
12 / 3	資本主義の阻害
12 / 4	租税回避の促進
Conclusion	

TOPIC
9 Should minors receive life imprisonment for serious crimes?

モデルエッセイ 👍 Affirmative   🎧 229

　　I believe that, in some cases, minors should receive life imprisonment for serious crimes. Mental age is difficult to measure, and it is less important than a criminal's intentions. Also, strict punishments can lead to less crime.

　　First, when deciding punishments for crimes, criminals' intentions are important. For example, according to the law, people rarely receive life imprisonment for accidentally killing another person. But when a crime is intentional, then life imprisonment is sometimes justified. Likewise, heavy penalties should be imposed on minors if they understood the results of their actions.

　　Furthermore, the details of some crimes show that minors can be capable of making adult decisions. Countries have specific age numbers to divide children from adults, but in reality these numbers should vary for each person. Some children develop more quickly than others. This means that sometimes a 16-year-old "child" has the mental capacity of a 20-year-old "adult."

　　Finally, having strict consequences will prevent future crimes. Several studies have shown that establishing strict punishments for crimes helps to stop them. It is possible that some minors may commit serious crimes because they expect to get special treatment if they are caught. This is unacceptable. We should make sure that there are always serious consequences for serious crimes.

　　For the reasons mentioned above, I believe that sentencing minors to life imprisonment for serious crimes is sometimes justified.

(227 words)

訳 **9** 未成年者は重犯罪で終身刑を受けるべきか
👍 Affirmative

　未成年者は、場合によっては、重罪について終身刑を受けるべきだと思う。精神年齢を測ることは難しく、またそれは犯罪者の意図よりも重要ではない。それに、厳罰は犯罪の減少につながることがある。

　まず、犯罪に対して刑罰を決める際には、犯罪者の意図が重要だ。例えば、法によれば、人は故意ではなく他人を殺してしまった場合、終身刑を受けることはまれだ。しかし、犯罪が意図されたものである場合は、終身刑が正当とされることがある。同じように、自分の行為の結果が理解できている場合には、未成年者にも重罰を科すべきだ。

　さらに、いくつかの犯罪を詳細に見ると、未成年者が成人と同じ判断力を備えている例もあることがわかる。各国は未成年と成人を区分する具体的な年齢を定めているが、現実にはこの年齢は人によって異なるはずだ。ほかの人々よりも発達が早い子どももいる。これはつまり、16歳の「子ども」が20歳の「大人」の思考力を持つこともあるということだ。

　最後に、厳しい結果を設けることは、犯罪を未然に防ぐことになるだろう。複数の研究で、犯罪に厳罰を設けることは犯罪の抑止につながると示されている。捕まっても特別な扱いを受けられると思っているために、重罪を犯す未成年者がいる可能性はある。これは受け入れられないことだ。我々は重罪には常に厳しい結果が待ち受けていることを明確にしておくべきだ。

　上述の理由から、私は未成年者に対し、重罪について終身刑を言い渡すことは正当な場合があると考える。

Vocabulary
□ imprisonment 投獄（life imprisonmentで「終身刑」の意味になる）　□ strict punishment 厳罰
□ unacceptable 受け入れられない、容認できない　□ sentence 〜に判決を下す

解説　未成年犯罪者に終身刑を認めるべきかという内容の設問。ここで終身刑というのは厳罰の象徴と考えるべきで、細かい量刑の話をすることに意味はない。日本でも「少年法」の厳罰化などをめぐり、さまざまな議論がなされている。

　終身刑を認めるべきだとする立場のモデルエッセイでは、犯罪の故意性こそが重要である点、成人と子どもの線引きの難しさ、そして犯罪抑止の観点をトピックとして挙げている。被害者の心情などをトピックとすることも可能だろう。

● Structure

Introduction
③⑥ 犯罪者の意図と刑罰
③⑦ 未成年者と成人の線引き
オリジナル 厳罰化による犯罪抑止
Conclusion

TOPIC 9 Should minors receive life imprisonment for serious crimes?

モデルエッセイ ♠ Negative

　　　Minors should not receive life imprisonment for serious crimes. Young people's mental states and environments have a large influence on their decisions. Also, there is usually still hope for rehabilitating them.

　　　First, young people's brains have not finished developing. Research has shown that the decision-making part of the brain continues to develop until an individual's mid-20's. So young people's brains are not as quick at making good decisions. This must be taken into account when considering punishments for minors.

　　　Furthermore, statistics show that a large percentage of juveniles committing crimes have witnessed violence in their own homes, and many of them witness violence on a weekly basis in their neighborhoods. Growing up in this type of environment can have negative effects on a child's psychological well-being. This must be considered before deciding a crime's punishment.

　　　Last, there is a high chance that minors who commit crimes can be rehabilitated. Young people's behavior can change drastically if they receive proper guidance. Rather than spending millions of dollars keeping minors in prisons, governments should invest in better support and education systems for these young people.

　　　In summary, minors should not receive life sentences for serious offenses. Instead, their life circumstances, still-developing brain structures, and possible futures should be taken into consideration.

(209 words)

ワンポイントアドバイス

第4パラグラフ第1文の ... who commit crimes can be rehabilitated は ... who commit crimes can learn from their mistakes などと言い換えてもよい。

訳 **9　未成年者は重犯罪で終身刑を受けるべきか**
　　　🌧 Negative

　未成年者は重罪について終身刑を受けるべきではない。若者の精神状態と環境は、彼らの決定に大きく影響する。また、若者には更生する希望が残されていることが多い。

　まず、若い人々の脳は発達を終えていない。意思決定に関わる脳の部位は20代半ばまで発達し続けることが、調査で示されている。つまり、若者の脳は、（大人ほど）素早く適切な判断を下すことができない。このことは、未成年者の刑罰を考える際に考慮されなければならない。

　さらに、統計では、罪を犯す未成年者の大多数が家庭で暴力を目にしており、その多くが毎週のように近隣で暴力を目にしていることが示されている。このような環境で育つと、子どもの健全な心理状態に悪影響が及びかねない。このことは、罪に対する刑罰を決定する前に配慮されなければならない。

　最後に、罪を犯した未成年者が更生できる可能性は高い。若者の行動は、適切な指導を受ければ大幅に変わりうる。未成年者を刑務所に入れておくのに何百万ドルも費やすより、政府は、こうした若者をより手厚くサポートし、教育する制度にお金を使うべきだ。

　まとめると、未成年者は重罪に対して終身刑を受けるべきではない。そうではなく、生活環境や発達途上の脳の構造、可能性のある未来を考慮に入れるべきだ。

Vocabulary

□ rehabilitate 〜を更生させる、社会復帰させる　□ juvenile 年少者、子ども

解説　今度は未成年者に厳罰を科すことに反対する立場で考える。未成年者に成人とは異なる刑事処分を下す法制は、日本の少年法に限らず世界各国にあるが、これは未成年者の精神的発達が成人の域に達しておらず、またその未成熟さゆえに人格に変化の可能性がある、つまり更生の可能性があると見なされるためである。

　モデルエッセイでは、罪を犯す未成年者の多くが目にして育つ暴力的な家庭環境を考慮に入れるべきだという点を上記の2点に加えて三つのトピックとした。

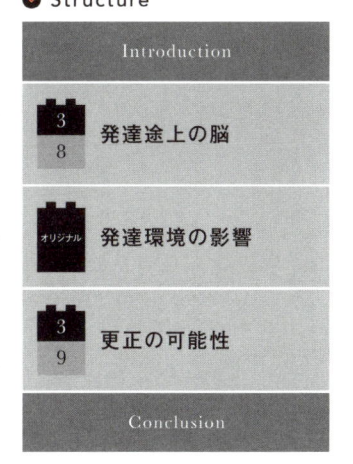

Structure

Introduction
3/8 発達途上の脳
オリジナル 発達環境の影響
3/9 更正の可能性
Conclusion

TOPIC

10　Agree or disagree: Hosting international sporting events is good for local communities

モデルエッセイ 👍 Affirmative

　　　　I agree that hosting international sporting events is good for local communities. It improves the economy, generates new jobs, and leads to improvements in infrastructure.

　　　　First, large events have economic benefits for local communities. During an international sporting event, there is a huge increase in the number of visitors. This means that local businesses can sell more goods and services. There is almost no negative economic effect for local communities because usually the extra costs for these events are paid by the government.

　　　　Second, hosting an international sporting event leads to the creation of new jobs. These events require investment in building stadiums and hotels. This creates more jobs for the local community. Although not all of these jobs are permanent, some of them last for multiple years, and the local people are able to acquire new skills and save money.

　　　　Third, investment in infrastructure benefits local people significantly. For example, improvements to public transportation are usually required before hosting a major sporting event. After the event is over, this improved infrastructure makes people's lives easier. Also, it makes the area a more attractive place to do business.

　　　　In conclusion, I am of the opinion that hosting international sporting events benefits local communities. It helps both the economy and the employment rate. Plus, local residents can make use of improved infrastructure and new facilities for many years.　　(227 words)

訳 10 賛成か反対か：国際スポーツイベントの開催は地域社会にとって有益である
👍 Affirmative

　国際スポーツイベントを開催することは地域社会にとってよいことだと思う。経済を上向かせ、新たな雇用を創出し、インフラの改善につながる。

　第一に、大規模なイベントは地域社会に経済的な恩恵をもたらす。国際スポーツイベント中には、来訪者数が大幅に増加する。これはつまり、地域の企業が販売できる物やサービスが増えるということだ。こうしたイベントに付帯するコストは、通常、政府が支払うため、地域社会には経済的な悪影響はほとんどない。

　第二に、国際スポーツイベントを開催することは、新しい雇用の創出につながる。こうしたイベントには、スタジアムやホテルの建設への投資が必要だ。これにより、地域社会により多くの働き口が創出される。こうした仕事のすべてが永続的であるわけではないが、数年は続くものもあり、地元の人々は新たなスキルを身につけ、お金を貯めることができる。

　第三に、インフラへの投資は、地元の人々に多大な恩恵を与える。例えば、大きなスポーツイベントを開催する前には、通例、公共交通機関の改善が必要となる。イベントが終わったあと、この改善されたインフラは人々の暮らしを楽にする。また、事業を行うにもより魅力的な場所になる。

　結論として、私は国際スポーツイベントを開催することは地域社会に恩恵をもたらすという意見だ。それは経済と雇用を改善する。それに、地域住民は改善されたインフラと新しい施設を長年にわたり活用することができる。

Vocabulary

□ permanent 永続的な、恒久的な

解説　国際スポーツイベントとしてはオリンピックやサッカーのワールドカップを思い浮かべればよい。2020年に東京オリンピックを開催する日本にとっても身近なテーマと言える。一口に地域社会と言っても、自治体、企業、住民といったさまざまなレベルでのメリット・デメリットがあることを頭に入れておくと、トピックが探しやすいだろう。

　国際スポーツイベントの開催が地域社会にとって有益だとする立場のモデルエッセイでは、地域の産業が潤う、新たな雇用が創出される、インフラが整備されるといったトピックを挙げた。

● Structure

| Introduction |
| 経済的恩恵 |
| 雇用の創出 |
| インフラの整備 |
| Conclusion |

TOPIC
10 Agree or disagree: Hosting international sporting events is good for local communities

モデルエッセイ ♠ Negative　　　MP3 232

　　Hosting international sporting events is not good for local communities. Failure to host an event well can harm the local community's image. Also, the costs of preparing for an event and keeping it safe are too high.

　　One negative effect of hosting an international sporting event is the possibility of generating bad publicity. Some local communities are not well-suited to handle these major events, and as a result they sometimes fail to do a good job of hosting them. This can harm the local community's international reputation.

　　Furthermore, the costs of preparing for a major event are astronomical. In addition to building hotels and stadiums, most areas also need to improve their transportation systems and infrastructure. This can cost billions of dollars. Because of this, many countries lose a significant amount of money by hosting major sporting events.

　　Moreover, improving security for these events is costly and problematic. Due to the increased danger of terrorism, security must be strengthened significantly. For large events, several thousand security guards need to be hired. This is extremely expensive. Also, it is difficult to manage security because many security guards are not well-trained. So the safety of the local people also goes down.

　　For the reasons mentioned above, local communities do not benefit from hosting international sporting events.　　(214 words)

訳 10 賛成か反対か：国際スポーツイベントの開催は地域社会にとって有益である
♣ Negative

　国際スポーツイベントを開催することは地域社会にとってよいことではない。イベントをうまく開催できなかった場合、地域社会のイメージを傷つける可能性がある。また、イベントの準備と安全に開催するための費用が高くつきすぎる。

　国際スポーツイベントを開催する悪影響の一つは、悪評を生んでしまう可能性があることだ。こうした大きなイベントを運営するのに適していない地域もあり、その結果、イベントをうまく主催できない場合がある。このことは、その地域の国際的な評価を傷つけることになりかねない。

　さらに、大きなイベントの準備にかかる費用は莫大だ。ホテルやスタジアムの建設に加え、ほとんどの地域は交通網とインフラを改善する必要がある。これには何十億ドルもかかるかもしれない。このため、多くの国が、大きなスポーツイベントの開催により、多額の資金を失っている。

　さらに、こうしたイベントに向けた安全対策の強化にも費用がかさみ、問題をはらむ。テロの危険性が高まっているので、安全対策は大幅に強化されなければならない。大きなイベントでは、数千人の警備員を雇う必要がある。これには極めて高額な費用がかかる。また、警備員の多くは十分な訓練を受けていないため、安全を確保することも難しい。そのため、地域住民の安全性もまた低下する。

　上述の理由から、地域社会は国際スポーツイベントの開催から恩恵を受けることはない。

Vocabulary
- publicity 評判、知名度
- well-suited 適した
- international reputation 国際的な評価
- problematic 問題のある

解説
　今度はスポーツイベントを開催するデメリットについて考える。すぐに思いつくのは開催にかかる莫大な経費だろう。政府から助成金が交付される場合はあるが、整備するのは競技場や宿泊施設だけではない。交通網などのインフラ整備にかかる費用は、極めて大きいものになるだろう。また警備など、ソフト面での経費も考慮に入れる必要がある。モデルエッセイでは、こうした点に加え、大きなイベントは世界中の注目を集めるため、成功すればメリットも大きいが失敗すると世界的に評判を落としてしまうリスクをトピックとして挙げた。

● Structure

Introduction
オリジナル　国際評価の低下
9/19　開催費用
9/20　安全保障の強化
Conclusion

問題　解答時間：1問につき25分

2　国際問題

CHAPTER_3

- Write an essay on the given TOPIC.
- Give THREE reasons to support your answer.
- Structure: Introduction, main body, and conclusion
- Suggested length: 200–240 words

TOPIC

1. Should Japan have more lenient immigration policies?

　　　　　　　　　　　　　　　　　解答・解説は204-207ページ

2. Agree or disagree: International terrorism will never be eliminated

　　　　　　　　　　　　　　　　　解答・解説は208-211ページ

3. Should nuclear weapons be outlawed worldwide?

　　　　　　　　　　　　　　　　　解答・解説は212-215ページ

4. Agree or disagree: World hunger will decrease in the future

　　　　　　　　　　　　　　　　　解答・解説は216-219ページ

5. Should import taxes be abolished?

6. Agree or disagree: The use of military force is sometimes justifiable

TOPIC

1 Should Japan have more lenient immigration policies?

モデルエッセイ 👍 Affirmative

Immigration policies in Japan should be more lenient because workers are decreasing, and companies need to consider new ways to innovate and increase profits.

Due to Japan's aging population, the younger generation will eventually need to support the older generation. The government will have a difficult time providing financial support for its citizens without forcing young people to work longer hours. However, Japan could get more workers by accepting more immigrants into the country.

Second, if Japan has more lenient immigration policies, it will attract skilled workers from abroad. There are millions of highly talented, hard-working people in the world that would love to live and work in Japan. If they were allowed into the country, they could contribute to Japanese society in many ways.

Finally, decades of research performed by scientists in a number of fields have shown that socially diverse groups are more creative and harder-working. This makes sense, because people with different backgrounds bring new information and viewpoints. Also, individuals have to work harder to effectively present their differing ideas and opinions to team members.

In conclusion, some cultural and economic problems facing Japan today may be resolved by accepting immigrants, and, for these reasons, closed immigration policies are likely harmful to the future of Japan.

(209 words)

訳 1 日本はより寛容な移民政策をとるべきか
👍 Affirmative

　日本の移民政策はもっと寛容にすべきである。なぜなら、労働者は減少しており、企業はイノベーションをもたらして利益を増やす新たな方策を考える必要があるからだ。

　日本では、人口の高齢化のため、若い世代がいずれ上の世代を支えなければならなくなる。若者に長時間労働を強いることなく、政府が国民を経済的に支援するのは困難になる。しかし、国内にもっと多くの移民を受け入れれば、日本は労働者を増やすことができるだろう。

　第二に、もし日本が寛容な移民政策をとれば、海外から技能を備えた労働者が集まるだろう。世界には日本に住んで働きたいと思っている有能で勤勉な人が何百万人もいる。もし彼らが入国を許されれば、彼らはさまざまな形で日本社会に貢献することだろう。

　最後に、さまざまな分野の科学者が行った数十年にわたる研究で、社会的に多様性を持つ集団のほうが、より創造的でよく働くということが示されている。これは当然である。なぜなら、背景の異なる人々は新しい情報と視点をもたらすからだ。それに、個々人は、チームのメンバーに異なる考えや意見を効果的に伝えるためにいっそうの努力が必要とされる。

　結論として、日本が今日直面している文化的課題と経済的課題のいくつかは、移民を受け入れることで解決できる可能性がある。そしてこれらの理由から、閉鎖的な移民政策は、恐らく日本の将来に悪影響を及ぼすだろう。

Vocabulary
□ innovate 刷新する、新生面を開く　□ contribute to ～ ～に貢献する　□ make sense 理にかなっている
□ viewpoint 観点、見方

解説
　世界の人口が増え続ける一方で、日本は少子高齢化、そして人口減少の問題に直面している。それは、労働力不足や社会保障制度の維持の問題へもつながっている。移民政策の寛容化に賛成の立場で答える場合、労働力不足の解決は思いつきやすい論点だろうが、それだけでは議論が行き詰まってしまうので、外国人労働者を受け入れた場合のメリットについてさらに考える必要がある。モデルエッセイでは、優秀な人材の確保、そして社会の活性化のポイントを挙げたが、日本人の閉鎖性の打破といった論点も考えられるだろう。

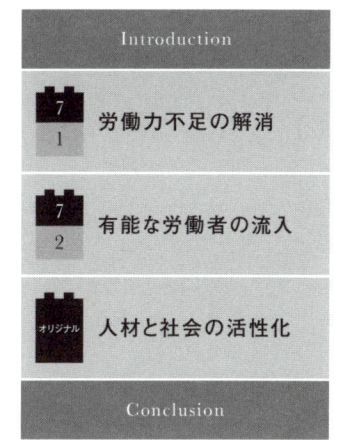

Structure
- Introduction
- ¶1 労働力不足の解消
- ¶2 有能な労働者の流入
- オリジナル 人材と社会の活性化
- Conclusion

TOPIC

1 Should Japan have more lenient immigration policies?

モデルエッセイ ◆ Negative　　　　　　　　　　MP3 234

　　Some argue that recent problems in Japan can be solved by more lenient immigration policies. However, immigration is often harmful to natural born citizens, as salaries decrease and more people enter the country illegally. Also, better solutions are emerging for the problems facing Japan.

　　Research shows that increases in migrant workers lead to decreased wages for the poorest workers. This means that natural born citizens are forced to work for lower salaries in order to compete with migrant workers. Companies have no reason to pay higher salaries when foreign workers are willing to work for lower wages.

　　Second, lenient immigration policies would lead to higher taxes because there would be more illegal immigrants. Even illegal immigrants benefit from public services like emergency medical care, high-quality roads, and law enforcement. However, they do not pay enough taxes to fund these. Instead, legal citizens are forced to pay higher taxes.

　　Finally, some believe that accepting more immigrants is necessary to fix Japan's aging population problem, but this is not true. Recent research shows that robots are likely to replace nearly half of workers over the next few decades. This means that even a small number of young workers should be able to support the elderly population.

　　When considering these problems, it seems that more lenient immigration policies would only lead to more problems for Japan overall.

(224 words)

ワンポイントアドバイス

「調査が示すところによれば」は Research shows that ... か One study shows that ...。この場合 research は不可算名詞なので、A research としないように注意。

訳 1 日本はより寛容な移民政策をとるべきか
🌧 Negative

　日本の昨今の諸問題は、より寛容な移民政策をとることによって解決できると主張する人もいる。しかし、賃金が低下し、不法に入国する人が増えるので、移民は日本で生まれた国民にしばしば悪影響を及ぼす。また、日本が直面する諸問題には、よりよい解決策が生まれつつある。

　調査によれば、移民労働者の増加は、最貧層の労働者の賃金低下につながるという。これは、自国民が移民労働者と競争力を保つために、さらに低い賃金で働かざるをえないということを意味する。外国人労働者が低賃金で働くのをいとわないのであれば、企業が高い賃金を払う理由はない。

　第二に、寛容な移民政策をとると、不法入国者が増えるために税の引き上げを招くだろう。不法入国者も救急医療や質の高い道路、警察などの公共サービスを受ける。しかし彼らはこうしたサービスをまかなうのに十分な税を支払わない。代わりに合法的な在住者がより高い税金を支払わなければならなくなる。

　最後に、日本の高齢化社会の問題を解決するには移民の受け入れを増やすことが必要だと考える人もいるが、それは真実ではない。最近の調査では、今後数十年間でロボットが労働力の半分近くに置き換わる可能性があることが示されている。これはつまり、若い労働者が少なくても、高齢人口を支えられるはずだということだ。

　これらの問題を考慮すると、より寛容な移民政策は、日本全体としては、さらに多くの問題につながるだけのように思える。

Vocabulary

□ illegally 違法に　□ emerge 現れる　□ migrant 移住の　□ compete with ~ ~と競う
□ law enforcement 法の執行、警察による取り締まり

解説　今度は日本の移民政策の緩和に反対する立場で考える場合。

　賛成する立場では、移民を、労働人口が減少する今後の日本の「労働力不足の解決策」と考えたが、それは裏を返せば賃金の安い競争者が流入してくることでもある。

　また日本が移民の厳しい規制をやめれば、不法入国者の数は急増する可能性も出てくるだろう。不法入国者の数が増えるとどんな影響が出るかについても考えよう。

　人口が減ればその分食糧供給が容易になるといった別の論点を提起することも可能だろう。

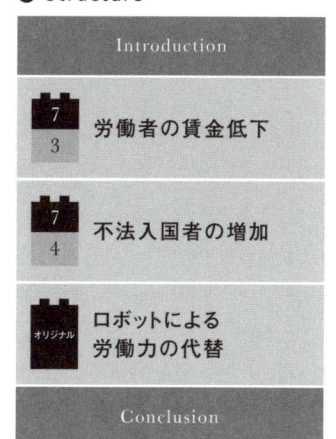

● Structure

| Introduction |
| 7/3 労働者の賃金低下 |
| 7/4 不法入国者の増加 |
| オリジナル ロボットによる労働力の代替 |
| Conclusion |

TOPIC

2 Agree or disagree: International terrorism will never be eliminated

モデルエッセイ 👍 Affirmative

I agree with the view that international terrorism will never be eliminated. Governments, the media, and globalization continue to contribute to terrorism. Also, the causes of terrorism are virtually impossible to remove.

First, international terrorism cannot be destroyed, because governments and the media unintentionally give power to terrorists. The goal of a terrorist is to cause widespread fear in a population. This cannot be done through terrorist attacks alone. Terrorists need governments and the media to publicize the attacks. From this perspective, the "War Against Terrorism" is terrorism's greatest supporter.

Second, globalization will continue to make terrorism one of the most effective forms of warfare. Thanks to advances in technology, people around the world can share news and information in seconds. This means that a small terrorist attack can instantly be shared with millions—even billions—of people. As globalization continues, it will become even easier for terrorists to get media coverage.

Third, the main causes of terrorism are inequality and misunderstanding, and these will always exist in human society. All people want freedom, safety, and fair treatment. When people do not have these, they become angry—and sometimes violent. Unfortunately, it is unlikely that all people will ever have these basic human rights, especially with the world's increasing population and decreasing resources.

In conclusion, unless society-wide changes are made to governments, the media, and inequality, destroying terrorism will be impossible.

(231 words)

訳 2 賛成か反対か：国際テロが根絶されることはない
　　　👍 Affirmative

　国際テロはなくならないだろうという見解に賛成だ。政府やメディア、グローバリゼーションは、テロを助長している。またテロの原因をなくすのは、事実上不可能だ。

　第一に、国際テロは撲滅できない。政府とメディアが意図せずしてテロリストに力を与えているからだ。テロリストの目的は、人々に広く恐怖を与えることだ。このことはテロ攻撃だけでは不可能だ。テロリストは、政府とメディアを使って、その攻撃を公に知らしめる必要がある。この観点からすると「対テロ戦争」はテロ行為を助長する最大の原因である。

　第二に、グローバリゼーションにより、テロ行為は最も有効な戦争行為の一形態であり続けるだろう。技術の発達のおかげで、世界中の人々は、ニュースや情報を瞬時に共有できる。これはつまり、小さなテロ攻撃を一瞬にして何百万人――何十億人さえ――もが知るということだ。グローバリゼーションが進むにつれ、テロリストはますますメディアで取り上げられやすくなっていくだろう。

　第三に、テロの主な原因は不平等と誤解であり、これらは今後も人間社会からなくなることはない。すべての人は自由と安全、公平な扱いを望む。これらを受けられないとき、人は怒り、時に暴力的になる。残念ながら、このような基本的な人権をすべての人が持つようになるとは考えにくい。特に世界人口が増加し、資源が減っていく中ではなおさらだ。

　結論として、社会全体の変化が政府やメディア、不平等に対して起こらない限り、テロ撲滅は不可能だろう。

Vocabulary

□ eliminate 〜を根絶する　□ virtually 事実上、実質的に　□ unintentionally 意図せずに　□ publicize 〜を公にする、公表する　□ warfare 戦争、戦争行為　□ get media coverage メディアで報道される

解説　頻繁に報じられる国際テロ。まず、その国際テロが根絶されることはないという意見に賛成する立場から考える。国際的な批判や武力攻撃を受けても終息しないテロの背景を考えよう。

　テロリズムとは「政治的な意図のもとに、一般人を巻き込む無差別の暴力や威嚇によって広く恐怖状態を作り出す行為」であり、その恐怖が広まることで効果を上げているとすれば、テロ事件を周知している政府やメディア、さらにその広がりを助長するグローバリゼーションが、実はテロリズムを利する結果になっていると考えられるだろう。

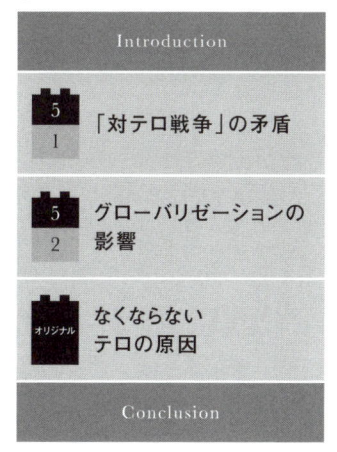

● **Structure**

- Introduction
- 5-1 「対テロ戦争」の矛盾
- 5-2 グローバリゼーションの影響
- オリジナル なくならないテロの原因
- Conclusion

TOPIC

2 Agree or disagree: International terrorism will never be eliminated

モデルエッセイ ♣ Negative 　MP3 236

  I disagree with the opinion that international terrorism will never be eliminated. Better equality, education, and government monitoring will all lead to the end of terrorism sometime in the future.

  One reason that terrorism is likely to disappear is that governments are becoming highly skilled at stopping terrorism. In recent years, governments have been able to prevent dozens of terrorist attacks. As government technology advances, it will become increasingly difficult for terrorists to organize attacks without being noticed.

  Another reason that terrorism will decrease is higher-quality education. Terrorists are, without exception, extremists. They have extremely biased views on a number of political issues. This is partly because their education has been one-sided. Because of the Internet, though, more and more people will come to have a balanced education. This may reduce terrorism overall.

  Finally, improved international equality will lead to the disappearance of terrorism. Better living conditions and political policies are resulting in less discrimination and more opportunities for minority groups. If more people feel that they are being treated fairly, then fewer of them will become terrorists.

  It is impossible to say when terrorism will be eliminated, but I believe that it will happen eventually. Humans have many flaws, but we all want peace and freedom, and we will never stop working for these.

(215 words)

訳 2 賛成か反対か：国際テロが根絶されることはない
🌧 Negative

国際テロが撲滅されることはないという意見には反対だ。平等と教育、政府による監視の向上はすべて、いずれテロ行為の終焉へとつながるだろう。

テロ行為がなくなるだろうと思われる一つの理由は、各国政府がテロ行為を阻止する高度な技術を獲得しつつあることだ。近年では、政府は何十件ものテロ攻撃を防ぐことができた。政府の技術の向上に伴い、テロリストが秘密裏に攻撃を企てることはますます難しくなるだろう。

テロが減るであろうもう一つの理由は、より質の高い教育だ。テロリストは例外なく過激主義者だ。彼らは多くの政治的問題について極度に偏った見方をしている。これは一つには、彼らの受けた教育が偏っているためだ。しかし、インターネットのおかげで、バランスのとれた教育を受けられる人は増えていくだろう。このことは、テロを全体として減らすだろう。

最後に、世界の平等が改善されることはテロの消滅につながるだろう。生活環境と政策の向上により、少数派に対する差別は減り、少数派に与えられるチャンスは増大している。もし、公平な待遇を受けていると感じる人が増えれば、テロリストになる人は少なくなる。

テロがいつなくなるかを言うことはできないが、いずれはそうなると思う。人間には多くの欠点があるが、我々はみな、平和と自由を望んでおり、そのために努力することをやめることはないだろう。

Vocabulary

☐ extremist 過激主義者、過激派　☐ flaw 欠点、欠陥

解説 今度は、テロはいずれ根絶されるだろうとする立場の答案。ここでもやはりテロの背景について考えることが大切だ。

モデルエッセイでは、各国政府のテロ対策が奏功しつつある点を指摘したうえで、テロリストたちが偏った教育を受けている（に違いない）ということ、生活に恵まれないことが背景にあると考え、それらの原因がなくなればテロリストも減っていくだろうと論じているが、対テロの国際ネットワークの拡充やテロ組織への資金流入の阻止といった論点を挙げることもできるだろう。

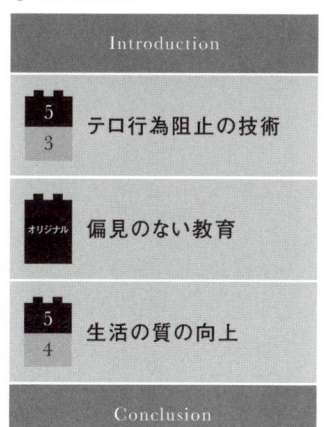

● Structure

| Introduction |
| 5-3 テロ行為阻止の技術 |
| オリジナル 偏見のない教育 |
| 5-4 生活の質の向上 |
| Conclusion |

TOPIC

3 Should nuclear weapons be outlawed worldwide?

モデルエッセイ 👍 Affirmative

🎧 237

　Nuclear weapons should definitely be outlawed worldwide. These weapons are a danger to every person on the planet, and it is risky to continue holding them. In addition, they waste precious taxpayer money.

　The main reason that nuclear weapons should be banned is that they threaten all life on the planet. If two nations used nuclear weapons against each other, it would lead to catastrophic climate change. Smoke from fires would block out the sun for months, causing widespread famine and possibly billions of deaths.

　Second, nuclear weapons are dangerous to develop and maintain. Although a nuclear weapon has never been detonated accidentally, the possibility does exist. One mistake could result in the loss of thousands of lives. This is particularly true in less developed nations, which have limited access to professional equipment and trained professionals.

　Last, nuclear weapons are a waste of money. Countries that possess these weapons spend billions of dollars every year to develop and maintain them. This is an even bigger problem in poor countries. For example, in North Korea the welfare of many citizens is sacrificed for investments in developing weapons.

　When considering the points mentioned above, it is clear that nuclear weapons should be banned worldwide. There will never be a justifiable reason to use nuclear weapons, and possessing them is expensive and dangerous.

(220 words)

訳 **3** 核兵器は世界的に禁止すべきか
👍 Affirmative

　核兵器は絶対に世界中で禁止されるべきだ。こうした兵器は、地球上のあらゆる人々にとって危険であり、保持し続けることは危険をはらむ。それに加え、核兵器は納税者の貴重な税金を無駄にする。

　核兵器を禁止するべき主な理由は、地球上のすべての生命を危険にさらすからだ。もし、二つの国家が互いに核兵器を使用すれば、壊滅的な気候変動につながるだろう。火災から出る煙は何か月も太陽を覆い隠し、飢饉が広がって、何十億人もの人々が死亡するかもしれない。

　次に、核兵器を開発、維持するのは危険である。これまで核兵器が誤って爆発させられたことはないが、その可能性は確実に存在する。一つの間違いが数千の人命の喪失につながってしまう。このことは途上国においてはとりわけ切実だ。こうした国では専門的な機器と訓練された専門家が不足している。

　最後に、核兵器は資金の無駄である。核兵器を保有する国々では、その開発と維持に毎年何十億ドルも費やしている。このことは、貧しい国々ではなおさら大きな問題だ。例えば北朝鮮では、多くの国民の福祉が、兵器開発への投資の犠牲にされている。

　上述の論点を考えると、世界中で核兵器が禁止されるべきであることは明らかだ。核兵器を使用することを正当化できる理由はなく、核兵器を保有することは高い費用がかかり、また危険である。

Vocabulary

□ outlaw ～を(法的に)禁止する、非合法化する　□ threaten ～を脅かす　□ catastrophic 破壊的な、大惨事の　□ detonate〈爆弾など〉を爆発させる

解説　核兵器の（法的）禁止の是非を問う問題。ここでは禁止するべきだという立場で考えよう。

　大量破壊兵器である核兵器の危険性は思いつきやすい論点だろう。モデルエッセイではさらに、開発・維持における危険性、つまり保持するだけでも危険であることに加え、経済的なデメリットも挙げている。

　その他、実験設備の確保の問題や国際関係の悪化などをトピックにすることもできるだろう。

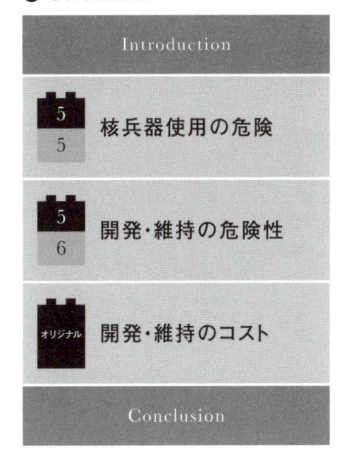

● Structure

Introduction
5/5 核兵器使用の危険
5/6 開発・維持の危険性
オリジナル 開発・維持のコスト
Conclusion

TOPIC

3 Should nuclear weapons be outlawed worldwide?

モデルエッセイ ♠ Negative

  I do not believe that nuclear weapons should be outlawed. History has shown that nuclear weapons help to deter military conflicts, and there is not a realistic method for removing nuclear weapons from the world.

  First, nuclear weapons are one of the few weapons in the world that actually prevent wars. There has not been a large-scale violent conflict between two major nations since the first nuclear bombs were dropped in Hiroshima and Nagasaki. This is because world leaders know that a nuclear war would be catastrophic.

  Second, nuclear weapons do not only prevent wars, but they also encourage diplomatic relations. Major world powers will always have conflicts and disagreements. Since war is not a reasonable option, their only choice is to negotiate when a disagreement arises. When countries and their allies have nuclear weapons, then, they will be respected in negotiations.

  Finally, outlawing nuclear weapons worldwide is unrealistic. The two nations with the most nuclear weapons—Russia and the United States—are unlikely to get rid of them in the near future, because it would decrease their level of security. Instead, they are more likely to improve defenses and make it clear that they can deal with nuclear attacks if necessary.

  For the reasons mentioned above, I am against outlawing nuclear weapons. Nuclear weapons are frightening, but that is one of the reasons that they actually make the world a safer place.　(233 words)

ワンポイントアドバイス

第4パラグラフ第2文の get rid of them [＝ nuclear weapons] は disarm（軍備を縮小する、武装解除する）としてもよい。

訳 3　核兵器は世界的に禁止すべきか
　　● Negative

　核兵器を禁止すべきではないと思う。核兵器が軍事衝突を抑止するのに役立つことは歴史が示すところであり、また世界から核兵器をなくす現実的な方法はない。

　第一に、核兵器は実際に戦争を防ぐ世界で数少ない兵器の一つだ。初の核爆弾が広島と長崎に投下されて以来、二つの主要国間での大規模な武力衝突は起きていない。これは、世界の指導者たちが、核戦争は破滅をもたらすだろうということを知っているからだ。

　第二に、核兵器は戦争を阻止するだけでなく、外交関係を推進する。世界の大国間には常に対立や不和があるだろう。戦争という選択肢は考えられないため、不和が起きても彼らには交渉するという選択肢しかない。（当事）国やその同盟国が核兵器を持っていれば、交渉において一目置かれる。

　最後に、世界中で核兵器を禁止することは非現実的だ。最も多くの核兵器を保有する2か国——ロシアとアメリカ——が近い将来核兵器を廃絶する可能性はないだろう。核兵器を廃絶すれば、安全保障レベルが下がるからだ。核兵器を廃絶するのではなく、両国は防衛能力を高め、必要があれば核攻撃に対処できるということを明確にする可能性のほうが高い。

　上述の理由から、私は核兵器を禁止することには反対だ。核兵器は恐ろしいものだが、そのことこそが世界をより平和な場所にしている理由の一つなのだ。

Vocabulary
□ deter 〜を抑止する　□ ally 同盟国　□ frightening 恐ろしい、ぞっとさせる

解説　今度は、核兵器を法的に禁止するべきかという問いにNoで答える立場の答案。禁止すべきでないという立場をとる以上、核兵器の積極的な意味づけができなければならない。

　一番思いつきやすいのは、戦争の抑止力として働くというものだろう。モデルエッセイの第2パラグラフで取り上げられた論点だ。その他、モデルエッセイの第4パラグラフでは、そもそも核兵器を禁止することが非現実的だというトピックを挙げている。米ロを中心とした軍縮の歴史を概観しておくとその難しさが感じられるだろう。

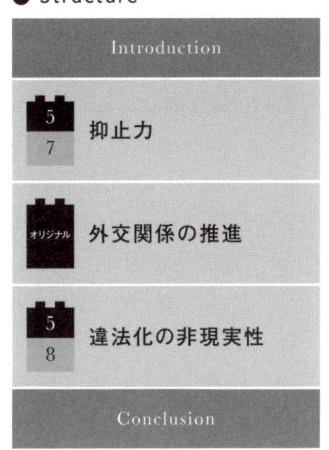

Structure

| Introduction |
| 5/7 抑止力 |
| オリジナル 外交関係の推進 |
| 5/8 違法化の非現実性 |
| Conclusion |

TOPIC
4 Agree or disagree: World hunger will decrease in the future

モデルエッセイ 👍 Affirmative

Although world hunger is currently a difficult and problematic issue, it is likely to decrease in the future thanks to high levels of production, technological developments, and local farming.

The real cause of world hunger is not scarcity of food, as research has shown that humans already produce enough food to feed 10 billion people. Rather, the problem is making this food available and affordable to those living in poverty. Since there is already sufficient food, world hunger should decrease as transportation and production costs go down.

One key to combating world hunger is lowering production and transportation costs. Technology is improving the likelihood of this. The development of automated farming tools has the potential to save billions of dollars annually, and this technology is improving rapidly. With more efficient transportation also emerging, it will not be long before cheap food can reach the world's poor individuals.

Finally, large agricultural production is not the only answer, as new forms of sustainable farming are developing. Using a combination of solar power, hydroponics, and careful planning, individual families can grow enough food to support themselves in virtually any environment, as long as they have access to the training and tools for growing food sustainably.

Considering humans' capacity for producing large amounts of food, coupled with improving technology, world hunger should decrease in the near future. Solving this problem completely, however, will take the cooperation of everyone on the planet.

(235 words)

訳 4 賛成か反対か：将来、世界の飢餓は減少する

👍 Affirmative

　世界の飢餓は現在、困難で厄介な問題だが、高いレベルの生産量、技術の発展、地域での農業により、将来、飢餓は減少するだろう。

　世界の飢餓の真の原因は食糧不足ではない。研究では、人類はすでに100億人を養うのに十分な食糧を生産していることが示されている。むしろ問題は、その食糧を貧しい暮らしをしている人々のもとに行き渡らせ、無理なく買える価格にすることである。すでに十分な食糧があるのだから、輸送コストと生産コストが減少するにつれて、世界の飢餓は軽減されるはずだ。

　世界の飢餓と闘ううえで鍵となる点の一つは、生産コストと輸送コストを下げることだ。技術によりその可能性は高まっている。自動化された農器具の開発により、年間何十億ドルというコストを節減できると見込まれており、この技術は急速に進歩している。より効率的な輸送方法も現れつつあり、世界の貧しい人々が安価な食糧を手にするようになるのに、そう長くはかからないだろう。

　最後に、新しい形の持続可能な農業が発達してきているので、大規模な農業生産は唯一の答えではない。太陽光発電と水耕栽培と周到な計画を組み合わせて活用し、食糧を持続可能な方法で育てるための訓練と器具を得られさえすれば、ほぼどんな環境でも各家庭で自給するのに十分な食糧を育てることができる。

　大量の食糧を生産する人類の能力を考えると、技術の改良も相まって、世界の飢餓は近い将来、減少するはずだ。しかし、この問題を完全に解決するには、地球上のすべての人々の協力が必要だろう。

Vocabulary

□ scarcity 不足、欠乏　　□ hydroponics 水耕栽培　　□ coupled with 〜に加えて、〜と相まって

解説　世界飢餓をテーマとした設問。世界の人口が増え続ける中で非現実的に聞こえるかもしれないが、国連の発表によれば2015年の世界の飢餓人口は8億人を切り、25年前から2億人以上減少している。今後もこの傾向が続くためには何が必要かを考えよう。

　モデルエッセイでは、流通手段の確保、生産・輸送コストの削減、農業技術の発展をトピックとした。結論の最終文で触れた「すべての人々の協力」、具体的には先進国の経済的投資などをトピックとすることもできるだろう。

● Structure

Introduction
4・5　世界の飢餓の真の原因
4・6　技術による生産・輸送コストの削減
オリジナル　持続可能な農業の発展
Conclusion

TOPIC

4 Agree or disagree: World hunger will decrease in the future

モデルエッセイ ● Negative

It is unlikely that the problem of world hunger will be solved or improved anytime soon. Increasing population, limited resources, and self-centered government policies all contribute to this problem.

The human population is currently growing at an alarming and unsustainable rate. Experts estimate that the ideal population for humans on earth is under 2 billion people, but there are already over 7 billion people on the planet, and that number is likely to reach about 10 billion by 2050. Our planet cannot sustain such a great number of people.

As the world's population grows, the earth's resources are also disappearing. According to scientific calculations, humans are already using more resources than the earth can continue to produce. With our current consumption patterns, we are likely to deplete the world's supply of fossil fuels, wildlife areas, and, in turn, food supply.

With increasing population and decreasing resources, the only way to maintain and improve the earth's food supply is through global cooperation and strict control of precious resources. Sadly, this does not seem likely to happen. Developed countries continue to promote reckless consumerism, so most people do not recognize or acknowledge these issues.

Unless some sort of groundbreaking solution to world hunger is discovered, due to growing populations, dwindling resources, and widespread consumerism, my prediction is that this problem will actually worsen in the future.

(224 words)

ワンポイントアドバイス

最後のパラグラフの冒頭はAlthough some might argue that decreasing world hunger in the future is possible（将来、世界飢餓を減らすことは可能だと論じる人もいるが）、あるいはAlthough decreasing world hunger in the future may be theoretically possible（将来、世界飢餓を減らすことは理論上は可能かもしれないが）などとしてもよい。

| 訳 | **4** 賛成か反対か：将来、世界の飢餓は減少する
　　　Negative

　世界飢餓の問題は近いうちに解決や改善が見込めるものではなさそうだ。人口の増加、限られた資源、自己中心的な政府の政策のすべてがこの問題の原因となっている。

　人口は現在、驚異的かつ持続不可能なペースで増加している。専門家は、地球の理想的な人口は20億人以下だと推定しているが、すでに地球上には70億人以上の人々がおり、その数は2050年までに100億人近くに達すると見込まれる。地球はこれほど多くの人々を支えることはできない。

　世界の人口が増加するにつれて、地球上の資源もまた消えつつある。科学的な試算によると、人類はすでに地球が継続して生産できる量を上回る資源を使っているという。私たちの現在の消費パターンでは、世界の化石燃料供給量を使い尽くし、野生生物の生息域を激減させ、その結果、食糧供給を枯渇させるだろう。

　人口が増加し資源が減少する中で、地球の食糧供給量を維持し改善する唯一の方法は、国際協力と貴重な資源の厳格な管理だ。残念ながら、これは起こりそうにもない。先進国は分別のない消費主義を推し進める一方なので、ほとんどの人はこうした問題を認識せず、認めてもいない。

　世界の飢餓に対して何らかの抜本的な解決策が見つからない限り、増加する人口と減少する資源、まん延した消費主義のために、この問題は将来、実際には悪化するだろうというのが私の予測である。

Vocabulary

☐ unsustainable 持続不可能な　☐ deplete ～を使い果たす　☐ reckless 無謀な、見境のない
☐ consumerism 消費主義　☐ groundbreaking 革新的な、画期的な　☐ dwindling 減少する、低下する

| 解説 | 　前の答案では、世界飢餓が減少しつつあると述べたが、この先この傾向が続くかどうかは別の問題だ。今度は、将来、世界飢餓は減少しないとする立場で考える。

　モデルエッセイでは、急激に増え続ける世界人口、枯渇しつつある資源、唯一の解決策である国際協力と資源の管理は期待できそうにないことの三つを挙げてトピックとしている。最後のトピックをより具体的に、紛争が終わりそうにない、富裕な国からの十分な投資が見込まれないなどと展開してもいいだろう。

Structure

Introduction

4〜7 世界の人口増加

4〜8 資源の枯渇

オリジナル 消費主義のまん延

Conclusion

TOPIC

5 Should import taxes be abolished?

モデルエッセイ 👍 Affirmative　　　　　　　　　MP3 241

I am in favor of abolishing import taxes, as they are harmful in several ways. They lead to fewer jobs for citizens, lower quality companies and products, and problems for other businesses.

The main disadvantage of import taxes is that they harm employment rates. Proponents of import taxes say they are needed so that local companies do not go out of business and raise unemployment. But tariffs actually increase unemployment rates. This is because import taxes cause prices to rise, and the market stagnates.

Furthermore, tariffs promote the emergence and growth of ineffective companies. When companies are protected by a tariff, they have less competition from foreign businesses. Thus, they have less incentive to create higher quality products at lower prices. Ultimately, this creates a market where domestic consumers overpay for inferior products from companies that cannot compete internationally.

Last, tariffs actually hurt the majority of businesses. For example, if there is a tariff on raw materials like steel and rubber, then domestic producers of those goods can control the market and raise prices. This causes major problems for companies that need to obtain these materials at competitive rates to produce their own products cheaply.

In conclusion, it is clear that import taxes are damaging overall. (206 words)

訳 **5** 輸入税は撤廃されるべきか
👍 Affirmative

　輸入税はいろいろな面で有害であるため、私はこれを撤廃することに賛成だ。輸入税は、国民の雇用の減少、企業と製品の質の低下、ほかの事業にとっての問題につながる。

　輸入税の主な欠点は、雇用率を低下させることだ。輸入税に賛成する人々は、地元の企業が倒産して失業率が上がることがないようにするために、輸入税が必要だと言っている。しかし実際には、関税は失業率を上げている。それは、輸入税は物価を上げ、市場を低迷させるからだ。

　さらに、関税は無能な企業の出現と成長を助長する。企業が関税で守られると、海外の企業との競争が少なくなる。そのため、そうした企業には、より低価格で、より高品質な製品を製造する意欲が生まれにくい。これは最終的に、国内の消費者が、国際的な競争力を持たない企業から質の悪い製品を高すぎる金額で購入する市場を生み出してしまう。

　最後に、関税は、実は大多数の事業にダメージを与えている。例えば、スチールやゴムのような原材料に関税をかければ、それらの製品を製造している国内のメーカーは、市場をコントロールして価格を上げることができる。このことは、自社製品を安く製造するために、安い価格でこうした原材料を入手する必要のある企業に、大きな問題をもたらしている。

　結論として、輸入税が概して有害であることは明らかだ。

Vocabulary

☐ proponent 支持者（＝people in favor）　☐ go out of business 倒産する、廃業する　☐ tariff 関税
☐ stagnate 停滞する、不活発になる　☐ overpay 払いすぎる

解説　輸入税とは輸入品に対してかけられる税で、関税はその一つ。ただ輸入税と関税はほぼ同義として回答して問題ない。輸入税がなければ、自由貿易状態になる。TPP、AIIBなどの経済圏問題の根幹でもあるので、基本的な考え方を押さえておきたい。

　モデルエッセイでは、輸入税が失業率を上げ、質の悪い商品を高い値段で流通させ、多くの事業にダメージを与えると述べている。輸入税を撤廃すれば失業率が上がるという見解もありうるが、この答案では輸入税が物価を上昇させて景気が停滞する結果、失業率が上がると判断している。

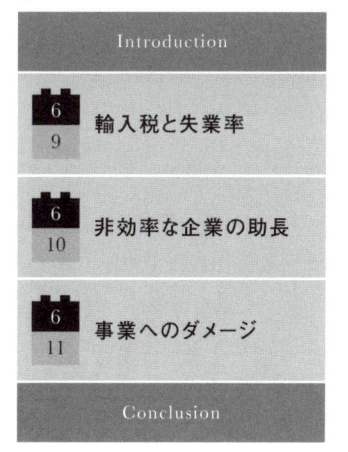

Structure

| Introduction |
| 6 / 9 輸入税と失業率 |
| 6 / 10 非効率な企業の助長 |
| 6 / 11 事業へのダメージ |
| Conclusion |

TOPIC

5 Should import taxes be abolished?

モデルエッセイ ◆ Negative

I believe that import taxes are good for a country overall and that they should not be abolished. These taxes increase the popularity of domestic companies' products, which saves jobs for many people. Also, import tariffs can strengthen and support important industries.

One of the primary benefits of import taxes is that they protect local jobs and companies. Some foreign countries have extremely low labor costs. As a result, their companies can sell products at lower prices than domestic competitors. This can cause local companies to go out of business, which would cause citizens to lose their jobs.

Yet another positive aspect of import tariffs is that they can strengthen vital industries. This is important for national security. It is impossible to predict what will happen in the future. It is theoretically possible that trade with many countries will stop due to war or natural disasters. If this happens, nations need to be able to produce the products that their citizens require.

Aside from import taxes needed for security, governments can also use temporary tariffs to support infant industries. For example, if a developing country wants its automobile industry to grow, then it can place tariffs on foreign automobiles. New, local automobile companies will then have a better chance of competing. Once the domestic automobile industry matures, the government can lower or remove this import tax.

In conclusion, the advantages of import taxes outweigh the disadvantages.

(236 words)

訳 5 輸入税は撤廃されるべきか
☔ Negative

　輸入税は概して国にとって望ましく、撤廃されるべきではないと私は考える。こうした税は、国内企業の製品の人気を高め、多くの人々の雇用を守る。また、輸入関税は重要な産業を強化し、支援する。

　輸入税の主な利点の一つは、地元の雇用と企業を保護することだ。海外には、労働コストが極めて低い国もある。その結果、そうした国々の企業は国内の競合他社よりも安い値段で製品を販売することができる。これが原因で、地元企業が倒産する可能性もあり、それによって国民が仕事を失うことになるかもしれない。

　さらに、輸入関税の別のよい側面は、重要な産業を強化できることだ。これは、国内の安全保障にとって重要だ。将来、何が起こるか予測するのは不可能だ。多くの国々との貿易が戦争や自然災害で止まることも、理論上はあり得る。もしこのようなことが起こった場合、国は国民が必要とする製品を生産できなければならない。

　輸入税は安全保障に必要であるほか、政府は新興産業を支援するために一時的な関税を活用することもできる。例えば、ある発展途上国が、国内の自動車産業を成長させたい場合、外国製の自動車に関税をかけることができる。そうすれば、新しい現地の自動車メーカーは競争に勝てる見込みが大きくなる。新たな国内の自動車産業が成熟したら、政府はこの輸入税を下げる、あるいは撤廃することができる。

　結論として、輸入税の利点は短所を上回る。

Vocabulary

□ competitor 競合企業　□ national security 国家安全保障　□ temporary 一時的な、暫定的な
□ infant industry 幼稚産業、未成熟産業　□ outweigh ～よりまさる

解説　輸入税のメリットとは、基本的に海外からの安い商品の流入に一定の歯止めをかけられることだ。

　安い商品が入ってくれば、市場原理でものの値段は下がるので、競争に耐えられずに倒産する企業や廃業する農家などが出てくる。国家レベルで見ても失業率が上がり、自給率が下がることは望ましくないだろう。輸入税はそうした事態の抑制になっていると考えられる。

　モデルエッセイでは、国内企業の保護、産業の強化、新興産業の育成をトピックとして挙げた。

● Structure

| Introduction |
| 6/7　地元企業の保護 |
| 6/8　重要な産業の強化 |
| オリジナル　新興産業の育成 |
| Conclusion |

TOPIC

6 Agree or disagree: The use of military force is sometimes justifiable

モデルエッセイ 👍 Affirmative　　　　　　　　　　　MP3 243

I agree that the use of military force is sometimes justifiable. Military force is occasionally necessary for protection, saving people in danger, and preventing the loss of human lives.

First, in some situations, military force is necessary for self-defense. For example, if it is clear that another country is likely to attack in the near future, then a preemptive strike can be justified. Everyone has a right to safety and security, and everyone also has a right to fight for safety and security. There are almost no leaders in the world against using a military for self-defense.

Second, there are times when military force is needed to protect people who are weak and in danger. In other words, the militaries of developed countries should act as the police of the world. One example where military force should have been used is in Rwanda in 1994. Powerful militaries did not intervene in the conflict, and as a result over 1 million people were brutally murdered.

Finally, the well-planned use of military force can prevent the loss of human lives. For example, when there is a conflict between two small countries, a powerful military could prevent them both from fighting. Some lives would be lost, but fewer than if nothing was done.

In conclusion, it is acceptable for a nation to use military force in some cases. (225 words)

ワンポイントアドバイス
第2パラグラフ第2文のa preemptive strike（先制攻撃）は、もし思い浮かばなければattacking first（先に攻撃すること）といってもよい。

訳 **6** 賛成か反対か：軍事力の行使は時に正当化される
　　👍 Affirmative

　軍事力の行使は正当化できる場合があるという意見に賛成だ。軍事力は時として、防衛のため、危険にさらされた人々を守るため、人命が奪われることを防ぐために必要となる。

　第一に、軍事力は自衛のために必要な場合がある。例えば、もし近い将来に他国が攻撃してくることが明らかであれば、先制攻撃は正当化されうる。すべての人々には、安全と安心を確保する権利があり、また安全と安心のために戦う権利がある。自衛のために軍隊を使うことに反対する指導者は、世界で皆無に等しい。

　次に、軍事力は、弱い人々や危険にさらされた人々を守るために必要な場合がある。言い換えれば、先進国の軍隊は世界の警察の役割を務めるべきである。軍事力が行使されるべきだった一例は、1994年のルワンダでのことだ。強力な軍隊が紛争に介入しなかったために、結果として100万人以上の人々が虐殺された。

　最後に、入念に計画された軍事力の行使は、犠牲者が出ることを防ぐことができる。例えば、二つの小国間に対立が起こった場合、強力な軍隊は両国が戦闘をするのを防ぐことができる。失われる命もあるかもしれないが、何もしなかった場合よりも少ないだろう。

　結論として、場合によっては国家が軍事力を行使することは認められる。

Vocabulary

☐ self-defense 自衛　☐ preemptive strike 先制攻撃　☐ intervene 介入する　☐ brutally 残忍に、残酷に

解説　場合によっては軍事力の行使は認められるとする立場から。真っ先に思い浮かぶのは、他国から攻撃を受けたときに自国を守るために起こす軍事行動、つまり自衛のための軍事力行使だろう。モデルエッセイでは、自国の防衛以外で許容すべき軍事行動として、ルワンダ虐殺を例に、弱者に対して残忍な行為がなされている場合の軍事力の行使、また戦争を防止するための軍事力の行使を挙げている。

　なお日本は建前上、軍隊を有していないことになっているが、自衛隊（Japan Self-Defense Forces）はおよそ25万人の自衛官を擁する防衛組織である。

● **Structure**

Introduction
5/9　自衛のための武力行使
5/10　弱者保護のための武力行使
オリジナル　戦争防止のための武力行使
Conclusion

TOPIC

6 Agree or disagree: The use of military force is sometimes justifiable

モデルエッセイ ● Negative　　　MP3 244

　　I disagree with the opinion that the use of military force is sometimes justifiable. Killing is fundamentally wrong, and refraining from violence can still be effective in conflicts. Also, military force is no longer necessary for modern, developed nations.

　　The main reason that military force is not justifiable is that it always results in the deaths of innocent people. It is terrible for soldiers to kill one another. However, it is even worse when average people suffer due to war, and innocent people are always harmed as a result of military force.

　　Another reason that military force is not necessary is that nonviolent resistance is just as effective—if not more effective. The best example of this is India's fight for independence from Great Britain. Led by Mahatma Gandhi, the Indian people obtained independence without violence.

　　Additionally, due to advances in technology and globalization, the primary "wars" between developed nations are now economic and digital. For example, leaders in both China and the U.S. understand that going to war would be a disaster. Therefore, they choose to "fight" using economic policies and various forms of cyber warfare.

　　When taking the points mentioned above into consideration, it becomes apparent that the use of military force is not justifiable.

(207 words)

訳 6 賛成か反対か：軍事力の行使は時に正当化される
🌧 Negative

軍事力の行使が正当化される場合があるという意見には反対だ。殺人は根本的に誤りであり、暴力を控えることは紛争においても効果がある。また、軍事力は、現代の先進国にはもはや必要ない。

軍事力を正当化できない主な理由は、軍事力は常に罪なき人々の死という結果を招くからだ。兵士が殺し合うことは悲惨である。しかし、普通の人々が戦争のために苦しむのはさらに悲惨で、軍事力を行使すれば必ず罪のない人々に被害が及ぶのである。

軍事力が必要でないもう一つの理由は、非暴力の抵抗が軍事力と同等の――軍事力以上のとは言わないまでも――効果があるからだ。この最もよい例が、イギリスからのインドの独立闘争だ。マハトマ・ガンジーによって率いられ、インドの人々は暴力なしで独立を獲得した。

加えて、技術の発展とグローバリゼーションによって、先進国間の主な「戦争」は今や経済上のものとデジタルなものになった。例えば、中国とアメリカの首脳はどちらも、戦争に突入すれば壊滅的な結果となることを理解している。そこで、両国は経済政策やさまざまな形態のサイバー戦争で「戦う」ことを選んでいる。

上述の論点を考慮に入れると、軍事力の行使は正当化できないことが明らかとなる。

Vocabulary
□ fundamentally 根本的に　□ refrain from ～ ～を差し控える

解説

軍事力の行使はいかなる場合にも認められないとする立場。軍事力が不要であるとする理由を考えよう。

モデルエッセイでは、そもそも殺人、とりわけ一般市民の犠牲は許されない、暴力を使わない抵抗にも武力行使と同じだけの効果がある、現代は物理的な武力の破壊力が高まりすぎたため、戦いの場面が軍事から経済・デジタルの場面に移っている、という3点をトピックとして挙げている。

国連（安全保障理事会）に紛争解決を委託するのは、国連の軍事力行使を認めることになるのでここではトピックとしては使えない。

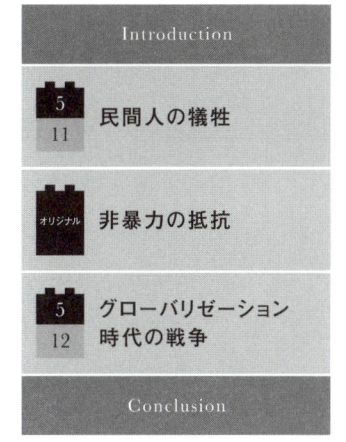

Structure

Introduction	
5-11	民間人の犠牲
オリジナル	非暴力の抵抗
5-12	グローバリゼーション時代の戦争
Conclusion	

3 サイエンス

- Write an essay on the given TOPIC.
- Give THREE reasons to support your answer.
- Structure: Introduction, main body, and conclusion
- Suggested length: 200–240 words

TOPIC

1. Should the use of genetically modified crops be banned?
   > 解答・解説は 230-233 ページ

2. Do the benefits of technological improvements outweigh any negative side effects?
   > 解答・解説は 234-237 ページ

3. Should animal testing be banned?
   > 解答・解説は 238-241 ページ

4. Agree or disagree: Improving space-related technology is a good investment
   > 解答・解説は 242-245 ページ

5. Can society eliminate its dependence on fossil fuels such as oil and gas in the near future?
   > 解答・解説は 246-249 ページ

6. Agree or disagree: All nuclear power plants should be shut down
   > 解答・解説は 250-253 ページ

7. Should cloning research be banned?
   > 解答・解説は 254-257 ページ

8. Agree or disagree: Improvements in medical technology are always beneficial to society
   > 解答・解説は 258-261 ページ

9. Is enough being done to protect the world's wilderness areas?
   > 解答・解説は 262-265 ページ

解答・解説

TOPIC

1 Should the use of genetically modified crops be banned?

モデルエッセイ 👍 Affirmative　　　MP3 245

　　　I believe that the use of genetically modified crops should be banned. The scientific community still does not know enough about the potentially harmful effects of genetically modified organisms (GMOs). Also, GMOs are only necessary when pursuing unsustainable farming practices.

　　　First, we do not have enough information about GMOs at this time. A large number of the scientific studies regarding GMOs have been funded by the large biotechnology companies that manufacture them. Reliable safety data can only be released by scientists without a conflict of interest, but such data is not yet available.

　　　Second, most of the supposed benefits of GMOs become unnecessary with sustainable farming. Large agricultural crops are vulnerable to insects and diseases because they are grown in monocultures. Farms that grow diverse, strategically located crops, however, have the capacity to these issues, even without GMOs.

　　　Third, producers of genetically modified crops use too many herbicides. One of the reported benefits of GMOs is that they are resistant to chemicals that kill weeds. This means that farmers can spray more of these chemicals onto genetically modified crops, which may be unhealthy for human consumption.

　　　In conclusion, I believe that genetically modified crops should be banned. Their safety cannot be guaranteed. Also, they promote unsustainable farming methods and the use of herbicides.

(213 words)

訳 1 遺伝子組み換え作物の使用は禁じられるべきか
👍 Affirmative

　遺伝子組み換え作物の使用は禁止されるべきだと思う。科学界では、遺伝子組み換え作物（GMO）の潜在的な弊害はまだ十分にわかっていない。また、遺伝子組み換え作物が必要となるのは、持続不可能な農業慣行を行う場合だけだ。

　第一に、私たちには遺伝子組み換え作物について、現時点で十分な情報がない。遺伝子組み換え作物に関する科学研究の多くは、遺伝子組み換え作物を製造している大手のバイオテクノロジー企業によって資金提供を受けてきた。信頼できる安全性についてのデータは、利害関係のない科学者にしか出せないものだが、そのようなデータはまだ入手できない。

　第二に、遺伝子組み換え作物について想定されている利点のほとんどは、持続可能な農法には必要ない。大規模農業による作物は、単一栽培で育てられるため、虫や病気に弱い。しかし、計画的に作物の位置を決めて多品種を栽培する農場では、遺伝子組み換え作物がなくても、こうした問題に対応することができる。

　第三に、遺伝子組み換え作物の生産者は過剰な除草剤を使う。遺伝子組み換え作物について報告されている利点の一つは、雑草を枯らす化学物質に耐性があることだ。これはつまり、農業従事者はこうした化学物質をより多く遺伝子組み換え作物に散布できるということで、人間が摂取するには不健康である可能性がある。

　結論として、私は遺伝子組み換え作物は禁止されるべきだと思う。遺伝子組み換え作物の安全性を保証することはできない。そのうえそれは、持続不可能な農法と除草剤の使用を促進するのである。

Vocabulary

□ genetically modified crop 遺伝子組み換え作物　□ unsustainable 持続不可能な　□ vulnerable 弱い、(病気に)かかりやすい　□ monoculture 単一栽培、単式農法　□ herbicide 除草剤　□ resistant 抵抗力がある

解説　遺伝子組み換え作物の使用を禁止すべきかを問う問題。遺伝子組み換えは、農作物だけでなく医療の分野でも研究が進められているホットなテーマなので、関連する問題に対して自分はどう答えるか、いくつかのトピックを考えておく必要があるだろう。

　禁止を肯定する（つまり使用に反対する）立場で書かれた上のモデルエッセイでは、安全性が確認されていないこと、代替農法があるのでそもそも必要でないこと、除草剤が多用され人間に有害である可能性があることをトピックとして挙げた。

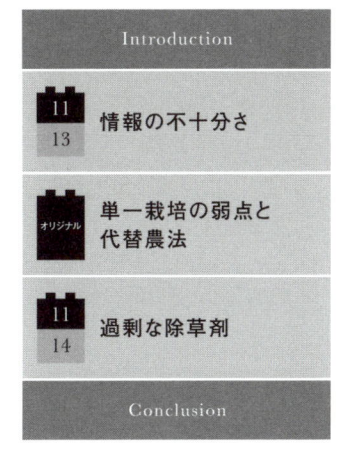

● Structure

| Introduction |
| 情報の不十分さ (11/13) |
| 単一栽培の弱点と代替農法 (オリジナル) |
| 過剰な除草剤 (11/14) |
| Conclusion |

TOPIC

1 Should the use of genetically modified crops be banned?

モデルエッセイ ● Negative   MP3 246

In recent years, an increasing number of people are against the use of genetically modified organisms (GMOs). I believe that GMOs are beneficial, however, because they can help feed the world's growing population, protect large crops from harmful insects, and improve the economy.

Without the use of genetically modified crops, we may be unable to feed all of the people on Earth. The human population is expected to reach around 10 billion by 2050. Experts predict we will need 70% more agricultural production to feed all of these people. Because of this growing number, we need to do everything we can to increase food production.

Second, genetically modified crops allow farmers to grow more food on less land, while using less water and pesticides. Since they require less water, GMOs are actually beneficial to the environment. Also, reducing the use of pesticides is important for the health of consumers. Globally, genetically modified crops have reduced pesticide spraying considerably.

Finally, GMOs help keep food production costs down, which results in lower prices for consumers. Genetically modified crops are reliable, consistent, and highly resistant. This means that genetically modified crops are easier to harvest, so farms using genetically modified crops can save money on labor. In turn, this saves money for customers, too.

In conclusion, I believe that the use of genetically modified crops is both necessary and justifiable.

(227 words)

訳 **1** 遺伝子組み換え作物の使用は禁じられるべきか
　　☂ Negative

　近年、遺伝子組み換え作物（GMO）の使用に反対する人が増えている。しかし、遺伝子組み換え作物は、増加する世界の人口を養い、大量の作物を害虫から守り、経済を促進するのに役立つので、有益だと思う。

　遺伝子組み換え作物の使用がなければ、地球上のすべての人々を養うことはできないだろう。人口は2050年までに約100億人に達すると予想されている。専門家は、このすべての人々を養うには農業生産を70％増やす必要があると予測している。この人口増加のため、我々は食糧生産を増やすためにできるあらゆることをする必要がある。

　次に、遺伝子組み換え作物は、農業者が水と殺虫剤の使用を減らしつつ、より少ない土地でより多くの食糧を生産できるようにする。必要とする水の量が少ないため、遺伝子組み換え作物は実際には環境によい。また、殺虫剤の使用を減らすことは、消費者の健康にも重要だ。世界全体で遺伝子組み換え作物は、殺虫剤の散布を大幅に減らした。

　最後に、遺伝子組み換え作物は、食糧生産コストを低く抑えるので、結果的に消費者が支払う価格は安くなる。遺伝子組み換え作物は、信頼性があり、安定しており、耐性が高い。つまり遺伝子組み換え作物は収穫が容易で、遺伝子組み換え作物を使う農家は労働コストを抑えることができる。このことは結局、消費者にとってお金の節約にもなる。

　結論として、遺伝子組み換え作物の使用は必要であり、かつ正当化できるものだと私は思う。

Vocabulary

□ pesticide 殺虫剤　□ justifiable 正当化できる

解説　遺伝子組み換え作物の是非について問う問題。ここでは禁止に対して否定する立場で考えてみよう。

　遺伝子組み換え作物のメリットとして一般に挙げられるのは、酷暑や寒さに強く、安定した供給が見込めること、害虫に耐性があるため、農薬の量を減らせることなどである。モデルエッセイでは、これらのメリットを、人口問題、環境問題、農作物の価格の問題と結びつけて論じた。そのほか、保存性の問題などを挙げることもできるだろう。

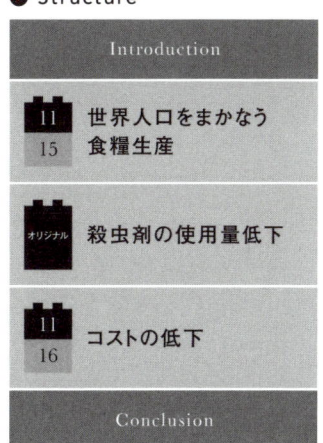

● Structure

| Introduction |
| ℓ1-ℓ5　世界人口をまかなう食糧生産 |
| オリジナル　殺虫剤の使用量低下 |
| ℓ11-ℓ16　コストの低下 |
| Conclusion |

TOPIC

2 Do the benefits of technological improvements outweigh any negative side effects?

モデルエッセイ 👍 Affirmative　　　MP3 247

　　　　Technology has made people educated and healthier, and it provides them with more free time. For these reasons, I believe it is safe to say that technological improvements are good for society overall.

　　　　First, technology now allows people to learn a great deal of things by themselves. The average person with a smartphone today has access to more information than the President of the United States had only 15 years ago. As the amount of information available increases, people have more opportunities to learn.

　　　　Second, thanks to technology, people are healthier than ever before. Since 1900 the global average life expectancy has more than doubled. Also, women are far less likely to die from childbirth than before, and new babies are far more likely to survive. All of these improvements are due to technology.

　　　　Finally, developments in technology are lessening the amount of work that people are required to do. Innovations in robotics will likely lower the number of hours that citizens in developed countries need to work. This extra time can be spent enjoying hobbies, learning, and sharing knowledge and resources with less fortunate people.

　　　　Improvements in technology can have some negative consequences. But technology also gives healthier, more educated people more free time to work on solving these problems. For this reason, I believe the benefits of improvements in technology outweigh any negative side effects.　　　　　　　　　　　　　　　(231 words)

ワンポイントアドバイス
第2パラグラフのlearn a great deal of things by themselvesはobtain an amazing amount of information by themselves、あるいはeducate themselves an incredible amountなどということもできる。

訳 2 科学技術の進歩の利点はいかなるマイナスの副次的影響にもまさるか
👍 Affirmative

科学技術は人に教養を与え、健康にし、自由な時間を増やす。こうした理由から、科学技術の進歩は社会全体にとってよいことだと言って間違いないと思う。

第一に、科学技術は現在、人々がさまざまなことを一人で学べるようにしている。スマートフォンを持っている今日の平均的な人は、わずか15年前のアメリカの大統領よりも多くの情報にアクセスすることができる。情報量が増えるにつれて、人は学ぶ機会が多くなる。

第二に、科学技術のおかげで、人は以前よりも健康になった。1900年以降、世界の平均寿命は2倍以上になった。また、女性が出産で死亡する確率は以前よりもずっと少なくなり、新生児の生存率ははるかに高まった。これらの改善はみな科学技術のおかげだ。

最後に、科学技術の発達は、人々がしなければならない仕事の量を減らしている。ロボット工学におけるイノベーションのおかげで、先進国の市民が働かなければならない時間は減るだろう。これによって生まれる余剰の時間を、人々は趣味を楽しみ、学習し、自分たちよりも恵まれていない人々と知識や富を分かち合って過ごすことができるようになる。

科学技術の進歩は、マイナスの影響をもたらすこともある。しかし、科学技術はまた、より健康になり、教養を高めた人々に、こうした問題の解決に取り組むより多くの時間をもたらしてくれる。そのため、科学技術の発展の利点は、いかなる副次的なマイナスの影響をも上回ると思う。

Vocabulary
□ outweigh 〜にまさる　□ educated 教養のある　□ have access to 〜〈もの・情報など〉を入手[利用]できる　□ available 利用できる　□ life expectancy 寿命　□ innovation 刷新、革新　□ fortunate 幸運な、恵まれた

解説 科学技術の進歩の是非を問う問題。いいことに決まっているように思えるが、具体的に論点を絞ってまとめないと説得力のある解答にはならない。

モデルエッセイでは、IT、医療、ロボットの例を挙げたが、環境問題（省エネ家電など）や災害の予知、宇宙開発など、いろいろな論点を挙げることが可能だ。解答に当たっては、単に論点を挙げるだけでなく、それらの技術が進歩したことによってどのような利点が生じたのかについても触れていくことが肝心だ。

Structure

Introduction
10-1　情報へのアクセスの飛躍的な進歩
10-2　医療的な進歩
オリジナル　労働時間の低減
Conclusion

TOPIC

2 Do the benefits of technological improvements outweigh any negative side effects?

モデルエッセイ ♣ Negative

 I believe that the negative side effects of technological advances outweigh their benefits. Technology is leading to overpopulation, destroying traditional practices, and causing huge damage to our planet.

 The human population is expected to be around 10 billion by 2050. Unfortunately, the Earth cannot support so many people. Living organisms tend to expand and consume resources as much as possible. Usually nature prevents them from getting out of control. Because of technology, however, humans have not been stopped by nature, and the outcome may be disastrous.

 Next, developments in technology are destroying many of the world's traditional practices. For example, most people in modern, developed countries do not know how to farm or raise livestock anymore. As a result, many people get unhealthy, GMO-packed food from giant agricultural companies. This also decreases people's appreciation for nature and the animals and plants that provide food.

 Finally, we often do not realize the negative effects of new technology. For example, for years scientists in the U.S. have been trying to understand why the country's honeybee populations have been disappearing. Recently researchers at Harvard University discovered that one cause may be pesticides used by farmers. The complete loss of bees would cause huge damage to humans' food supply.

 In conclusion, the benefits of technological improvements do not outweigh the negative side effects. Technological advances are leading to overpopulation, loss of traditional skills, and countless unknown issues.

(233 words)

訳 2 科学技術の進歩の利点はいかなるマイナスの副次的影響にもまさるか
☂ Negative

科学技術の進歩による副次的なマイナスの影響はメリットを上回ると思う。科学技術は人口過剰につながり、伝統的な習わしを破壊し、地球に甚大なダメージを及ぼしている。

人口は2050年までに100億人近くに達すると予想されている。残念ながら、地球はこれほど多くの人々を支えることができない。生物は可能な限り拡大し、資源を消費できるだけ消費する傾向がある。通常なら、自然は生物が抑制不可能にならないようにしている。しかし、科学技術があるために、人類には自然による抑制がきかず、結果は破滅的になるかもしれない。

次に、科学技術の発達は、世界の伝統的な慣行の多くを破壊してきた。例えば、現代的な先進国のほとんどの人々が、今では作物や家畜の育てかたを知らない。その結果、多くの人は大手農業企業がつくった遺伝子組み換え原料が詰まった不健康な食品を買うようになった。これにより、自然や、食べ物を与えてくれる動植物に対する人間の感謝の気持ちも減っている。

最後に、私たちは新しい科学技術のマイナスの影響に気づいていないことが多い。例えば、アメリカの科学者たちは何年にもわたり、国内からミツバチがいなくなってきている理由をつかもうとしてきた。最近、ハーバード大学の研究者たちは、一因は農家が使っている殺虫剤の可能性があることを突き止めた。ハチが完全にいなくなれば、人類の食糧供給に大きなダメージが生じる。

結論として、科学技術の発展によるメリットが、副次的なマイナスの影響にまさることはない。科学技術の進歩は、人口過剰と伝統的な技術の損失につながり、未知の問題は数えきれない。

Vocabulary

□ overpopulation 人口過剰　□ practice 実践、習わし　□ livestock 家畜　□ GMO(=genetically modified organism) 遺伝子組み換え生物(作物)　□ pesticide 殺虫剤

解説

現実世界には多様な問題があり、それが科学技術の進歩によって引き起こされている点に焦点を当てて考えれば、科学技術の進歩におけるマイナスの側面を中心に解答することも十分可能だ。

モデルエッセイでは、人口問題、伝統的な農業・牧畜業の慣行の衰退、そして原因不明の問題が発生している事例を挙げてトピックとしている。当然のことながら、環境問題や生命倫理のような問題を取り上げることもできるだろう。

● Structure

- Introduction
- 10-3 自然の抑制からの逸脱
- 10-4 伝統的慣行の破壊
- オリジナル ミツバチの減少
- Conclusion

TOPIC

3 Should animal testing be banned?

モデルエッセイ 👍 Affirmative

I am of the opinion that animal testing should be banned. Aside from the fact that animal testing is unreliable, there are also more promising methods for testing products and medicines. Further, animal testing is unethical, and people need to respect animals more.

The main reason that animal testing should be banned is that it is not reliable. Animals and humans are very different organisms. Because of this, some products that are harmful to humans are not harmful to animals, and vice versa. In fact, most potential pharmaceutical drugs that are shown by animal testing to be effective and safe do not pass clinical tests.

Next, there are already more promising methods for testing goods. For example, testing methods that use human cells and tissues combined with special computer programs are more reliable. These methods can even be used to test the effects of various substances on specific organs and cells, which leads to more accurate results.

Finally, animal testing is unethical. According to a recent study, each year over 100 million animals die in the laboratories of chemical and pharmaceutical companies, universities, and research institutes. This is just one example of mankind's lack of respect for other animals, which is one of modern society's greatest problems.

Due to the reasons mentioned above, I believe that animal testing should be banned. (221 words)

ワンポイントアドバイス

第2パラグラフの3文目にある vice versa はラテン語から来た表現で「逆もまた真実で」という意味。A is B, and vice versa. で「AはBである。そしてその逆（BはAである）もまた真実だ」という意味を表す。便利な表現なので覚えておきたい。

訳 3　動物実験は禁止すべきか
　　　👍 Affirmative

　私は、動物実験は禁止されるべきだと考えている。動物実験は信頼性がないという事実に加え、製品や薬品を試験するもっと確実な方法も存在する。また、動物実験は非倫理的であり、人間はもっと動物を大切にするべきだ。

　動物実験が禁止されるべき主な理由は、信頼性に乏しいことである。動物と人間はかけ離れた生物だ。このため、人間に有害でも動物には無害な製品もあり、その逆もある。実際、動物実験では効果があり、安全であると示された開発中の医薬品のほとんどが、臨床試験を通過しない。

　次に、製品を試験するのにはもっと確実な方法がすでに存在する。例えば、特別なコンピュータープログラムと組み合わせて人間の細胞と組織を使った実験方法は、より信頼性が高い。こうした方法は、特定の臓器や細胞への多様な物質の影響を実験するのに使うこともでき、さらに正確な実験結果をもたらす。

　最後に、動物実験は非倫理的である。最近の研究によると、化学メーカーや医薬品メーカー、大学、研究機関の実験室で毎年1億匹以上の動物が死亡しているという。この事実は、人間がほかの動物を大切にしていないことを示す一例にすぎず、これは現代社会で最大の問題の一つだ。

　上述の理由から、動物実験は禁止されるべきだと思う。

Vocabulary

□ unethical 非倫理的な　　□ pharmaceutical drug 薬剤、薬品　　□ clinical test 臨床試験
□ tissue 組織

解説　動物実験の是非は、動物福祉の観点から、生命倫理の大きなトピックの一つになっている。当然倫理的な観点は外せないが、単に「かわいそうだから禁止するべきだ」と感情的に反応するのではなく、なぜ動物実験をしなくていいのかの論拠を提示することが大切だ。

　モデルエッセイでは、前臨床試験としての動物実験は信頼性が乏しいことと、代替技術の発達の二つをトピックとして挙げている。なお、人間に対する試験についてはヘルシンキ宣言（1964年）で規範が示されている。

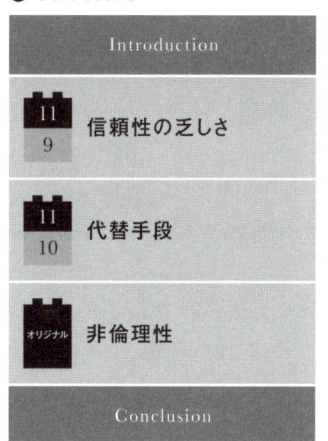

Structure

| Introduction |
| 11-9 信頼性の乏しさ |
| 11-10 代替手段 |
| オリジナル 非倫理性 |
| Conclusion |

TOPIC

3 Should animal testing be banned?

モデルエッセイ ♠ Negative

I do not think that animal testing should be banned. Animal testing saves human lives, which are more important than animals' lives. Also, there are limited alternatives.

The primary reason that animal testing should not be banned is that human lives are more valuable than animal lives. Before animal testing was introduced, humans used products without performing safety tests. This led to a considerable number of deaths and even more illnesses. Scientists do not wish to cause harm to animals, but it is a better option than allowing humans to be harmed.

Second, it is difficult to replace animal testing. The scientific community is working hard to find alternative testing methods and to reduce the number of animals used for testing each year. However, living organisms are very complicated, so our ability to perform reliable tests with only cell tissue and computer programs is still quite limited.

Last, animal testing leads to valuable scientific discoveries. Animal testing has contributed to medical breakthroughs related to diseases like cancer, AIDS, and diabetes. Also, experimenting with animals has taught psychology researchers a great deal of information about basic learning processes and motivational factors such as hunger, thirst, and reproduction.

As mentioned above, animal testing is currently a necessity for protecting the welfare of humans. Therefore, until a reliable replacement can be found for animal testing, I do not believe that it should be banned.

(231 words)

訳　3　動物実験は禁止すべきか
♠ Negative

　私は、動物実験を禁止するべきだとは思わない。動物実験は人命を救うが、人命は動物の命よりも重要である。また、代替手段は限られている。

　動物実験を禁止するべきではない第一の理由は、人命は動物の命よりも価値があるということだ。動物実験が導入される前、人間は安全性を確認する実験を行わずに製品を使っていた。死亡に至るケースも相当数あり、病気を招くケースはさらに多かった。科学者たちは動物に害を与えることを望んではいないが、人間に害を与えるよりは好ましい選択肢だ。

　次に、動物実験の代替手段を見つけることは困難である。科学界では、代替の実験方法を探すことに努め、毎年実験に使われる動物の数を減らそうと努力している。しかし、生物というものは大変複雑なので、我々が細胞組織とコンピュータープログラムのみで信頼できる実験を行う能力は、まだかなり限られている。

　最後に、動物実験は貴重な科学的な発見をもたらす。動物実験はこれまで、がんやエイズ、糖尿病といった疾病に関する医学的な発見に貢献してきた。また、動物を使った実験は、心理学の研究者に、基本的な学習プロセスと飢えや渇き、生殖のような動機づけ要因について非常に多くの情報をもたらしてきた。

　上述のように、動物実験は現在のところ人間の幸福を守るために必要である。ゆえに、動物実験に代わる信頼できる手段が見つかるまでは、禁止されるべきではないと思う。

Vocabulary

□ alternative 代替(の)　□ breakthrough (科学上の)大発見、画期的な進歩　□ diabetes 糖尿病
□ reproduction 繁殖、生殖

解説

　動物実験の禁止に対して否定の立場をとる場合は、なぜ動物実験が必要かを考える。

　動物実験は臨床試験の前に行われる実験であり、人間への危険性を減らすためのものである。また、その実験からは多くの知見ももたらされる。

　モデルエッセイでは、さらに、倫理的な観点から犠牲になる動物の数を減らす努力はなされていると述べたうえで、代替手段が限られていることをトピックとして挙げている。

● Structure

Introduction
¶1 人命の優先
¶1 (オリジナル) 限られた代替手段
¶1/¶2 科学的な発見への寄与
Conclusion

TOPIC

4 Agree or disagree: Improving space-related technology is a good investment

モデルエッセイ 👍 Affirmative　　　　　　　🎧 251

　　　Many people argue that improving space-related technology has no direct benefit for life on Earth. However, space exploration creates a need for new technological innovations, and many useful technologies come from investing in space exploration, especially in the medical and environmental sciences.

　　　Scientists claim many useful technological innovations have been made by trying to help astronauts in the harsh conditions of outer space. For example, NASA's efforts to provide astronauts with nutrient-rich foods in space have led to improvements in commercial food for newborn babies.

　　　Space-related technology also helps improve medical science. One example is a robotic arm called the neuroArm, which is used to perform surgery. It was originally developed to help astronauts do heavy-lifting and maintenance in space. Today, the neuroArm allows surgeons to save the lives of patients who need surgery while inside an MRI machine.

　　　Space technology research even leads to benefits for people in developing countries. For example, water purification systems developed to sustain life in outer space are now used to change wastewater into safe drinking water. This technology provides poor communities around the world with access to clean drinking water.

　　　Just looking at these few innovations, we can see how dedicating time and money to space-related technologies is a good investment. Technologies developed to keep astronauts safe and healthy in space have a direct impact on daily life on Earth. (227 words)

訳 **4** 賛成か反対か：宇宙関連技術を向上させることはすぐれた投資である
👍 Affirmative

　多くの人が、宇宙関連技術の進歩は、地球上の生活に直接的な利益をもたらさないと主張する。しかし、宇宙探査は新たな技術革新の必要性を生み、宇宙探査への投資からは、特に医療と環境科学において、多くの有益な技術が生まれている。

　宇宙空間という過酷な環境にいる宇宙飛行士を助けようとして多くの有益な技術革新が生み出されたと、科学者たちは主張している。例えば、宇宙で宇宙飛行士に栄養価の高い食事を提供しようというNASAの取り組みは、新生児用の市販食品の改善につながった。

　宇宙関連技術は、医学の進歩にも役立っている。一例に、手術に使われるニューロアームと呼ばれるロボットアームがある。これは当初、宇宙飛行士が宇宙で重量物の運搬や保守作業をするのに役立てるために開発された。今日、ニューロアームのおかげで外科医は、MRI内で手術を受ける必要がある患者の命を救えるようになった。

　宇宙技術の研究は、発展途上国の人々にも恩恵をもたらしている。例えば、宇宙空間で生命を維持するために開発された浄水システムは、現在、廃水を安全な飲み水に変えるために活用されている。この技術のおかげで、世界中の貧しい地域の人々が清潔な飲み水を得られるようになっている。

　これらの少数の技術革新を見ただけでも、宇宙関連技術に時間と費用をかけることがどれほどよい投資であるかがわかる。宇宙空間で宇宙飛行士の安全と健康を維持するために開発された技術は、地球上の日常生活にも直接的な影響を与えている。

Vocabulary

□ harsh 過酷な　□ newborn baby 新生児　□ surgery (外科)手術　□ water purification system 浄水システム　□ sustain ～を維持する、持続する　□ dedicate ～をささげる

解説　宇宙関連技術の推進に対する賛否を問う問題。宇宙関連の話題に興味がないと何を書けばいいか途方に暮れてしまうかもしれないが、宇宙そのものに関する知識を問うているわけではないので、賛成の立場で書く場合は、それをどう地上の世界の問題と結びつけられるかを考えよう。

　モデルエッセイでは、宇宙関連技術が、地上での生活に関わる食品や医療技術などの開発につながった事例を挙げているが、宇宙が過酷な環境であることを考えれば、原発事故の際に使用できるロボットの開発などの例を考えることも可能だろう。

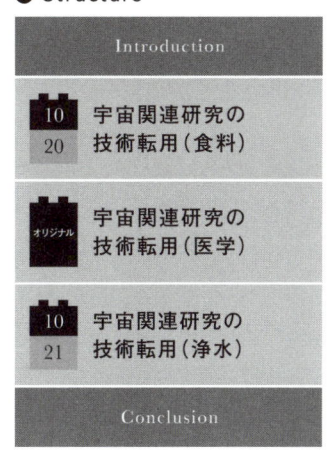

● Structure

Introduction
10 / 20　宇宙関連研究の技術転用（食料）
オリジナル　宇宙関連研究の技術転用（医学）
10 / 21　宇宙関連研究の技術転用（浄水）
Conclusion

TOPIC

4 Agree or disagree: Improving space-related technology is a good investment

モデルエッセイ ♣ Negative

I disagree with the opinion that improving space-related technology is a good investment. Space technology is not useful to most people, and there are better ways to use this money, such as for ocean exploration.

First, space technology does not benefit the general public enough. Occasionally, proponents of investment in space technology argue that it leads to better technology for people on Earth. This is certainly true in some cases. But for the most part, space technology does not benefit average people.

Second, we could spend this money on more important things like developing renewable energy or decreasing world poverty. These investments would have a direct benefit on human lives. For example, it is simply not logical to spend money building spaceships when there are millions of people in the world that are starving or do not have clean water.

Third, exploring our oceans is more important than exploring space. Several experts claim that exploring and studying the ocean might lead to many important discoveries. For example, it is believed that some of the creatures living in the ocean could be used to develop cures for many diseases. Discoveries like this are unlikely in space.

Considering the points mentioned above, I believe it is fair to state that investing in space-related technology is not a good idea.

(217 words)

訳 **4** 賛成か反対か：宇宙関連技術を向上させることはすぐれた投資である
🌧 Negative

　宇宙関連技術を向上させることはよい投資であるという意見には反対だ。宇宙技術はほとんどの人にとっては無益であり、この資金には、例えば海洋探査など、もっと適切な使い道がある。

　第一に、宇宙技術は一般の人々には十分なメリットがない。宇宙技術への投資を支持する人々は、地球上の人々によりよい技術をもたらすことにつながると主張することがある。これは確かに当てはまるケースもある。しかし多くの場合、宇宙技術は普通の人々にはメリットがない。

　第二に、私たちはこの資金を、再生可能エネルギーの開発や世界の貧困の低減など、もっと重要なことに使うことができる。こうした投資は、人間の暮らしに直接的な恩恵をもたらす。例えば、世界では何百万人もの人々が飢えていたり、清潔な水が手に入れられなかったりする一方で、宇宙船の建造に費用を投じるというのはまったく理にかなっていない。

　第三に、海洋探査は宇宙探査よりも重要だ。海洋を探査し研究することは、たくさんの重要な発見につながる可能性があると、複数の専門家が主張している。例えば、海に生息する生物の中には、多くの病気の治療薬を開発するのに使うことができるものもあると考えられている。このような発見は宇宙では見込みが薄い。

　上述の論点を考慮すると、宇宙関連技術に投資することはよい考えではないと言えると思う。

Vocabulary

☐ proponent 支持者、提案者　☐ renewable energy 再生可能エネルギー　☐ starve 飢える

解説　宇宙関連技術にあまり関心がない場合は、反対の立場で書くほうがはるかに容易だろう。なぜならば、そのような開発を行う労力や費用はもっと有益なものに使うべきだと論じればいいからだ。

代わりに投資すべきものを列挙しただけでは、答案としては単調になる。モデルエッセイでは、宇宙関連技術は日常生活にはあまり役に立たないこと、もっと緊急を要する問題がたくさんあること、海洋開発には具体的なメリットがあることを挙げてトピックとしている。

Structure

Introduction

オリジナル：一般人に対するメリットのなさ

10/22：資金のより有効な使い道

10/23：より優先度の高い研究

Conclusion

TOPIC

5 Can society eliminate its dependence on fossil fuels such as oil and gas in the near future?

モデルエッセイ 👍 Affirmative　　　MP3 253

　In my opinion, it is possible for society to eliminate its dependence on fossil fuels such as oil and gas. There are already many good alternative energy sources, and their costs are dropping. In addition, environmental crises will motivate people to abandon fossil fuels.

　First, the world is already capable of replacing fossil fuels. Scientists have presented detailed plans showing how the entire world could theoretically be powered by wind, solar, and water sources. The technology already exists. The only problem that remains is getting it adopted by the general public.

　Second, thanks to developments in technology, sustainable energy sources are becoming more cost-effective. For example, recently in Australia it was found that producing wind energy was cheaper than using coal or natural gas. Also, solar panels become cheaper every year. Eventually, renewable energy sources will be so cheap that everyone starts using them.

　Last, it is likely that several crises related to power, resources, and the environment will occur in the near future. For example, many scientists believe that the Earth's increasing temperature will soon result in serious droughts, heat waves, typhoons, and other disasters. These will likely lead to more adoption of renewable energy sources.

　Based on the points mentioned above, I believe that society can eliminate its dependence on fossil fuels in the near future.

(218 words)

訳 5 近い将来、社会は石油やガスのような化石燃料への依存をなくせるか
👍 Affirmative

　私の意見では、社会が石油やガスといった化石燃料への依存をなくすことは可能だ。すでに適切な代替エネルギー源が多数あり、それらのコストは下がっている。さらに、環境危機は化石燃料の使用中止を促すだろう。

　第一に、世界にはすでに化石燃料を別のものに置き換える能力がある。科学者たちは、風力、太陽光、水力によって理論上いかにして世界全体に電力を供給できるかを示す詳細な計画を提示してきた。この技術はすでに存在する。残る唯一の課題は、一般市民に受け入れられることだ。

　第二に、技術の発展のおかげで、持続可能なエネルギー源の費用効率は高まってきている。例えばオーストラリアでは最近、風力エネルギーを生み出すことは石炭や天然ガスを使うよりも安いことがわかった。また、太陽光パネルも年々安くなっている。いずれ、再生可能エネルギーは非常に安くなり、誰もが使い始めるだろう。

　最後に、電力や資源、環境に関する複数の危機が近い将来に起こる可能性がある。例えば、多くの科学者たちが、地球の気温上昇は近いうちに深刻な干ばつ、熱波、台風などの災害を引き起こすだろうと考えている。これは再生可能エネルギー源の導入の増加につながるだろう。

　上述の論点に基づいて考えると、社会は近い将来、化石燃料への依存をなくすことができると私は思う。

Vocabulary

□ alternative energy 代替エネルギー　□ theoretically 理論上は　□ sustainable 持続可能な
□ drought 干ばつ

解説　化石燃料と地球温暖化に関する問題は、環境関連の中でも代表的な問題。基本的な論点をきちんと押さえておきたい。

　化石燃料の使用をなくすためには、それに代わるエネルギー源の見込みが立たなければならない。モデルエッセイでは、代替エネルギー（再生可能エネルギー）の存在、その費用効率化、そして化石燃料の使用をやめざるを得ない現状をトピックとして挙げた。

Structure

Introduction
8-1　代替エネルギー
8-2　再生可能エネルギーの費用効率
オリジナル　化石燃料の使用を断念せざるを得ない状況
Conclusion

TOPIC

5 Can society eliminate its dependence on fossil fuels such as oil and gas in the near future?

モデルエッセイ ● Negative

I do not believe that society can eliminate its dependence on fossil fuels in the near future. Shifting to new sources of energy is a slow, expensive process, and it requires support from both governments and the general public.

First, society in general is not motivated to quit using fossil fuels. Scientists have shown that it is possible, in theory, to replace fossil fuels with renewable energy. But the implementation of such theories would require trillions of dollars in investment, extensive public education, and support from both governments and individuals. Organizing all of these is not likely in the near future.

Second, society is still too dependent on fossil fuels. Even respected environmentalists have acknowledged that the world will continue relying on natural gas for many years. Additionally, technology is making it easier to drill for oil, which is increasing supply and making it cheaper. As long as there is an affordable supply, dependence will not decrease.

Finally, removing fossil fuels will be a lengthy, complex process. Back in the 19th century, for example, it took over 50 years for coal to replace wood as the main source of energy. Replacing gas and oil may take much longer because such a large number of machines use these resources.

For these reasons, I do not believe that society will be able to eliminate its dependence on fossil fuels anytime soon. (229 words)

訳 5 近い将来、社会は石油やガスのような化石燃料への依存をなくせるか
🌧 Negative

社会が近い将来、化石燃料への依存をなくすことはできないと思う。新しいエネルギー源への移行は、ゆっくりとしたお金のかかるプロセスであり、政府と一般市民両方からの支援を必要とするだろう。

第一に、社会は全体として、化石燃料の使用をやめる動機づけがない。科学者は、化石燃料を再生可能エネルギーに置き換えることは、理論上可能だと示している。しかし、このような理論を適用するには何兆ドルという投資と、広範な市民教育、政府と個人両方からの支援が必要となる。これらすべてを準備することは、近い将来に実現しそうにない。

第二に、社会は化石燃料に頼りすぎている。尊敬を集める環境保護活動家でさえも、世界は今後何年もの間、天然ガスに頼り続けるだろうと認めている。それに加え、石油の採掘は以前よりも技術的に容易になっており、その結果石油の供給は増え、価格は下がっている。手ごろな価格の供給がある限り、依存が減ることはないだろう。

最後に、化石燃料をなくすことは時間のかかる複雑なプロセスになるだろう。例えば、19世紀にさかのぼると、主要なエネルギー源が木材から石炭に代わるのに50年以上かかった。ガスと石油の代替化は、これらの資源を使用する機械がこれほど多数ある以上、はるかに長い時間がかかるだろう。

こうした理由から、社会は近いうちに化石燃料への依存をなくすことはできないと私は思う。

Vocabulary
□ implementation 実現、実行　□ affordable 手ごろな[手の届く]価格の

解説 設問文のin the near future(近い将来)を論拠に、化石燃料の使用はなくならないとする立場の答案。過去問でも、設問文にin the coming decades(この先数十年の間)のような限定がついたことがある。「近い将来には」なくならない、と言えれば、設問に答えたことになる。

モデルエッセイでは、第2、第4パラグラフで、再生可能エネルギーへの移行には膨大な資金、時間、援助が必要だと述べた。また第3パラグラフでは、シェールガス[オイル]のような非在来型の化石燃料の開発によって生産量が増えている事実も論拠とした。

● Structure

Introduction
⑧③ エネルギーの移行を阻む諸事情
⑧④ 化石燃料への過剰な依存
⑧⑤ 化石燃料廃止にかかる時間
Conclusion

TOPIC

6 Agree or disagree: All nuclear power plants should be shut down

モデルエッセイ 👍 Affirmative

I believe that all nuclear power plants should be shut down. Both the plants themselves and the waste they produce are too dangerous.

First, nuclear power plants are too vulnerable to disasters and attacks. The nuclear catastrophe that occurred in Fukushima in 2011 shows the danger of these facilities. They may be a target for attacks by terrorists and other governments. In fact, cyber-attacks have already taken place at nuclear facilities in Korea and Iran.

Second, disposing of radioactive waste is a major problem. Nuclear fuel remains highly radioactive for thousands of years after it is no longer useful. There is no way to know what might happen in the next few thousand years. Because of this, it is impossible for governments to design a reliable process for disposing of this waste.

Third, there are several good alternatives to nuclear power being developed. Renewable sources of energy such as wind and solar do not generate as much power. However, they do not produce large amounts of hazardous waste or endanger local people, either. This is why countries like Germany are working to phase out nuclear power and replace it with renewable energy sources.

There is plenty of evidence to show that nuclear power plants are unsafe and problematic in the long run. For this reason, nuclear power plants should be gradually shut down and replaced by renewable energy sources.

(229 words)

訳 6 賛成か反対か：すべての原子力発電所は停止すべきである
👍 Affirmative

　すべての原子力発電所は停止されるべきだと思う。原発そのものも、原発が生む廃棄物も、あまりにも危険だ。
　第一に、原発は災害や攻撃に対してあまりにも脆弱だ。2011年に福島で起きた原発の大事故はこれらの施設の危険性を示している。それらはテロリストや他の政府の攻撃対象になるかもしれない。実際、韓国やイランの原子力施設ではサイバー攻撃が起きている。
　第二に、放射性廃棄物の処理は大きな問題だ。核燃料は使用できなくなってから何千年もの間、高い放射性を保持する。今後数千年の間に何が起こるかを知るすべはない。このため、政府が放射性廃棄物の信頼できる処理プロセスを策定するのは不可能だ。
　第三に、原子力に代わる適切な代替手段がいくつか開発されている。風力や太陽光などの再生可能エネルギー源は、発電量は劣る。しかし、これらは大量の危険な廃棄物を排出せず、地元の人々を危険にさらすこともない。そのため、ドイツのような国々は原発を段階的に廃止し、再生可能エネルギー源に切り替える取り組みを行っている。
　原子力発電所が、長期的には危険で問題の多いものであることを示す証拠は数多くある。そのため、原子力発電所を徐々に停止し、再生可能エネルギー源に切り替えるべきだ。

Vocabulary

- vulnerable 脆弱な、（攻撃・被害を）受けやすい
- dispose of ～ ～を処分する
- radioactive waste 放射性廃棄物
- hazardous 危険な
- phase out ～を段階的に廃止する

解説　すべての原発を停止すべきだという立場の答案。福島原発事故でも明らかになったように、原発は非常に危険性の高い施設である。だが、単に危険だから停止すべきだというのでは解答にならない。

　モデルエッセイでは、自然災害とテロや外国からの攻撃に対する脆弱性、放射性廃棄物の危険性と代替手段としての再生可能エネルギーをトピックに挙げたが、経年劣化の問題や活断層の存在などを挙げることも可能だろう。

　また今後の原発建設に関する設問であれば、廃炉にかかる費用などもトピックになるだろう。

Structure

- Introduction
- 原発の危険性
- 放射性廃棄物の問題
- 代替手段としての再生可能エネルギー
- Conclusion

TOPIC

6 Agree or disagree: All nuclear power plants should be shut down

モデルエッセイ ♣ Negative   MP3 256

I disagree with the view that all nuclear power plants should be shut down. Nuclear power is reliable and has low pollution. Also, it has a promising future.

Although nuclear power is not a renewable source of energy, it is relatively friendly to the environment. It produces significantly less greenhouse gases than power generated using fossil fuels such as coal, oil, and gas. This helps to curb global warming.

In addition, nuclear power is more reliable than other power sources. Renewable energy sources such as solar and wind energy are dependent on weather conditions, which can change at any time. But nuclear power plants can generate energy consistently over long periods of time. Moreover, the fuel to run these power plants will last much longer than fossil fuels.

Last, nuclear power research is very promising. Nuclear power plants currently use nuclear fission to generate power. But scientists are working to generate power using nuclear fusion, which is a process that occurs naturally in stars. If scientists succeed in doing this, the world will finally have an unlimited source of clean, renewable energy.

Taking the above points into consideration, it is clear that nuclear power plants should not be shut down. Rather, we should put more efforts into researching and improving nuclear power. (212 words)

訳 6　賛成か反対か：すべての原子力発電所は停止すべきである
☂ Negative

　すべての原子力発電所は停止されるべきだという見解には反対だ。原子力は安定していて、汚染が少ない。また、原子力には有望な未来がある。

　原子力は再生可能なエネルギー源ではないが、環境には比較的やさしい。石炭、石油、ガスのような化石燃料を使った発電よりも温室効果ガスの排出は著しく少ない。このことは地球温暖化の抑止に役立つ。

　加えて、原子力は他のエネルギー源よりも安定している。太陽光や風力のような再生可能エネルギー源は天候に左右されるが、天候は不安定なものだ。しかし、原子力発電所は長期間一定して発電できる。さらに、これらの発電所を稼働するための燃料は、化石燃料よりもずっと長く使える。

　最後に、原子力発電の研究はとても有望だ。原子力発電所は現在、発電に核分裂を使っている。しかし、科学者たちは恒星で自然に起こっているのと同じプロセスである核融合を使っての発電に取り組んでいる。もし、科学者たちがこれに成功すれば、世界はついに、クリーンで再生可能な無限のエネルギー源を手にすることとなるだろう。

　こうした点を考慮すると、原子力発電所は停止されるべきでないことは明らかだ。むしろ、原子力を研究し、改善していくことにもっと力を注ぐべきだ。

Vocabulary
□ curb 〜を抑制する　□ nuclear fission 核分裂　□ nuclear fusion 核融合

解説　今度は、原発停止に反対する立場の答案。

モデルエッセイでは、火力発電と比べて温室効果ガスの排出量が少なく、温暖化防止に役立つこと、再生可能エネルギーと比べて安定して発電できること、そして研究が進められている核融合発電をトピックとして挙げたが、原発を止めれば電気代が上がり、経済が低迷するといった論点を挙げることもできるだろう。

◆ Structure

| Introduction |
| 温暖化の防止 |
| 原発の安定性 |
| 新タイプの原発 |
| Conclusion |

TOPIC

7 Should cloning research be banned?

モデルエッセイ 👍 Affirmative

     I believe that cloning research should be banned. Aside from being unnatural, it is also dangerous for a species and has an extremely low success rate.

     The main reason that cloning should be banned is that it is not natural. If people used cloning to produce and modify humans, then it would cause unnatural changes to the human species in general. There would likely be class divisions between cloned and non-cloned humans. Also, determining the traits of new generations upsets the natural balance of the world.

     Second, decreases in genetic diversity are hazardous to animals. Plenty of scientific studies have shown that genetic diversity makes a species stronger. This is part of the evolutionary process. With cloning, however, plants and animals lose their genetic diversity, making them more vulnerable to problems such as diseases.

     Third, cloning technology is unreliable. In particular, there is a danger of cell mutation when performing cloning. This is why more than 90 percent of cloning attempts fail. Instead, unhealthy, mutated organisms are produced. Then, after a short and painful existence, they die. This type of scientific research is extremely unethical.

     Mentioned above are just some of the reasons that cloning research should be banned. As technology develops, it is important for humans to pursue scientific research that is ethical and safe. Cloning research is neither of these.   (222 words)

訳 **7** クローン研究は禁止されるべきか
👍 Affirmative

　クローン研究は禁止されるべきだと思う。自然に反しているだけでなく、生物種にとって危険でもあり、成功率が極めて低い。

　クローン技術が禁止されるべき主な理由は、自然に反するからだ。もし、クローン技術をヒトの繁殖や改変に使えば、ヒトという種全体に不自然な変化が起こることになる。クローンで生まれた人間とクローンでない人間の間に階級区分も生じるだろう。また、新しい世代の形質を決定することは、世界の自然なバランスを乱してしまう。

　第二に、遺伝的多様性の低下は、動物にとって危険である。遺伝的多様性は種をより強固にしていると多くの科学研究が示している。これは進化のプロセスの一部だ。しかしながら、クローン技術によって動植物は遺伝的多様性を失い、このことで病気などの問題に対してより脆弱になる。

　第三に、クローン技術は信頼できない。特に、クローンを作成する際に、細胞の突然変異の恐れがある。クローン作成の試みの90％以上が失敗するのはこのためだ。むしろ、突然変異した不健康な生物が生み出される。そしてその後、その生物は、短命で苦痛に満ちた存在として生きたあと、死ぬ。このような科学研究は極めて非倫理的だ。

　上述したことは、クローン研究が禁止されるべき理由の一部に過ぎない。技術の発展に伴い、人は倫理的で安全な科学研究を追求することが重要だ。クローン研究は倫理的でも安全でもない。

Vocabulary

□ modify ～を(部分的に)変える　□ class division 階級区分　□ trait (遺伝)形質　□ mutation 突然変異　□ mutate ～を突然変異させる　□ unethical 非倫理的な

解説　クローン研究の禁止に賛成する立場の答案。

　クローン研究を批判的に論じる場合は、倫理的な側面が中心になってくる。クローン羊「ドリー」の例で知られるように、哺乳類でもクローン動物ができることは明らかになっており、それを推し進めてヒトのクローンを考えたときの不自然さは、思いつきやすいトピックだろう。モデルエッセイでは、遺伝的多様性の喪失が動植物を脆弱にする点、成功率の低さから生じる非倫理性を残りのトピックとしている。

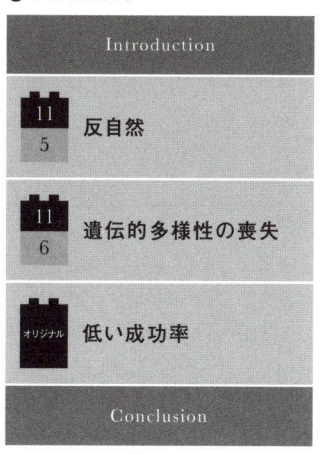

Structure

- Introduction
- 11/5　反自然
- 11/6　遺伝的多様性の喪失
- オリジナル　低い成功率
- Conclusion

TOPIC 7 Should cloning research be banned?

モデルエッセイ ♠ Negative　　　258

　　I do not believe that cloning research should be banned. People need to understand that cloning research and cloning humans are separate issues. Also, cloning research produces many desirable results.

　　Although most would agree that fully cloning a human is not right, this is not a justifiable reason to ban cloning research. Instead, we should only restrict the cloning of humans. This way, scientists would still be free to study cloning and improve their understanding of genetics, which could be beneficial to mankind.

　　The main advantage of cloning research is its potential contribution to medical science. For example, it is theoretically possible that scientists could use cloning technology to replace organs such as kidneys and hearts. This type of technology would save countless lives, but it will be difficult to develop if cloning research is banned.

　　Finally, it is possible that cloning could be used to build populations of endangered and extinct animals. It is estimated that between 200 and 2,000 animal species become extinct every year. There is no denying that humans are largely responsible for this. With cloning, we can repair some of the damage that humans have caused.

　　When considering the benefits of cloning research, it becomes clear that banning it is not a good idea.　　(209 words)

ワンポイントアドバイス

第2パラグラフの2文目はInstead, we should just set up laws that ban scientists from cloning humans.（そうではなく、我々は科学者がヒトをクローン化することを禁じる法律をつくるべきなのだ）と言い換えることもできる。

訳 7 クローン研究は禁止されるべきか
　　　　　Negative

　私はクローン研究が禁止されるべきだとは思わない。人々はクローン研究とヒトのクローン作成が別問題であることを理解する必要がある。また、クローン研究は多くの望ましい結果を生み出す。

　ヒトの完全なクローンを作成することは正しくないということにはほとんどの人が同意するだろうが、これはクローン研究を禁止する正当な理由にはならない。そうではなく、我々はヒトのクローン作成だけを規制するべきなのだ。そうすれば、科学者は自由にクローン技術を研究し、遺伝学の理解を深めることができる。このことは人類にとって有益なものとなりうる。

　クローン研究の主なメリットは、医学に貢献する可能性があることだ。例えば、科学者がクローン技術を使って、腎臓や心臓といった臓器を取り換えることは、理論的には可能だ。このような技術ができれば無数の生命が救われるだろうが、クローン研究が禁止されれば開発は困難になる。

　最後に、絶滅危惧種や絶滅種の動物の個体数を増やすために、クローン技術を使用することが可能だ。毎年、200から2000種の動物が絶滅していると推定されている。人間がこの主たる原因となっていることは否定できない。クローン技術があれば、人間が引き起こしたダメージのいくつかを修復することができる。

　クローン研究のメリットを考えれば、それを禁止するのがいい考えでないことは明らかになる。

Vocabulary

□ genetics 遺伝学　□ extinct 絶滅した　□ There is no denying that ～ ～ということを否定することはできない

解説　クローン研究の禁止に反対する立場の答案。

　クローン研究はクローン人間をつくることとはまったく別問題だと問題を峻別したうえで、その利点を挙げていく方針だ。モデルエッセイでは、遺伝学の理解の深化という学術的な側面のほか、移植用の臓器確保といった医学への貢献、絶滅危惧種と絶滅種の個体数増加をトピックとして挙げているが、ほかに良質な食用家畜の増産などのトピックを考えることもできるだろう。

Structure

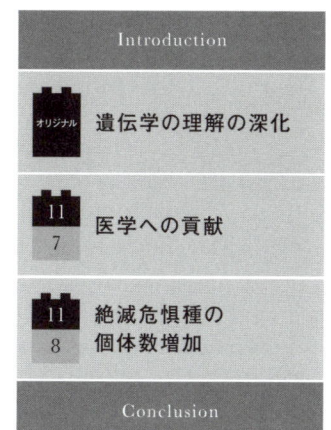

- Introduction
- オリジナル：遺伝学の理解の深化
- ¶7：医学への貢献
- ¶8：絶滅危惧種の個体数増加
- Conclusion

TOPIC 8

Agree or disagree: Improvements in medical technology are always beneficial to society

モデルエッセイ 👍 Affirmative

I agree that improvements in medical technology are always beneficial to society. Thanks to medical technology, more people can now stay healthy, live longer, and afford effective medical care.

The most obvious reason that medical technology is always beneficial to society is that it allows us to live longer. Every year, we find new cures and treatments for diseases, and the life expectancy of developed nations continues to increase. This means that we can spend more time with our family and friends.

Second, improvements in medical technology allow people to live more comfortably. For example, some people with knee problems live in constant pain. It is difficult for them to do daily activities and almost impossible to exercise. Thanks to developments in medical 3D printing technology, however, it is now possible to eliminate this pain by building perfectly sized replacements for their knees.

Finally, as medical technology improves, it also becomes much cheaper, and more people can receive proper care. Right now many advanced medical treatments are still so expensive that only the world's richest people have access to them. However, thanks to the development of medical technology, we are approaching an era in which affordable healthcare is available to everyone.

In summary, I am of the opinion that improvements in medical technology are always a good thing for society. (220 words)

ワンポイントアドバイス

第4パラグラフの第3文はHowever, this is gradually changing as medical technology improves. In the future, affordable healthcare will be available to everyone. (しかし医療技術が発達するにつれてこの状況は徐々に変わってきている。将来、誰もが手ごろな費用で医療を受けられるようになるだろう) のように2文に分けてもよい。

訳 8 賛成か反対か:医療技術の発達は常に社会にとって有益である
👍 Affirmative

医療技術の発達は常に社会に有益であると思う。医療技術のおかげで、より多くの人々が今では健康を保ち、長生きし、効果的な医療を受けられるようになった。

医療技術が常に社会に有益である最も明白な理由は、そのおかげで私たちは長生きできるようになったということだ。毎年、病気の新しい治療薬と治療法が発見され、先進国の平均寿命は延び続けている。このことは、私たちがより長い時間を家族や友人と過ごせるということを意味している。

次に、医療技術の発展は、人々をより快適に生活できるようにする。例えば、ひざに問題のある人々は常に痛みを抱えて生きている。日常的な活動をすることは難しく、運動はほぼ不可能だ。しかし、医療における3Dプリンター技術の発展のおかげで、ひざにぴったりのサイズの代替物をつくることによって、現在ではこの痛みを除去することが可能になった。

最後に、医療技術が発達するにつれて、費用も大幅に下がり、適切な手当てを受けられる人が増える。現在は、多くの先進医療はまだとても高額で、世界で最も裕福な人々しか治療を受けることができない。しかし、医療技術の発展のおかげで、誰もが手ごろな費用で医療を受けられる時代が近づいている。

要約すると、私は医療技術の発達は常に社会にとってよいことだという意見だ。

Vocabulary

□ life expectancy 平均余命、寿命　□ replacement 代替物　□ era 時代

解説 医療技術の発達は常に社会に有益だとする立場の答案。

医療技術の発達が有益だというのはごく当たり前のことのように感じられるが、かえって適切なトピックを見つけるのが難しいということもある。

モデルエッセイでは、寿命が延びるという誰もが思いつきやすいトピックに続き、3Dプリンターによる装具の開発という周辺器具に関するトピック、医療費の低下という経済的トピックを挙げている。第3パラグラフの事例では、痛みからの解放ということで、「生活の質」(quality of life)の向上について触れることもできるだろう。

● Structure

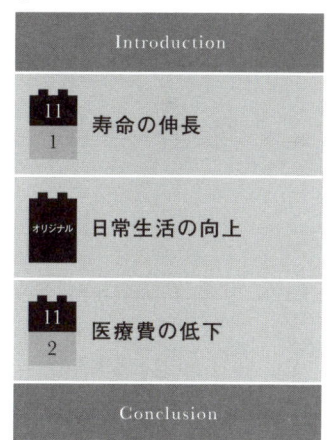

| Introduction |
| 11-1 寿命の伸長 |
| オリジナル 日常生活の向上 |
| 11-2 医療費の低下 |
| Conclusion |

TOPIC

8 Agree or disagree: Improvements in medical technology are always beneficial to society

モデルエッセイ ◆ Negative

Improvements in medical technology are not always a good thing. They can lead to unnatural scientific experimentation, dangerous illnesses, and the loss of traditional healing techniques.

First, some medical technology is unethical. One example of this is genetic modification. In the near future, it is possible that parents will be able to choose their children's genetic characteristics. They may even be able to clone themselves. This is unnatural, and it could cause a number of ethical and scientific problems.

Second, the more we create drugs for some illnesses, the worse they become. For example, antibiotics that fight bacterial infections can promote the development of drug-resistant bacteria, sometimes referred to as "superbugs." In other words, our drugs are making bacteria stronger and more dangerous. This could potentially lead to a disease that cannot be controlled, which could kill billions of people.

Last, as we continue to rely on medical technology, more traditional healing methods are being ignored or forgotten. For example, many doctors give their patients various medications for illnesses that could be healed naturally with herbs, proper nutrition, and rest. Nowadays, most people do not acknowledge the power of natural healing methods, but many of them have been used effectively for thousands of years.

In light of the points mentioned above, I disagree with the claim that improvements in medical technology are always beneficial to society.

(226 words)

| 訳 | 8 | 賛成か反対か：医療技術の発達は常に社会にとって有益である |

◆ Negative

　医療技術の発達が常によいこととは限らない。医療技術の発達は、自然に反する科学実験や、危険な病気、伝統的な治療技術の喪失につながる可能性がある。

　第一に、医療技術の中には非倫理的なものもある。その一例は、遺伝子操作だ。近い将来、親は子の遺伝的特性を選ぶことができるようになる可能性がある。親は自分のクローンをつくることさえできるようになるかもしれない。これは自然に反しており、数多くの倫理的かつ科学的問題を引き起こす可能性がある。

　第二に、治療薬をつくればつくるほど、悪化する病気もある。例えば、細菌の感染に対処する抗生物質は、時に「スーパーバグ」と呼ばれる抗生物質に耐性を持つ細菌を出現させることがある。言い換えると、私たちの医薬品が、細菌をさらに強く危険にしているのだ。このことは、コントロール不可能な病気を発生させかねず、何十億人もの人々が死亡するかもしれない。

　最後に、私たちが医療技術への依存を続けると、伝統的な治療法が見過ごされ、忘れられていく。例えば、多くの医師は、薬草や適切な栄養、休養をとれば自然に治る病気に対して、さまざまな医薬品を患者に与える。最近では、ほとんどの人が自然療法の力を認めていないが、その多くは数千年もの間、効果的に活用されてきたものなのだ。

　上述の点を踏まえ、医療技術の発展が常に社会にとって有益であるという主張に私は反対である。

Vocabulary

□ genetic modification 遺伝子組み換え、遺伝子操作　□ antibiotic 抗生物質　□ infection 感染
□ drug-resistant 薬物抵抗性の

| 解説 | 医療技術の発達が常に有益だとは認めない立場の答案。

やや意外に感じられるかもしれないが、トピックの立て方次第ではこの立場での回答も十分に可能だ。

モデルエッセイでは、遺伝子操作のような非倫理的な医療、薬品に耐性を持った細菌の出現、伝統的な治療法の喪失を挙げているが、保険のきかない先端医療の出現で、受診できる人とできない人の格差が広がるといった社会的な側面を挙げることも可能だろう。

● Structure

| Introduction |
| オリジナル 非倫理的な医療 |
| 11-3 細菌の耐性 |
| 11-4 伝統的な治療法 |
| Conclusion |

TOPIC

9 Is enough being done to protect the world's wilderness areas?

モデルエッセイ 👍 Affirmative　　　MP3 261

　　　I believe that enough is being done to protect the world's wilderness areas. Reforestation and conservation efforts are improving, and awareness about these issues is high.

　　　First, governments, large corporations, and individual volunteers have begun to invest a significant amount of time and money into planting trees around the world. Recently, there was an event in Ecuador where over half a million trees were planted in a single day. Activities like this show that great efforts are being made to preserve nature.

　　　Second, nations around the world are doing more to protect their forests. For example, Brazil, which contains a large percentage of the Amazon rainforest, has managed to decrease deforestation significantly in recent years. In addition, the United Nations Forum on Forests now meets regularly to plan and promote the sustainable management and protection of forests all over the world.

　　　Finally, awareness about environmental issues is particularly high right now. Political leaders, famous celebrities, TV show hosts, and even ordinary people frequently discuss the importance of protecting wilderness areas and the environment. There is no denying that humans have destroyed far too many wilderness areas. But the fact that most people are aware of this is a sign that things will change soon.

　　　In conclusion, it seems that current efforts to protect wilderness areas are satisfactory. It is certainly an important issue, but luckily many people are already working hard to solve it.　　(234 words)

訳 **9** 世界で自然が残る地域を守る取り組みは十分に行われているか
👍 Affirmative

　世界で自然が残る地域を守る取り組みは十分に行われていると思う。森林再生と保全の取り組みが進んでおり、こうした課題についての関心は高い。

　まず、政府、大企業、個人のボランティアは、世界中で木を植えることにかなりの時間と資金を投じ始めた。最近では、エクアドルで50万本以上の木を1日で植えるイベントがあった。このような活動は、自然を守るために多大な努力がなされていることを示している。

　次に、世界中の国々が、森林を保護するためにいっそうの取り組みを行っている。例えば、アマゾンの熱帯雨林の大部分が国内にあるブラジルは、近年、森林破壊を著しく減らすことができた。加えて、国連森林フォーラムは現在、世界中の森林の持続可能な管理と保護の計画を策定し促進するために、定期的に会合を開いている。

　最後に、環境問題への関心はまさに今、非常に高まっている。政界のリーダーや著名人、テレビ番組の司会者、また、一般の人々までもが、自然の残っている地域と環境を守る重要性について頻繁に話し合っている。人類があまりにも多くの自然を破壊してきたことは否定できない。しかし、ほとんどの人がこのことを認識しているという事実は、近いうちに状況が変わる兆しだ。

　結論として、自然が残っている地域を保護する現在の取り組みは十分だと思われる。確かに重要な課題ではあるが、幸い、多くの人々がすでに、この解決に向けて努力をしている。

Vocabulary
- wilderness area 自然が残る地域、自然保護区域
- deforestation 森林伐採、森林破壊
- celebrity 有名人

解説　wilderness area は「未開拓地、自然保護区域、原生自然環境保全地域」などと訳されることもあるが、要するに wilderness（野生、未開）が残る地域で、例えばアマゾンの原生林を思い浮かべればいいだろう。

　モデルエッセイでは、森林再生（reforestation）や森林保護の活動を取り上げ、また環境問題への関心の高まりを論拠として挙げながら、自然保護の取り組みは十分になされていると論じている。

Structure

| Introduction |
| 8/13 始まった植林 |
| 8/14 各国の施策 |
| オリジナル 関心の高まり |
| Conclusion |

TOPIC 9 Is enough being done to protect the world's wilderness areas?

モデルエッセイ ● Negative

　　　In my opinion, current environmental preservation efforts are not sufficient. Due to human activities, an extremely high number of animals are going extinct. High consumption and population increases are making this ongoing problem even more serious.

　　　First, humans are causing tens of thousands of species to go extinct every year. The main cause of this is habitat loss, which is considered to be the primary threat to most of the world's endangered animals. Unless we act now to protect wilderness areas, thousands of the world's animal species will continue to disappear from this planet.

　　　Second, the human population continues to increase, and consumption levels are too high in developed countries. Thus, people are required to exploit an unsustainable amount of the planet's resources, and forests all over the world are destroyed. We need to find a sustainable solution for managing this rapid growth and high consumption as soon as possible.

　　　Third, although many nations have begun to adopt environmental conservation policies, and the rate of deforestation is slowing, positive change is not happening quickly enough. Until humans are consistently consuming less resources than the planet can sustain, then environmental efforts should be considered a failure overall. Consequently, all people should come together to reverse these problems.

　　　For the reasons mentioned above, it is clear that more should be done to protect this planet's natural habitats. (225 words)

ワンポイントアドバイス
第2パラグラフの第3文は We must do more to protect wilderness areas, or we will continue to lose more and more of the planet's biodiversity [animals; species]. などとしてもよい。

訳 9 世界で自然が残る地域を守る取り組みは十分に行われているか
🌧 Negative

　私の意見では、現在の環境保護活動は不十分である。人類の活動が原因で、極めて多くの動物が絶滅しようとしている。大量消費と人口増加は、進行中のこの問題をさらに深刻にしつつある。

　第一に、人類は毎年、何万種という生物を絶滅に追いやっている。この主な原因は生息地の減少で、世界の絶滅危惧種の動物のほとんどにとって、最大の脅威だと考えられている。私たちが今、自然が残された地域を守るために行動しない限り、世界中の何千という動物種が、これからも地球から消え続けるだろう。

　第二に、人口は増加を続け、また先進国における消費レベルは高すぎる。このため、人々は持続不可能な量の地球の資源を使わざるを得ず、世界中の森林は破壊されている。私たちは、この急速な（人口の）増加と大量消費に対処できる持続可能な解決策をできるだけ早く見出す必要がある。

　第三に、多くの国々は環境保護政策をとり始め、森林破壊のスピードは鈍化しつつあるが、好ましい変化の速さは十分ではない。人類が一貫して、資源の消費を地球が持続できる量に抑えるようにならなければ、環境保護の取り組みは、概して失敗と見なすべきだ。したがって、すべての人々がこの問題を一転させるために協力すべきだ。

　上述の理由から、地球の自然環境を守るために、もっと多くの取り組みがなされるべきであることは明らかだ。

Vocabulary

□ ongoing 進行中の　□ habitat 生息地　□ endangered 絶滅の危機に瀕した

解説　自然保護の取り組みが不十分だと論じる場合は、具体的にどんな問題が進行中か（あるいは悪化しつつあるか）、改善しなければどんなことが起きるかを考えてポイントを立てよう。

　モデルエッセイでは、止まらない生物種の喪失、持続不可能な消費活動、そして森林破壊のスピードは鈍化しつつあるもののまだ効果は十分に出ていない点をトピックとして挙げている。

　森林の二酸化炭素吸収力を考えれば、森林破壊が地球温暖化を加速させているといった論点を挙げることもできるだろう。

Structure

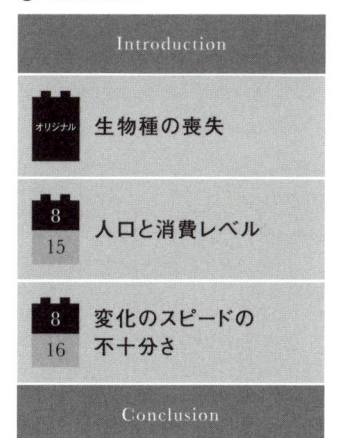

| Introduction |
| オリジナル　生物種の喪失 |
| 8 / 15　人口と消費レベル |
| 8 / 16　変化のスピードの不十分さ |
| Conclusion |

4 教育・IT・ビジネス

問題 ⏰解答時間：1問につき25分

CHAPTER_3

- Write an essay on the given TOPIC.
- Give THREE reasons to support your answer.
- Structure: Introduction, main body, and conclusion
- Suggested length: 200–240 words

TOPIC

1 Should the number of weekly working hours be decreased?

> 解答・解説は 268-271 ページ

2 Should children be allowed to own and use smartphones?

> 解答・解説は 272-275 ページ

3 Does the mass media have a negative effect on society?

> 解答・解説は 276-279 ページ

4 Agree or disagree: The value of a college education will continue to decrease as technology improves

> 解答・解説は 280-283 ページ

5 Does the Internet have a beneficial effect on society?

解答・解説

TOPIC

1 Should the number of weekly working hours be decreased?

モデルエッセイ 👍 Affirmative　　　　　MP3 263

　　　The number of weekly working hours should be decreased, as happy and healthy workers with specific time constraints can increase a company's productivity and profits, and there are always freelance workers available online to assist during busy periods.

　　　Several studies have shown that happy, well-rested workers are more productive, engaged and successful at their jobs. Also, happy workers take fewer sick days than unhappy workers, and employees that get adequate sleep are less likely to make mistakes. For this reason, decreasing weekly working hours will make offices more efficient.

　　　Second, increased working hours do not result in higher outputs. According to Parkinson's Law, work expands and contracts to fill the time allowed to complete it. This means that giving employees limited hours to work is more effective. With strict time management, companies can maintain productivity and profits while also giving employees more freedom.

　　　Finally, when full-time employees cannot complete jobs on their own, companies can employ skilled freelancers to assist them. Thanks to advances in technology, millions of skilled workers are available for short-term projects online. This new system of work has been shown to increase company profits in many situations.

　　　Considering the proven benefits of giving employees more freedom and specific time constraints, along with the newly emerged online freelance market, society's current average working hours seem to be too long.　　　　　　　　　　　　　　　　(222 words)

訳 1 1週間の労働時間は短縮すべきか
👍 Affirmative

　週の労働時間は減らされるべきだ。満足度が高く、健康で、一定の時間的制約がある労働者は、会社の生産性と利益を上げることができ、また忙しい時期には、いつでもオンラインでフリーランスワーカーにサポートを依頼できるからだ。

　満足していて休息がよくとれている労働者は、より生産性が高く、積極的で、仕事に成功していると、複数の研究が示している。また、満足している労働者は、不満を抱えた労働者よりも病気での欠勤が少なく、睡眠時間が十分な従業員のほうがミスをする可能性が低い。こうした理由から、週の労働時間を減らすことは、職場の効率を高める。

　第二に、労働時間を増やしても生み出される結果が増えるわけではない。パーキンソンの法則によれば、仕事はその完遂のために与えられた時間を満たすように伸び縮みする。これはつまり、従業員に与える仕事の時間を制限すれば、効率が上がるということだ。時間管理を厳しくすれば、企業は従業員により多くの自由を与えながら、生産性と利益を維持することができるのだ。

　最後に、正社員が自力で仕事を完了することができない場合、企業はフリーランスの熟練労働者を活用して正社員をサポートしてもらえばいい。技術の進歩により、インターネットを通じて、何百万もの熟練労働者に短期間のプロジェクトを依頼することができる。この新しい仕事のシステムは、さまざまな状況で企業の利益を増すことが示されている。

　従業員により多くの自由と一定の時間的制約を与えることによる明らかな利点と、新たに登場したオンラインでのフリーランス市場を考えれば、現在の社会の平均労働時間は長すぎるように思われる。

Vocabulary

□ constraint 制約、強制　□ well-rested よく休息をとった　□ freelancer フリーランサー

解説　労働時間を減らしてその分作業量が減ってしまうのであれば、企業の業績は下がるだろう。したがって、肯定の立場では労働時間の減少を補う手段を考える必要がある。

　モデルエッセイでは、労働者の生活の充実、およびパーキンソンの法則（一定の仕事を終わらせるのにかかる時間と作業スピードは反比例する）による作業効率の向上を第1、第2のトピックとして挙げた。また効率向上だけでは不十分な場合の手段として、第3のトピックでは、オンラインでフリーランサーを雇う方法を取り上げている。

● Structure

Introduction
12/15 効率の向上
オリジナル 効率の向上
12/16 フリーランサーの活用
Conclusion

TOPIC

1 Should the number of weekly working hours be decreased?

モデルエッセイ ◆ Negative　　　　　　　　　MP3 264

　　The number of weekly working hours should not be decreased because it would damage the economy and increase work-related stress. Also, it would result in a decrease in salaries and benefits.

　　The main reason that the number of weekly working hours should not be decreased is that it would hurt the economy. In a healthy economy, workers produce more value than they consume. If people worked less, then they would create less value for society. In other words, decreasing working hours would not be beneficial for the economy.

　　Second, if there are too many limitations on working hours, people will feel more stressed and less satisfied at their jobs. Good employees want to help their coworkers and accomplish many things. With fewer working hours, though, it would be more difficult to produce positive results at work. Over time, this would lead to feelings of dissatisfaction and stress.

　　Last, even if the working hours are reduced, the amount of work that needs to be completed will not decrease. In order to get all of this work completed, companies would be forced to hire more employees, and their profit margins would decrease. This would most likely lead to lower salaries and fewer benefits for companies' employees.

　　In conclusion, I do not think that the number of weekly working hours should be decreased.　　　　　　　　　(220 words)

訳 1 1週間の労働時間は短縮すべきか
🌧 Negative

経済にダメージを与え、仕事関連のストレスが増えるため、週の労働時間は減らさないほうがよい。また、（労働時間が減れば）給与と手当も減少してしまうだろう。

週の労働時間を減らすべきではない主な理由は、経済に悪影響を及ぼすからだ。健全な経済では、労働者は消費するよりも多く生産する。人々の働く時間が減れば、社会にもたらす価値が少なくなる。言い換えれば、労働時間を減らすことは、経済に有益ではないだろう。

次に、勤務時間に関してあまり多くの制約があると、ストレスがたまり、仕事に満足が感じられなくなる。優れた従業員は同僚を助け、多くのことを成し遂げたいものだ。しかし労働時間が減れば、仕事で意味ある結果を生み出すことは難しくなる。時間がたつにつれて、このことは不満とストレスにつながるだろう。

最後に、仮に労働時間が減ったとしても行うべき仕事の量が減るわけではない。行うべき仕事すべてを終わらせるために、企業はより多くの従業員を雇わなければならなくなり、利幅は減るだろう。このことは結果的に従業員の給料を下げ、手当を減らすと考えられる。

結論として、週の労働時間を減らすべきだとは思わない。

Vocabulary
□ profit margin 利ざや

解説

労働時間が減ることで生じる一番わかりやすいデメリットは、作業量の減少だろう。減る時間が特定されていないので、肯定の答案のように労働時間の減少が作業効率の向上をもたらすと論じることも可能だが、労働時間が半分になっても作業スピードが倍になるわけではない。

モデルエッセイではほかに、十分な時間がなければ満足な仕事ができずに不満やストレスがたまること、一人の作業時間が減ればその分を他の人員で補うことになり会社の負担が増えることをトピックとして挙げた。

Structure

- Introduction
- 12/17 経済へのダメージ
- オリジナル ストレスの増大
- 12/18 会社の損失
- Conclusion

TOPIC

2 Should children be allowed to own and use smartphones?

モデルエッセイ 👍 Affirmative　　　　　🎵 265

　　I believe that children should be allowed to own and use smartphones. Aside from protecting children's safety, smartphones are also useful for building relationships and learning about technology.

　　First, children are safer when they have smartphones. For example, there are now apps that allow parents to track the location of their children at all times using GPS. Also, there are apps for storing important health information in phones, such as a child's allergies or medical conditions. With tools like these, smartphones could save children's lives.

　　Furthermore, smartphones are a great tool for interacting with friends and building strong relationships. Using smartphones, children can chat, play games, and even help each other with homework. Also, there is a chance that a child without a smartphone will be left out of social activities and possibly even bullied.

　　Finally, children must familiarize themselves with common forms of technology. Recently, a study found that Japanese people have below average computer skills. It is suspected that this is because most young people do not have access to a computer at home. Unless they are skilled at using many types of technological devices, young people will have fewer work opportunities and be unable to compete in the global economy.

　　For the reasons mentioned above, it is good for children to own and use smartphones. Owning a smartphone makes children safer and improves their social lives and technical skills.　　(232 words)

ワンポイントアドバイス

第2パラグラフの冒頭の文はFirst, possession of a smartphone has many safety benefits.などとしてもよい。

訳 **2** 子どもにスマートフォンの所有・使用を認めるべきか
👍 Affirmative

　子どもはスマートフォンの所有・使用を認められるべきだと思う。スマートフォンは子どもの安全を守るだけでなく、人間関係を築いたり技術を学んだりするのにも役に立つ。

　まず、子どもはスマートフォンを持っているほうが安全だ。例えば、今は、GPSを使って親が常時子どものいる場所をたどることができるアプリがある。また、子どものアレルギーや病状といった重要な健康上の情報を電話に保存するアプリもある。こうしたツールによって、スマートフォンは子どもの命を守ることができる。

　そのうえ、スマートフォンは友だちと交流し、堅固な人間関係を築く優れたツールだ。子どもたちはスマートフォンを使っておしゃべりをし、ゲームで遊び、宿題でお互いに助け合うことさえできる。また、スマートフォンを持っていない子どもが仲間はずれにされたり、場合によってはいじめられたりする可能性もある。

　最後に、子どもは技術の一般的な形態に慣れ親しむ必要がある。最近、ある研究で日本人には平均以下のコンピュータースキルしかないことが明らかになった。これは多くの若者が家でコンピューターに触れていないからではないかと考えられる。さまざまなテクノロジー機器を使いこなせない限り、若者の就業の機会は減り、グローバル経済の中で戦っていくことはできないだろう。

　上述の理由から、子どもがスマートフォンを所有し使用するのはよいことだ。スマートフォンを持っているほうが子どもは安全で、社会生活や技術のスキルが向上する。

Vocabulary

□ app アプリ　□ track ～の跡をたどる　□ bully ～をいじめる　□ familiarize *oneself* with ～ ～に慣れ親しむ、なじむ

解説　スマートフォンも普及が進み、これから出題される可能性の高いテーマだ。

　スマートフォンの特徴を考えると、インターネットが負担なく見られること、（パソコンに比べ）携帯性が高いこと、豊富なアプリがあることなどが挙げられるだろう。

　子どもがスマートフォンを所有・使用するメリットとして、モデルエッセイでは、子どもの安全管理に使えること、コミュニケーションツールとしての重要性、さらにデジタル機器に親しむ必要性の観点で論じている。

Structure

Introduction
9 / 11 　生活を守るスマートフォン
9 / 12 　人間関係を築くツール
オリジナル　デジタル機器への慣れ
Conclusion

TOPIC

2 Should children be allowed to own and use smartphones?

モデルエッセイ ♠ Negative

Children should not be allowed to own and use smartphones. Using the Internet is unsafe for children, and smartphones can be addictive. Additionally, it is not good for children to stare at screens all the time.

First, children should not be given access to the Internet by themselves, because it is too dangerous. Aside from the large number of websites with adult material that is not appropriate for children, it is also risky for children to interact with new people online. They could be deceived into meeting with a kidnapper or a child molester.

Second, studies have revealed that smartphone use can be addictive for some people. A lot of people are unable to maintain a normal lifestyle without access to their smartphones because they have become so dependent on them. This can often harm interpersonal relationships. Surely we should not give our children any devices that cause obsession and addiction.

Last, children already spend too much time staring at screens. In the past, children spent most of their free time outdoors doing various physical activities like sports. Today, however, far too many children spend their free time watching TV and playing on computers and smartphones. Studies suggest that children are getting physically weaker because of this change.

In conclusion, I do not think that children should be given smartphones. We can keep children safer and healthier by limiting their access to this technology.

(234 words)

訳 2 子どもにスマートフォンの所有・使用を認めるべきか
🌧 Negative

　子どもはスマートフォンの所有・使用を認められるべきではない。インターネットの使用は子どもには危険だし、スマートフォンは中毒になることがある。加えて子どもが常に画面を凝視しているのは好ましいことではない。

　第一に、子どもは自分でインターネットにアクセスする手段を与えられるべきではない。それはあまりにも危険だからだ。子どもにふさわしくない成人向けの内容のウェブサイトがたくさんあるだけでなく、知らない人とオンラインでやり取りをするのも危険だ。子どもがだまされて誘拐犯や児童性的虐待者に会ってしまうことにもなりかねない。

　第二に、人によっては、スマートフォンは中毒になりうるということが、研究で明らかになってきた。スマートフォンに過剰に依存し、それなしには普通の生活が送れない人が数多くいる。このことは人間関係に害を及ぼす可能性がある。子どもたちに強迫観念と中毒を引き起こすような機器を与えるべきではないのは明らかだ。

　最後に、子どもはすでにあまりにも長い時間、画面を凝視して過ごしている。以前、子どもは、屋外でスポーツのような体を動かすさまざまな活動をして自由時間の大部分を過ごしていた。しかし今日では、あまりにも多くの子どもが、テレビを見、コンピューターやスマートフォンで遊んで自由時間を過ごしている。研究により、この変化の結果、子どもの体が弱くなっているということが示されている。

　結論として、子どもにスマートフォンは与えられるべきではないと思う。この技術へのアクセスを制限したほうが、子どもの安全と健全さを保つことができる。

Vocabulary

- addictive 中毒性の、病みつきになる
- kidnapper 誘拐犯
- molester 痴漢、性犯罪者
- interpersonal relationship 対人関係
- obsession 強迫観念、とりつかれること

解説　肯定の立場の解説でスマートフォンの特徴を挙げたが、こうした特徴が子どもに問題を引き起こしていると考えることも可能だ。

　インターネットにアクセスできるため有害な情報に触れたり、危険な人間関係に巻き込まれたりする可能性があるし、どこにでも持ち歩け、ゲームなどのアプリも充実しているので、それを手離すことができなくなり、一日じゅうそれを見ているということにもつながる。使いかたによっては法外な通信料を請求される可能性に触れることも可能だろう。

● Structure

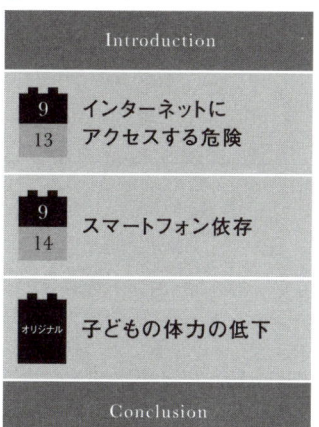

Introduction
9/13　インターネットにアクセスする危険
9/14　スマートフォン依存
オリジナル　子どもの体力の低下
Conclusion

TOPIC

3 Does the mass media have a negative effect on society?

モデルエッセイ 👍 Affirmative

　　The mass media certainly has a negative effect on society. It presents unreliable information, causes people to doubt their value, and promotes environmental destruction.

　　First, mass media news programs tend to be biased and misleading. News programs should be unbiased, honest, and free from government and sponsor controls. Unfortunately, this is not the case. For example, government regulations have caused Japan's press freedom ranking to drop to embarrassingly low levels in recent years.

　　Second, people cannot escape the influence of mass media advertising. This is a problem because a significant portion of advertising is designed to make people feel bad about themselves. For example, advertising often makes young girls overly self-conscious about their bodies. This has been linked to an increase in eating disorders such as anorexia, which is one of the most dangerous mental illnesses.

　　Third, the media is promoting a lifestyle that is harmful to the planet. The media works to convince people that acquiring wealth and possessions is necessary for happiness. This is part of the reason that humans are destroying the planet. About 20% of people are consuming 80% of our resources. This problem will get worse with further population increases and economic development.

　　When taking the above points into consideration, it is apparent that the mass media has an extremely negative effect on society. (219 words)

ワンポイントアドバイス

第4パラグラフ第2文はThe media idolizes rich people and encourages reckless consumption.（メディアは富裕層を偶像化し、無謀な消費を促進している）などとしてもよい。

訳 3 マスメディアは社会に対して悪影響があるか
👍 Affirmative

　マスメディアは確実に社会に悪影響を及ぼしている。マスメディアは信頼できない情報を提示し、自分の価値観に疑念を持たせ、環境破壊を促進する。

　第一に、マスメディアのニュース番組には偏りがあり、誤った認識を与える傾向がある。ニュース番組は公平、誠実で、政府やスポンサーのコントロールから自由であるべきだ。しかし残念ながら、現実はそうなっていない。例えば近年、政府の規制のために、日本の報道の自由度ランキングはあきれるほど低いレベルに落ちている。

　第二に、人はマスメディアの広告の影響から逃れることができない。広告のうちのかなりのものは人々に自信を失わせるように作られているので、これは問題である。例えば、広告は若い女性に自分の身体について過剰に意識させることが多い。これが、拒食症のような摂食障害の増加につながっている。拒食症は最も危険な精神疾患の一つだ。

　第三に、メディアは地球に害を及ぼすような生活様式を推進している。メディアは、富と財産を獲得することが幸福のためには必須だと人々に確信させるように働く。これは、人間が地球を破壊している一因となっている。約2割の人々が地球の資源の8割を消費している。この問題は、さらに人口が増加し、経済が発展するにしたがって悪化するだろう。

　上述の点を考慮に入れると、マスメディアが社会に極めて悪い影響を与えていることは明白だ。

Vocabulary

□ unbiased 偏りのない、公平な　□ be not the case 事実と異なる　□ regulation 規制　□ press freedom 報道の自由　□ embarrassingly 当惑するほどに　□ anorexia 拒食症

解説　一口に「マスメディア」と言ってもテレビ、ラジオ、新聞、インターネットなど多様だが、それらに共通する最大の特性は、情報が大衆に伝わることだ。この点を念頭に置いてトピックを考えよう。

　メディアが社会に悪影響を及ぼすとする上のモデルエッセイでは、メディアの偏向性、広告の影響、メディアが富の獲得と幸福とを結びつける問題をトピックとして取り上げた。メディアも私企業であり、利害関係から自由になれないこと、情報の過剰な提供によって政治的無関心を引き起こす可能性などもトピックになりうるだろう。

● Structure

Introduction	
12／5	情報の偏向
12／6	広告の影響
オリジナル	消費生活の助長
Conclusion	

TOPIC

3 Does the mass media have a negative effect on society?

モデルエッセイ ♠ Negative　268

　　I do not believe that the mass media has a negative effect on society. The media teaches and entertains people, and it is always improving.

　　The greatest benefit of the media is its educational value. Thanks to news programs, we can learn about what is happening in other areas of the world. Even popular dramas and comedies teach us an incredible amount of things. Plus, the media includes a wide variety of educational programs that teach about topics such as science and history.

　　In addition, the media contributes to society by entertaining people. Entertainment has been an important part of every human civilization. Humans need stories in their lives. Most people would not want to quit watching television or films forever. This is because the media makes their lives more enjoyable. Surely this is a positive thing.

　　Finally, the mass media is always getting better. Television programs and advertisements are often criticized for the way that they present information. But the history of media shows that it is gradually getting better. Only 50 or 60 years ago, news programs were extremely biased, and there were no regulations on advertisements for harmful products.

　　In conclusion, I disagree with the view that the mass media has an undesirable effect on society. The mass media makes us happier and more knowledgeable. Also, it is likely to continue improving in the future.　　　　　　　　　　　　　　　(228 words)

ワンポイントアドバイス

第3パラグラフの第1文はIn addition, the media provides valuable entertainment to people. などとしてもよい。

訳 **3** マスメディアは社会に対して悪影響があるか
　　　　 🌧 Negative

　マスメディアが社会に悪影響を及ぼしているとは思わない。メディアは人々を教育し、人々を楽しませ、絶えず向上している。

　メディアの最大の長所は教育的な価値があることだ。ニュース番組のおかげで、私たちは世界の他の地域で何が起こっているのかを知ることができる。人気のドラマやコメディでさえも、私たちに驚くほど多くの物事を教えてくれる。さらに、メディアには、科学や歴史などのテーマについて教えてくれる幅広い教育番組がある。

　加えて、メディアは人々を楽しませることによって社会に貢献している。娯楽は人類のあらゆる文明において重要な要素である。人間の暮らしには物語が必要だ。ほとんどの人は、テレビや映画を今後まったく見ないようにしたいとは思わないだろう。それは、メディアが人の生活をもっと楽しめるものにしているからだ。確かにこれは好ましいことだ。

　最後に、マスメディアは常に改善されている。テレビ番組や広告はよく、その情報の提示の仕方で批判されている。しかし、メディアが徐々によくなってきていることをその歴史は示している。わずか5、60年前には、ニュース番組は極めて偏っていて、有害な製品の広告に規制はなかった。

　結論として、私はマスメディアが社会に好ましくない影響を与えているという見解には同意しない。マスメディアは私たちをより幸せにし、知識を増やしてくれる。また、今後もマスメディアは向上を続けるだろう。

Vocabulary
□ incredible 信じられないほどの、途方もない　□ entertain 〜を楽しませる

解説　今度はマスメディアの利点について考えてみよう。この立場で考える場合は、もしもマスメディアが存在しなかったらと考えるとトピックが浮かびやすい。

　マスメディアが存在しなかった場合、一番大きい問題は情報が入ってこないことだろう。すなわち私たちは世間で、あるいは世界で何が起きているかを知ることができない。モデルエッセイでは、このトピックのほか、マスメディアが娯楽を提供していること、またメディアの偏向性が是正されつつあることを論点として取り上げた。

Structure

Introduction
12-7　教育的価値
12-8　娯楽の提供
オリジナル　メディアの改善
Conclusion

TOPIC

4 Agree or disagree: The value of a college education will continue to decrease as technology improves

モデルエッセイ 👍 Affirmative　　MP3 269

　　As technology evolves, the value of a college education will continue to decrease. Due to cost savings and course quality, online courses are a better alternative for many students. Also, students can still have a successful career without a college degree.

　　First, the quality of online education is improving rapidly. In particular, online courses may be better for learning a wide range of practical skills. To give just a few examples, there are excellent online courses for software engineering, graphic design, and even construction management. With focused courses that teach specific, valuable skills, students can make themselves more attractive to employers.

　　Second, traditional universities have several high costs. Tuition fees have risen consistently over the years. Additionally, students' time and money are required for commuting to campuses. For students that want to avoid spending too much and going into debt, this makes online alternatives very attractive.

　　Last, a university degree is no longer a requirement for a successful career. Companies are starting to realize that many high quality workers come from online schools, and they are likely to hire more of these people in the future. Moreover, many students are able to start freelance businesses using skills that they acquire online.

　　For the reasons mentioned above, I believe that improvements in technology will continue to reduce the value of a college education.

(222 words)

ワンポイントアドバイス

最後の文のカンマ以下は I believe that continual technological developments will cause the value of a college education to decline. あるいはもっとシンプルに I believe that college educations are becoming less valuable. などと表現を変えてもよい。

訳 **4** 賛成か反対か：大学教育の価値は技術の進歩に伴って減り続ける
👍 Affirmative

技術が進歩するにつれて、大学教育の価値は下がり続けるだろう。コスト節減とコースの高い質のために、オンラインコースは多くの学生にとってよりよい代替手段になる。また、学生は大学の学位がなくても仕事で成功することができる。

第一に、オンライン教育の質は急速に向上してきている。特に、オンラインコースは実用的な技能を幅広く身につけるにはかえって適しているかもしれない。少しだけ例を挙げると、ソフトウェアエンジニアリングやグラフィックデザイン、建設管理に至るまで、優れたオンラインコースがある。特定の価値の高い技能を教えるコースに的を絞れば、学生は雇用者にとって魅力的な人材になることができる。

次に、従来の大学にはいくつもの高い費用がかかる。学費は年々上がってきている。加えて、学生にはキャンパスに通学する時間とお金も必要だ。多額の出費をしたり借金を抱えたりしたくない学生にとって、このことは、オンラインによる代替手段をとても魅力的なものにしている。

最後に、大学の学位はもはや仕事で成功するための必須要件ではない。企業は、オンラインスクールが質の高い労働者を多数輩出していることに気づき始め、将来はこうした人々をもっと多く雇用するようになるだろう。そのうえ、多くの学生はオンラインで身につけた技能を活用して、フリーランスで仕事を始めることもできる。

上述の理由から、私は大学教育の価値は技術の向上に伴って下がり続けると思う。

Vocabulary

☐ alternative 代替案、代替手段　☐ consistently 絶えず、一貫して　☐ go into debt 借金に陥る
☐ requirement 必須条件

解説 設問中のasは「〜するにつれて」という意味。つまり、技術の進歩が大学教育の価値を低下させ続けるかを問う設問である。したがってオンライン教育と従来の大学の教育を相関的に捉える視点が必要だ。

モデルエッセイでは、オンライン教育の質の向上、コストの安さ、そして就職におけるメリットをトピックとして挙げている。ほかに学習内容の選択肢の豊富さや受講の時・場所を選ばないこと、学習ペースの融通が利くことなどをトピックとすることもできるだろう。

Structure

- Introduction
- オリジナル：オンライン教育の質の向上
- ⑨-1：大学教育のコスト
- ⑨-2：キャリアへの影響の低下
- Conclusion

TOPIC

4 Agree or disagree: The value of a college education will continue to decrease as technology improves

モデルエッセイ ● Negative　　　MP3 270

　　Although more people are taking college courses online these days, the value of a college education will never decrease. College is a good life experience. Also, degrees guarantee higher salaries, and new policies will likely lower costs in the future.

　　Attending a college campus allows students to meet new people every day. In university, students make friends they will know until they are old, which is very valuable. Moreover, knowing many people is helpful for getting a good job after graduation, so the conventional college experience is good for both personal and professional reasons.

　　In addition, studies show that people without degrees earn less money than those with degrees. University education is expensive, but college graduates make much higher salaries after a while. For this reason, the value of a college education is cost-effective. It just requires a larger initial investment.

　　Finally, policies that support lowering education costs are becoming more popular, especially in European countries. For example, Germany has completely removed higher education costs. As a result, students will be able to enjoy the benefits of a college experience while keeping fees as low as an online education.

　　Some people claim that all education will be online in the future. However, positive experiences, better salaries, and decreasing prices all prove that traditional education cannot be replaced completely. (218 words)

ワンポイントアドバイス
第2パラグラフ3文目のknowing many peopleはhaving many connections（多くのつながりがある）などと言い換えてもよい。

訳 **4** 賛成か反対か：大学教育の価値は技術の進歩に伴って減り続ける

🌧 Negative

　最近では、大学のコースをオンラインで受ける人が増えているが、大学教育の価値が下がることはないだろう。大学時代は素晴らしい人生経験だ。また、学位はより高い給料を保証し、さらに新しい政策によって将来、学費は下がると思われる。

　大学のキャンパスに通うことで、学生は毎日新しい人々と出会うことができる。大学で学生は、年を取るまで関係の続く友人ができる。これはとても価値のあることだ。また、多くの人と知り合いであることは、卒業後によい仕事に就くのに役立つので、従来の大学での経験は、個人としても、仕事の面でもよいことだ。

　加えて、学位を持たない人は、学位を持つ人よりも収入が少ないことが調査で示されている。大学教育は高くつくが、大学を卒業した人は、しばらくすればはるかに高い給料を得られる。このような理由で、大学教育は費用効果が高い。単により高額の初期投資が必要だということなのだ。

　最後に、教育費の低減を促す政策が、特にヨーロッパ諸国で一般的になってきている。例えば、ドイツは高等教育の学費を完全に撤廃した。その結果、学生はオンライン教育と同程度の安い学費で、大学での経験のメリットにあずかることができるだろう。

　すべての教育が将来、オンラインになるだろうと主張する人もいる。しかし、有意義な経験、より高い給与、費用の低下はいずれも、従来の教育を完全に置き換えることはできないということを証明している。

Vocabulary

□ conventional 従来の、伝統的な　□ cost-effective 費用効果が高い

解説　今度は技術が進歩しても大学の価値は低下し続けることはないという立場の答案。

　この問題は、要するに「リアル対デジタル（＝バーチャル）」のメリット・デメリットを問う問題であり、リアルのよさについて考えればモデルエッセイ第2パラグラフのトピックが出てくる。

　モデルエッセイでは、第3パラグラフで収入が少ないというオンライン教育の問題点、第4パラグラフで学費が高いという大学教育の問題点は解決されるという展望を取り上げた。ほかにオンラインでは強制力がないため学習を継続するのが難しいといったトピックも考えられるだろう。

● Structure

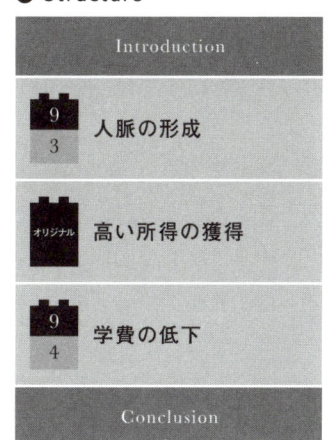

| Introduction |
| 9 / 3　人脈の形成 |
| オリジナル　高い所得の獲得 |
| 9 / 4　学費の低下 |
| Conclusion |

TOPIC

5 Does the Internet have a beneficial effect on society?

モデルエッセイ 👍 Affirmative 　　　　　　　　　　　　　MP3 271

> I am of the opinion that the Internet has a beneficial effect on society. In addition to strengthening interpersonal communication, the Internet also benefits global education, and it allows businesses to communicate with their customers more effectively.
>
> First, the Internet supports interpersonal communication. One common complaint is that online communication is not as healthy as face-to-face communication. However, online communication does not replace face-to-face meetings. Instead, it is a supplement to in-person communication, and it increases the overall volume of interaction. This additional method for staying in touch is especially valuable for friends and family members that live far apart.
>
> Second, the Internet is an important tool for worldwide education. Thanks to the Internet, individuals in developing countries with limited access to education can obtain high quality information and skills from experts in other countries. More education for a larger number of people will raise the number of individuals able to perform skilled jobs, which results in more innovation and improves the global economy.
>
> Last, almost all businesses in developed countries have an online presence, which gives them more ways to directly communicate with customers. As a result, businesses can better understand market trends and customer preferences, meaning they can provide their services more intelligently, which leads to higher customer satisfaction and profits.
>
> Due to the benefits the Internet provides for relationships, students, and businesses, it seems that the positive effects of Internet usage greatly outweigh the negatives.
>
> 　　　　　　　　　　　　　　　　　　　　　　　　　(238 words)

訳 **5** インターネットは社会に有益な影響をもたらすか
👍 Affirmative

　私は、インターネットは社会に有益な影響をもたらすと考える。インターネットは人と人とのコミュニケーションを補強するだけでなく、世界の教育にも恩恵をもたらし、企業がより効果的に顧客とコミュニケーションをとることを可能にする。

　第一に、インターネットは、人と人とのコミュニケーションをサポートする。よく聞かれる不満に、オンラインでのコミュニケーションは面と向かってのコミュニケーションに比べて健全でないというものがある。しかし、オンラインでのコミュニケーションは、直接会ってのコミュニケーションに置き換わるものではない。むしろ、対面のコミュニケーションを補助するものであり、交流の全体量を増加させるのだ。連絡を取り合うためのこの追加的な手段は、特に、遠く離れて暮らす友人や家族にとって利用価値が高い。

　第二に、インターネットは、世界の教育にとって重要なツールである。インターネットのおかげで、教育の機会が限られている発展途上国の人々は、他国にいる専門家から、質の高い情報とスキルを得ることができる。より多くの人々により多くの教育の機会が与えられれば、スキルの必要な仕事ができる人の数が増え、その結果、イノベーションが増して世界経済は向上する。

　最後に、先進国のほとんどすべての企業がオンラインサイトを活用し、顧客と直接コミュニケーションをとる方法を増やしている。その結果、企業は市場の動向と顧客の嗜好をよりよく理解できるようになっている。これはつまり、企業がサービスをよりスマートに提供できるということであり、顧客満足度と利益の向上につながっている。

　インターネットが人間関係や学生、企業に与えるメリットを考えれば、インターネット利用のプラスの影響は、マイナスの影響を大きく上回ると思われる。

Vocabulary
□ interpersonal 対人の、個人間の　□ supplement 補足、補完　□ customer satisfaction 顧客満足度

解説　今や社会に深く根づいているインターネットの功罪を問う問題。インターネットの特徴は、パソコンなどのデバイスを介して、世界中の人と、個人間であるいは不特定多数の人と、双方向的につながることができるという点だろう。またネット上にある情報量の多さは形容するのが難しいほどである。

　モデルエッセイでは、インターネットの否定的な側面とされる人間関係の間接性を、直接的な関係を補完するものだと反論することで一つのトピックとしている。

⚫ Structure

| Introduction |
| 10/10 連絡手段としてのインターネット |
| 10/11 教育のツール |
| オリジナル 顧客とのコミュニケーションツール |
| Conclusion |

TOPIC

5 Does the Internet have a beneficial effect on society?

モデルエッセイ ◆ Negative

While the Internet has many obvious societal benefits, it has many negative effects as well. Increased Internet usage among people and businesses damages interpersonal relationships. Also, personal information is more vulnerable to theft, and incorrect information is often posted.

Recent studies show that the majority of business executives prefer face-to-face interaction, arguing that it builds stronger and more meaningful relationships. Creating a positive emotional environment is a result of in-person communication, which benefits both personal and professional relationships. This cannot be replaced by online interaction.

Next, personal information posted online is often stolen. As Internet usage increases, more and more people feel comfortable purchasing products and entering private information online. As a result, the frequency of identity theft and credit card fraud is increasing. Experts estimate that the annual global cost of cybercrime is enormous.

Last, the Internet can be misleading for students and researchers. Information posted online is often incorrect or not officially verified, whereas information in books must be verified before publication. Since there are not standards for verifying online information, students and researchers should avoid relying on the Internet. Using incorrect information could lead to serious negative consequences.

In conclusion, the Internet has a negative effect on society overall. In addition to issues regarding security, privacy, and reliability, the Internet also has a harmful impact on personal and business relationships.

(223 words)

訳 5 インターネットは社会に有益な影響をもたらすか
🌧 Negative

インターネットには、明らかな社会的利益が数多くある一方で、マイナスの影響もたくさんある。個人および企業の間でインターネット利用が増えていることは、人と人との関係にダメージを与えている。また、個人情報は盗まれやすくなり、しばしば不正確な情報が掲載されている。

最近の研究によると、企業の重役の大多数が面と向かってのやり取りを好み、そのほうが強固で有意義な関係が築かれると主張しているという。望ましい感情的環境ができることは、直接のコミュニケーションの成果であり、個人間および仕事上の関係の両方でよい影響をもたらす。これにオンラインでの交流が置き換わることはできない。

次に、インターネット上に投稿された個人情報が頻繁に盗まれている。インターネット利用が増えるにつれて、ますます多くの人が、インターネットで商品を購入し、個人情報を入力することに違和感を覚えなくなっている。その結果、個人情報詐取とクレジットカード詐欺の数が増している。専門家は、サイバー犯罪による世界の年間被害額は巨額だと推定している。

最後に、インターネットは学生や研究者に誤った情報を与える場合がある。インターネット上に掲載された情報は正確ではない、あるいは正式に検証されていないことが多いが、書籍に掲載される情報は出版前に必ず検証される。インターネット上の情報を検証する基準がないため、学生や研究者はインターネットに頼るのを避けたほうがよい。不正確な情報を使うと、深刻なマイナスの結果につながりかねない。

結論として、インターネットは概して社会にマイナスの影響を及ぼしている。安全性、プライバシー、信頼性に関する問題に加え、インターネットは個人の関係と仕事上の関係にも悪影響をもたらしている。

Vocabulary
- face-to-face interaction 対面しての交流
- fraud 詐欺
- verify 〜を(真実であると)確認する

解説
肯定の解答の冒頭にインターネットの特徴を挙げたが、その特徴ゆえにインターネットにはデメリットも多い。

とりわけ誰とでもつながっているということは、不可抗力的に犯罪などに巻き込まれる可能性があるし、誰もが情報を発信できるということは不確かな情報がまん延するということでもある。これらの点はインターネットの有害性を論じるうえで強力なトピックとなる。

Structure

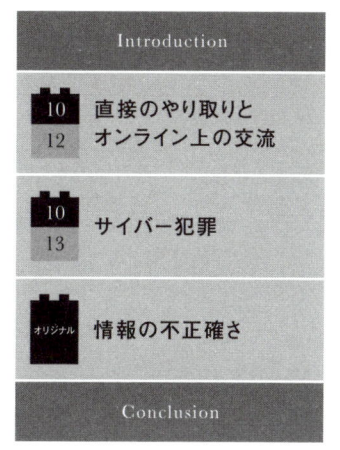

Introduction	
10 / 12	直接のやり取りとオンライン上の交流
10 / 13	サイバー犯罪
オリジナル	情報の不正確さ
Conclusion	

［編者紹介］
ロゴポート

語学書を中心に企画・制作を行っている編集者ネットワーク。編集者、翻訳者、ネイティブスピーカーなどから成る。おもな編著に『英語を英語で理解する 英英英単語 初級編／中級編／上級編／超上級編』、『最短合格! 英検®1級／準1級 英作文問題完全制覇』、『出る順で最短合格! 英検®1級／準1級 語彙問題完全制覇［改訂版］』、『出る順で最短合格! 英検®準1級〜3級単熟語EX』、『最短合格! 英検®2級英作文&面接 完全制覇』、『最短合格! 英検®準2級ライティング完全制覇』（ジャパンタイムズ出版）、『分野別IELTS英単語』（オープンゲート）、『TEAP単熟語Grip1500』（アスク出版）、『英検®準1級スーパーレベル問題集──本番がラクに解けるようになる』（テイエス企画）などがある。

最短合格! 英検®1級
英作文問題完全制覇

2016年9月5日　初版発行
2022年10月5日　第10刷発行

編者　　ジャパンタイムズ&ロゴポート
　　　　©The Japan Times, Ltd. & Logoport, 2016
発行者　伊藤秀樹
発行所　株式会社　ジャパンタイムズ出版
　　　　〒102-0082 東京都千代田区一番町2-2
　　　　　　　　　一番町第二TGビル2F
　　　　ウェブサイト　https://jtpublishing.co.jp/
印刷所　日経印刷株式会社

本書の内容に関するお問い合わせは、上記ウェブサイトまたは郵便でお受けいたします。
定価はカバーに表示してあります。
万一、乱丁落丁のある場合は、送料当社負担でお取り替えいたします。ジャパンタイムズ出版営業部あてにお送りください。
このコンテンツは、公益財団法人日本英語検定協会の承認や推奨、その他の検討を受けたものではありません。

Printed in Japan　ISBN 978-4-7890-1646-9

本書のご感想をお寄せください。
https://jtpublishing.co.jp/contact/comment/